PRAISE FOR
THE VAGINA BUSINESS

"In *The Vagina Business*, Marina Gerner takes you on a tour around the world to learn about the femtech products being designed and marketed today—from apps that track fertility and periods, to smart bras that tell women about their heart health, to new forms of contraception for women (and men). *The Vagina Business* is also an important story about the long-held taboos about women's bodies that have hindered research, education, and investment in women's health, and about the feminist innovators who are shattering these taboos to provide women what they want and deserve."

—**DEENA EMERA**, PhD, author of
A Brief History of the Female Body

"A smart, tech-savvy primer on not only the bottom-line business value of more inclusive research, but its whole-hearted worth for all humankind."

—**ABBY NORMAN**, author of
Ask Me About My Uterus

"Fascinating, infuriating, and exciting, *The Vagina Business* introduces some extraordinary female revolutionaries and the fantastic promise of tech to transform women's lives. Some scenes will make you want to scream. But others will have you jumping up and down in delight at the extent to which women are supporting women to innovate—and the vast scale of the sisterhood's imagination. Gerner renders complex science simple and makes venture capital thrilling. She is a strong writer with a gift for telling a story, and this is a great one. *The Vagina Business* is an important book, with significance for our understanding of the impact of structural discrimination on women's health. I hope it is bought and read by many, many people who then advocate for, research and invest in the fairer future that femtech offers".

—SOPHIE WALKER, activist and author of
Five Rules for Rebellion

"*The Vagina Business* is an eye-opening book that everyone needs to read. It shines a light on how women's needs have been routinely dismissed and ignored by science, medicine, and technology. Gerner offers us hope for the future, showing us how the world can be a better place for women when innovators in tech, science, and medicine begin to take our needs seriously."

—SARAH E. HILL, PhD, author of
This is Your Brain on Birth Control

"Marina Gerner's brilliant book should be titled *How to Make More Money Than You Ever Dreamed Possible* because she is handing all venture capitalists, investors, and corporations that opportunity on a plate. She has done all the due diligence they could ever want in this deeply researched, wide-ranging and utterly riveting study of the entrepreneurs pioneering in the sector that business, finance and tech are massively missing out on through sheer squeamishness: women's sexual and reproductive health. *The Vagina Business* is a must-read—and also, when you buy and read it, a must-display—to overcome the ridiculousness that is holding this sector back. Make sure you show the cover off when you're reading it on the Tube, on the plane, by the pool, on the beach, in the office. There's a huge amount of money to be made out of taking women seriously, and this book is the evidence. BUY IT NOW."

—CINDY GALLOP, founder & CEO, MakeLoveNotPorn

"If you care about your health and the health of all the women in your life, you should read this book. After reading it, I finally felt heard. I finally felt seen. And it felt so good. *The Vagina Business* is one of those books every woman should read multiple times in her life—the lessons in it are invaluable."

—MARIJA BUTKOVIC, entrepreneur, journalist, women's health advisor and consultant

"Marina Gerner's writing is electric, and *The Vagina Business* will leave you shocked and energized. It's a terrific page-turner that will transform how every reader sees the worlds of business and technology."

—JAKE KNAPP, author of the *New York Times* bestseller *Sprint*

"In a world where women's health and pleasure have been sidelined, *The Vagina Business* is a rallying cry for change. This book will expand your mind, and make you rethink how you open your wallet."

—RENA MARTINE, author of *The Sex You Want: A Shameless Journey to Deep Intimacy, Honest Pleasure, and a Life You Love*

THE VAGINA BUSINESS

THE INNOVATIVE BREAKTHROUGHS THAT COULD CHANGE EVERYTHING IN WOMEN'S HEALTH

MARINA GERNER

Published by Sourcebooks
P.O. Box 4410, Naperville, Illinois 60567–4410
(630) 961-3900
sourcebooks.com

Cataloging-in-Publication Data is on file with the Library of Congress.

Printed and bound in the United States of America.
MA 10 9 8 7 6 5 4 3 2 1

To my mother, obviously

CONTENTS

PART III: Out into the World

INTRODUCTION

SKIN IN THE GAME

Did he actually just say that? For a moment, she thought she'd misheard him. Farah Kabir had come to an island in the English Channel to pitch her company to a group of investors. Flying in from London, she had gone straight to a conference center hotel, the kind you see all over the world, with cold gray floors and lukewarm coffee. She straightened her clothes and felt her hands shake as she reached for a glass of water. It had taken blood, sweat, latex, and her life savings to get to this point.

The idea for her company had come to her a few years earlier when Farah came off the contraceptive pill. There were too many side effects: weight gain, mood swings, and greasy skin. "Hormonal contraception just wasn't working for me," she says. Condoms became her preferred option.

One day, she went to a shop on her lunch break at work to buy condoms. "You walk down the condom aisle, and you see they're garishly packaged, they promote a man's conquest, and you don't really know what the ingredients are," she says. With other products you apply to your body, you can usually see what they're made of, "But it's not like that with condoms. Either way you don't want to be down the condom aisle for too long." Which is exactly what happened.

As Farah rummaged around the condom aisle looking for information on ingredients, she bumped into her boss. "I was absolutely mortified. He would've seen the bright red pack in my hands." What was embarrassment at first turned into frustration. "Because internally I was thinking: why is it OK for me to take control of every other aspect of my health but not my sexual health?"

Over lunch, she told her friend Dr. Sarah Welsh, who is a gynecologist, about the awkward bump in with her boss, and asked: "Why isn't it acceptable for women to carry contraception?" Sarah was not surprised. In her line of work, she had seen women come into her clinic with hard-to-treat STIs and women who said they didn't carry protection because it was "a man's job" or they didn't want to be seen as promiscuous. "So, we had this light bulb moment there and then: why don't we create a condom designed with women in mind?"

The two women decided to take a closer look at the industry to see whether there were any condoms that had been created considering the preferences of female customers. "We were so shocked that nobody had done this in Europe," says Farah. Then, they surveyed two thousand women and discovered that when it comes to condoms, women care about the ingredients and sustainability. The women in their survey didn't like the smell of latex or garish packaging, but equally they didn't want something girly, pink, and floral. "We carved out a product from what our survey respondents wanted," says Farah. "Our condoms are vegan and biodegradable. They have no nasty chemicals in them like anesthetics that make a man last longer but are irritating to the walls of a vagina."

"We put all of our life savings into creating condoms," she says. To take their company Hanx further, they needed to raise money from investors. At her pitch, Farah was the only female founder facing a group of predominantly male investors that day. That's when she heard the question that threw her. One investor laughed and said: "Can you demonstrate how to put on a condom?"

She realized the question was meant to mock her. "They didn't take me seriously as a woman trying to raise investment for a business that currently is in a male-dominated industry," she says. It's a throwback to the classrooms of decades-old sex education, where teenagers laugh while pulling condoms over bananas. Who would have thought this attitude would carry on into investor board meetings led by men with silver hair?

It's *my* job to ask impertinent questions as a journalist. Over the last decade, I've been writing about business, technology, and culture. Stories like that of Farah drew my attention to a new field that's at the cusp of a revolution: female technology—femtech, which is technology focused on female bodies around maternity, birth, periods, sex, menopause, fertility, and contraception and beyond. The question I wanted to answer became: What stands in the way of such innovation? And how can this new generation of entrepreneurs succeed?

I set out to interview a range of female entrepreneurs in the space for an article. Every entrepreneur I spoke to told me outrageous stories about reactions from investors, who tend to be predominantly male. It's hard enough for female entrepreneurs in any industry to raise money, but for those with a vagina-centric innovation it's even harder. Not only do investors not relate to the issue at hand, but they are too embarrassed to discuss it in a business setting. It isn't proper, they think, twiddling their ties. It's not polite conversation. As one well-known venture capital investor put it: "I don't want to talk about vaginas in my Monday morning partner meeting."

My article was published in *Wired* magazine and went viral. It was read and shared by tens of thousands of people. Messages came flooding into my inbox from female entrepreneurs: "I loved your article. I think it really captured how particularly difficult it is for women." Perhaps more surprisingly, I received messages from younger, millennial male investors too. "Super cool article," one wrote. "As an investor, I definitely had that problem initially. Now, I am way past it." Like others who were squeamish at first, he was making a foray into femtech.

I realized this was just a flash of the ankle. The more founders I spoke to, the more I learned about the stigma they deal with, the censorship they face from mainstream media as well as social media platforms, and also, the tremendous potential they have in an industry that could capture 50 percent of the world's population. This, I knew, has to become a global movement.

Society has mostly overlooked female health—from the detrimental side effects of the birth control pill to a lack of groundbreaking innovation in childbirth and menopause. Designing technology—largely by women, for women—is a novel approach. After all, most technology is still designed by men, for men. This bias starts with ever-growing smartphones,

which don't fit into our hands, and extends to bigger tech, like
seat belts and the broad-shouldered, masculine car crash test
dummies, as Caroline Criado-Perez has shown in her groundbreaking book on the gender data gap, *Invisible Women*.
Prosthetics, voice recognition, and protective clothing for
healthcare professionals have all been designed for male bodies.
A world that was designed around a male default ultimately
impacts our health and safety.

The more I immersed myself in the world of femtech, and
its wider ecosystem, the more it puzzled me. Women make 80
percent of healthcare decisions in the United States, according
to the U.S. Department of Labor, but are hardly involved in the
design of the healthcare system. It was only in 1993 that women
and people of color were officially included in U.S. clinical trials,
and much of our current medical knowledge has been shaped
by earlier research. Women were long excluded from research
because of our cycles; even animal testing tends to exclude
female mice, because of their hormones.

In both puberty and perimenopause, hormone levels are chaotic.

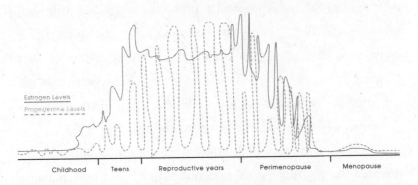

Perimenopause Lost, Professor Jerilynn C. Prior.

The consequences have been catastrophic. Women are 50 percent more likely than men to be given a wrong diagnosis after a heart attack. Across 770 types of diseases, women are diagnosed an average four years later than men. And a delayed diagnosis means women are more likely to suffer pain and complications.

Female-specific diseases are met with a raised eyebrow, as polycystic ovary syndrome (PCOS) is routinely misdiagnosed. It can take close to a decade to get a diagnosis for endometriosis. Even Oprah was repeatedly misdiagnosed when she had heart palpitations as part of menopause.

The dosage of most drugs is calculated based on studies overwhelmingly conducted on male participants, even though in women, drugs tend to linger longer, as our liver and kidneys process them differently.

Only 4 percent of all healthcare research and development is focused on women's health issues, according to PitchBook data. In the UK, less than 2.5 percent of publicly funded research is dedicated to reproductive health and childbirth. Women's health is both underfunded and underresearched.

This disparity has existed for millennia. In ancient Greece, people believed women's health problems were caused by our uterus wandering around our body; say if it got stuck in the chest, we'd have chest pain. In the nineteenth century, doctors blamed "hysteria," which comes from the Greek word *hystera* for "uterus," as a cause for female health issues. Today, women continue to be brushed off for "complaining."

Female pain has been normalized, from childbirth to menopause, as society shrugs and says "Welcome to being a woman" instead of coming up with better solutions. The terms we use are revealing. There's nothing quite like "morning sickness" to trivialize what can be a debilitating experience in pregnancy, confined not only to the morning. Another contender for outdated terms is "geriatric pregnancy," which sounds bleak and is also oxymoronic, as you can't be ancient and fecund. We don't say, "Here's your geriatric pack of Viagra."

Female bodies have long been shrouded in mystery, and those who work in related fields continue to face stigma. In a speech Virginia Woolf gave in 1931, she said it would still be decades before women could tell the truth about our bodies. To this day, our culture and the attitudes—of both men and women—stand in the way of innovation and of how we as women relate to our own bodies. As data is slowly catching up with reality, could a burgeoning group of innovators help to plug the gap?

Vagina innovation

Let's not forget that the business world is a reflection of our culture. Think about the way we use language. Calling somebody "a dick" is commonplace, but try shouting "vagina" in a pub. A figurative fear of vaginas can be traced back to folktales of the toothed vagina, the *vagina dentata*, throughout history. This fear was central to Freud's idea that men suffer from castration anxiety. Today, many femtech entrepreneurs I've spoken to encounter what they describe as "a fear of vaginas."

We can find "vagina ghosts" haunting ancient Japanese woodblock prints. But there's no direct Japanese word for "sexual wellness," notes Amina Sugimoto, the founder of Fermata, an online marketplace for femtech products in Japan and Asia.

While dick doodles grace public bathroom walls around the world, most people can't draw a clitoris.

To begin with, words like "vagina" are tricky for many people. Just by reading the word "vagina," you may feel awkward, excited—or both. Many of the entrepreneurs echo the words of Tracy MacNeal, CEO of Materna, a company that has developed a dilator that pre-stretches the vaginal canal to make vaginal birth easier and faster: "When I first saw the product, I thought, 'Don't be ridiculous. Do I want to be the CEO of Vagina?' But then my sister said, 'You just feel this way because society has not valued vaginas.' So, I realized I have to start with myself."

Despite my liberal upbringing, I'm not immune to societal norms either and catch myself participating in them. Why do I whisper the word "period"? When asked for a period pad at work in the past, I have passed it on surreptitiously in an envelope, as if I'm dealing drugs. Gloria Steinem imagined that if men had periods, "menstruation would become an enviable, boast-worthy, masculine event," but we still have some way to go. Businesses thrive when people recommend products to each other, when we tell our friends about this new meditation app or that massage hammer we enjoy. Of course, somebody's period is a private matter, but how can a business thrive in an area most people talk about in whispers, if at all?

Our prejudice runs deep. In an experiment, researchers at a university in Colorado recruited a group of participants aged seventeen to thirty-six, who were told they were part of a study on "group productivity." They were instructed that they would be solving a problem together with another person. What they didn't know was that this other person, a woman, was part of the experiment. At one point during the task, she reached into her handbag to get some lip balm and instead fumbled out one of two things onto the table: either a wrapped tampon or a hair clip. After the task, researchers asked participants to evaluate their partner. The women who dropped the tampon as opposed to the hairclip were rated to be less competent and less likable by participants.

Privacy is one thing; shame is another. Lift one strand of shame, and you'll be pulling up a whole web of it. In a survey, Dr. Ingrid Johnston-Robledo, a researcher on body shame, has found that women who agree with the statement "I am embarrassed when I have to purchase menstrual products" were also more likely to say, "I think pictures of women breastfeeding are obscene." Sadly, they were also less likely to have the ability to advocate for their own sexual pleasure. In other words, shame about the female body inhibits sexual agency. Entrepreneurs in the sextech space face a complicated web of shame that entraps potential customers, and this, in turn, influences how they conceive of and promote their products.

At the same time, there is a huge opportunity for companies to reach people who are looking for quality information and innovative products. Two-thirds of women between the ages of eighteen and twenty-four are too embarrassed to use the word "vagina" at a doctor's office, according to a survey by Ovarian Cancer Action, a British charity. It's likely that these same women would feel more comfortable if they could seek answers through an app or a community of like-minded people.

The other issue is that there is no legacy of knowledge. Information about pelvic floors, for instance, is not typically passed down the generations together with the family heirlooms. Instead of talking openly about pelvic floor issues like incontinence, people use euphemisms. "After I gave birth, my mum would say 'Lie down,' and she wouldn't tell me why," says Gloria Kolb, the founder of Elidah, which provides a noninvasive therapeutic device for stress urinary incontinence. "It wasn't until after I started my company that I found out she had two pelvic floor surgeries herself. I asked: 'How could you not have told me any of this?' She was just like, 'Eh, you don't talk about it.'"

"Nobody tells you, right? Nobody tells you about these phases in life until you're there and you don't even know what you don't know," said Dr. Mridula Pore, CEO and cofounder of the healthcare app Peppy, at a Women of Wearables event.

"People are realizing the same things over and over in each generation, but they're not putting it somewhere in black and white," says Rob Perkins, cofounder of OMGYes. This means companies in the space have an opportunity to provide access to trusted information, at a time when people turn to Google with mixed results.

If we continue to avoid talking about female bodies, by shrouding them in mystery, we rob women of pleasure and inflict them with pain. Juliana Garaizar of angel fund Portfolia was presenting Materna's birthing device to a group of investors in Houston. Shortly before the meeting, a colleague warned her, "There is no way we can put this slide on." But Garaizar insisted. "If there is one slide we should be showing—it is this one!"

As expected, the slide caused a ripple of giggles to run through the crowd. What they were shown was a photo of a vagina torn after childbirth compared to a healthy vagina. For too long, women's pain has been ignored, from endometriosis to childbirth and breastfeeding. We can no longer let giggles get in the way of female health. It's time for Eve's curse to become a blessing.

First-person power

It was Sigmund Freud who said that clitoral orgasms are infantile, while vaginal orgasms are mature. But Freud didn't have any skin in the game. He had no firsthand experience. Over the last decades, researchers have made great strides in discovering the origins and functioning of the female orgasm, and unsurprisingly, many of these researchers are women. Just like research and art, businesses and innovation often arise out of a problem the founder has experienced and wants to solve. Whenever I speak to founders, they talk about what it is that inspired their idea. Their personal stories, the risks they take, and their motivations are what the business world refers to as "skin in the game."

Dr. Lyndsey Harper sits in front of her bed, framed by two brass lamps, as I speak to her on Zoom. "My background is that I am an obstetrician gynecologist, and so I'm treating patients for women's health issues, contraception, pregnancy, pap smears, breast exams, all things from fertility to menopause," she tells me with a bright smile and the kind of upbeat voice that always endears me to American entrepreneurs.

"When I was in private practice, a lot of my patients would share with me—especially once we had gotten to know one another, you know, maybe after a couple of babies together—like, 'Hey, I love my partner, but I don't care if we ever have sex again.'"

"And I would hear that over and over every day," she says. "I literally had no idea what to do to help my patients. and I do not like feeling that way. I asked my partners in the practice, 'Hey, do y'all patients have these problems?' They said, 'We hear this all the time'. Unfortunately, in ob-gyn training and our wider culture, we're taught to think 'Oh, join the club, drink a glass of wine, or go on vacation'—it can be very dismissive. But for me, I know these women, right, I've taken care of their pregnancies, we've been through a lot together. So, for me these answers felt like a bad idea."

Harper realized that there was hardly any research on women's sexual dysfunction. "There are urologists who spend half of their time on men's sexual dysfunction. We know all about erectile dysfunction, premature ejaculation—these things are discussed at medical conferences, and we have medications for them. The same is not true for women, unfortunately. So, once I became aware of this disparity and learned that 43 percent of women have sexual problems, I became very interested and excited about learning as much as I could about women's sexual health." It inspired her to found Rosy, a platform offering women advice on sexual health and wellness.

For Lora DiCarlo, it all began with an orgasm. DiCarlo, who has a shock of curly black hair and the eyes of a leopard, experienced what she describes as a mind-blowing orgasm. "The convulsions made me roll off the side of the bed, and I was lying on the floor just thinking, 'Okay—how do I do that again?' and I'm looking at this person and I'm like, how do I do it again *by myself*? I want this power!" She tried to find a sex toy that would re-create the experience but soon realized that what she was looking for didn't exist. She would have to invent it herself.

Many founders describe realizing that technology is out of step with their needs. "I had this moment: I was sitting at my desk, I had my laptop, my Kindle, Apple Watch, iPhone—I had all these gadgets, everything was perfect and functional," says Eirini Rapti, the CEO of Inne. But these gadgets contrasted with the internal thermometer she used to chart her menstrual cycle—it was clunky and beeped through the night. "I was like, this is just bullshit," she says. "It needs to be on par with what the rest of technology offers us." A decade later, her company launched a cycle tracking device that can read progesterone levels through a daily spit test connected to an app.

It was when Colette Courtion, the CEO of Joylux, had her first child that she "learned firsthand what women truly go through when it comes to their vaginal health and wellness. No one—not even my doctor—shared with me that every time you sneeze or jump up and down, you would pee your pants, and I was mortified to learn of this." She discovered there were very few treatment options. "And I said to myself, there's got to be a better way."

A lot of what has held female technology back in the past is stigma. It was easier for obstetricians to think "just stitch her up" instead of developing a tool that would help with vaginal tearing. It was easier to release a mere contraceptive pill for women than to get men to accept the same side effects for themselves. It was easier to ban images of female pleasure in advertising than it was to counteract the damage done by exploitative porn. And without the first-person perspectives of women who innovate in the space, there's a risk it continues to be so.

Entrepreneurs of female well-being

How can a bra save lives? Could birth ever be painless? What's the future of contraception? In an age where female bodies are still the most sexualized and the least understood, I embark on a one-woman journey to answer these questions and to uncover the most revolutionary femtech innovation.

Some people take umbrage at the word "vagina," noting that "vulva" would be more anatomically accurate. The reason I call it "vagina-centric" rather than "vulva-centric" innovation is that I would like to continue the conversation that began with the *Vagina Monologues* and carries on with books like Dr. Jen Gunter's *The Vagina Bible* and Rachel E. Gross's *Vagina Obscura*—I believe there is value in creating a unified, go-to term, rather than getting lost in labia.

I'm interested in what I think of as "entrepreneurs of female well-being." To me, this encapsulates everything to do with vaginas, but it also goes beyond the ovaries. It includes innovation that helps us recognize the symptoms of heart attacks in women, which is the number one killer of women in the UK and United States. It includes companies that playfully educate people about female sexual pleasure. It includes not only apps that support new parents but also tech that alleviates the symptoms of menopause.

My intention is to focus on solutions that are pertinent to vast numbers of women. When we address female well-being, we better the well-being of all—of families, of workplaces, and of nations.

The term "femtech" was popularized by Ida Tin, the founder of Clue, a period tracking app, and it has been gaining traction ever since. People who have never encountered the term femtech before tend to mishear it as "fintech." Others yet assume that the "fem" excludes those who don't identify as women, but that's not reflective of the companies in this space.

This innovation is not just valuable to women; it can also help gender minorities including trans men, intersex people, and non-binary people, who have vaginas; some of these products can be used by everyone. Whatever your gender identity may be, I welcome you.

Equally, no woman is the same. Some menstruate, some don't. Some want children, some don't. Some women had their uterus or ovaries removed in medical interventions. Some women have high testosterone levels. None of this makes you more or less of a woman.

Another common misconception is that femtech refers to companies led by female founders. It's estimated that 80 percent of femtech companies are led by women, according to FemHealth Insights. Most entrepreneurs in this book are women, but it's not like we're Amazonian warriors who are surrounded only by women—I believe we get nowhere without getting everybody on board.

Many femtech innovations come out of first-person perspectives, but just as it's possible to be an excellent addiction therapist without being an addict, lived experience should not be a prerequisite for working in this industry. It's about compassion, which, as Martha Nussbaum puts it, is "a central bridge between the individual and the community."

The term "femtech" does have downsides: some products are more medical than tech, like contraceptives. Others hardly feel like tech at all, such as period underwear. That's why some prefer to use "women's health innovation" as an umbrella term.

In any case, terms like "femtech" evolve and new ones arise, but female well-being will always require innovation. What began in the period tracking world has since expanded to encompass aspects of health that impact women not only *solely*, like periods, but also *differently*, like heart health, or *disproportionately*, like bone health.

Some areas of female health receive far more attention than others if we look at the number of femtech companies.

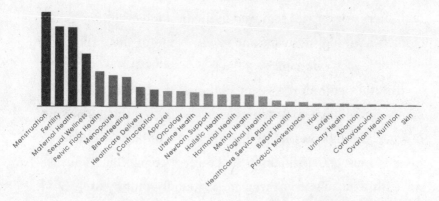

FemHealth Insights.

The diverse range of femtech entrepreneurs face stigma and censorship. They have seen it all: from being asked to demonstrate how to put on a condom to pitching panels of men whose faces turn the color of beetroot to being disinvited from conferences and banned on social media. At the same time, their ventures are far from niche, and femtech could have a market potential of $1 trillion.

In some countries, the innovation I write about is provided through public organizations, like the NHS or Medicaid, employers, or non-profits. Others are bought by consumers directly. The most powerful innovation needs to be accessible and affordable.

Many of the innovations in the space are subjective. Just like you might say, "I'd never wear an oversize lemon-yellow jacket" while I say, "I've always wanted one!" Just like some women want a delivery in a birthing pool, while others want an elective cesarean. Just as some like to meditate with an app, while others prefer to not meditate at all. At the end of the day, it's about having greater choice.

In many cases you'll have to decide for yourself: Is this empowering to me? Or is it useless? Either answer is fine, and let's not judge those women who make different choices.

I am, however, drawing some lines: I'm calling out any products that are damaging and unnecessary by design. The prime example of this is vagina cleaning and steaming products. Vaginas are self-cleaning, and unlike asparagus, they need no steaming.

There have always been, and there continue to be, companies that perpetuate and cash in on insecurities. Let's separate the "empowerment talk" from what a product actually is or does.

Technology is a tool. It can serve and it can exploit us. If societal values don't keep up with the pace of technology, the result is likely to be insidious. There's a huge difference between innovation that genuinely improves female well-being and products that reinforce and monetize women's vulnerabilities. There is, unfortunately, a long history of such products. And there is a large number of vendors who sell snake oil.

We need to be wary of anything that falls into the "pink tax" category—the classic examples are razors in pink packaging—that are sold to women at a markup price. My mother always told me to buy men's razors, which cost less and fulfill the same function. The pink tax permeates healthcare too when the painkiller ibuprofen is repackaged and sold at a higher price as "Feminax" for period pain.

For me, the definition of femtech is innovation that moves women's health forward. It's often consumer focused and digitally enabled. But I have seen people use femtech to encompass anything aimed at women, including beauty, hair removal, or even weight loss products. None of these fit my definition of femtech.

It's not that I dislike lipstick. Please. My bathroom shelf holds a pile of lipsticks as much as anyone else's. But I'm focused on health for a reason, rather than what to wear this season. What's hair removal got to do with health? Nothing. And I'm tired of having the thought "Wouldn't it be nice to lose a bit of weight?" live rent-free in my head—beauty takes on all shapes, sizes, and skin tones. The test to figure out whether something qualifies as femtech is simple: Does it advance female health?

Femtech products are as varied as their innovators. Whether they leave us feeling curious or laughing with embarrassment, they share a crucial goal: to better our understanding of female health. This goal is unusual in a business world that is still a male-dominated one. Until recently, there were more CEOs called John than female CEOs at big companies in the United States and UK. Executive boards are still populated with male names like Paul and George (but I have yet to see Ringo).

The femtech community is a powerful example of how women thrive when we support each other in business. In the femtech industry, the sisterhood is alive and ovulating. It's diverse and inclusive. It's time to draw a new portrait of the archetype of female entrepreneurship, one that does not require a deep voice or black turtleneck.

While interviewing female investors and entrepreneurs in other fields, they sometimes ask me: Why do you focus on femtech? Their first reaction is to think that focusing on femtech is another way of "keeping women in their place," of confining women to launching vagina-centric companies.

The reality is, as one interviewee put it, "If it's too vagina-related, investors clench up, but if it's too far removed from vaginas, clothes, and makeup, they're not interested either." That's because women are more likely to raise funding in "gender-congruent" fields like fashion and beauty while facing a "lack of fit" bias and less funding in male-dominated engineering and tech. Society wants women to look good; it's less interested in whether we feel well.

What's telling is that male-led ventures escape the "lack of fit" bias, as men are not pigeonholed in the same way. Consumers replicate this one-sided perception: craft beer made by women is evaluated less favorably, while cupcakes made by men are welcomed with open arms. Femtech founders therefore face two kinds of hurdles: they often operate in male-dominated fields, like condoms, or areas that are shrouded in taboos, like miscarriage.

Of course, women create and innovate across all fields. I'm very proud of the fact that my mother is an artist, that my grandmother is an engineer, that my great-grandmother was a doctor, and that my great-great-grandmother ran a small business. Of course, I believe that we should blaze trails and succeed in all parts of society. The reason I'm writing about femtech is that we urgently need more vagina innovation. One day, I hope that femtech will just be tech, but for now, we're not there yet.

A journey through the world of femtech

I am based in London. Together with New York, it's the city with the highest number of femtech companies, according to FemHealth Insights. There are about two thousand femtech companies globally. Over 50 percent of them are in the United States.

I have seen several maps that capture the geographical spread of femtech companies, and though definitions vary, the main hubs outside of the United States are the UK, Switzerland, France, Germany, India, Australia, Israel, Singapore, and Japan. My research reflects this global and diverse set.

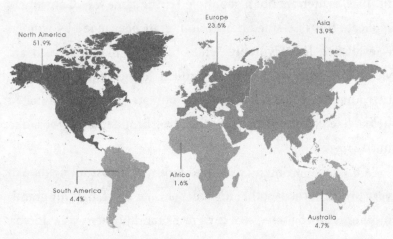

The global distribution of femtech companies.

FemTech Analytics report, 2021.

Every place has its own needs and characteristics. Laws, such as whether abortion is legal, vary by country. What is covered by the healthcare system, once again, varies by country. Regulatory approval varies by country. There's the CE Mark in Europe and FDA regulation in the United States. Some innovation is closely tied to its local context, while others swim the currents of globalization.

In the course of my research, I've come across many hundreds of entrepreneurs, researchers, medical professionals, and investors at conferences, webinars, pitches, and other industry events. In this book, I include about one hundred of them in over fifteen countries.

I am an experienced journalist, which means I chase experts with endless questions, hear what goes unnoticed, report, investigate, and dig deep to unearth stories. I am also a trained social scientist, having done a PhD on a scholarship in my early twenties, so I can interpret and evaluate scientific studies to turn them into accessible insights.

For each study or data point I write about, you can find a source in the endnotes, if you would like to delve further into a topic. Bear in mind that new evidence always continues to emerge on our health: that is the nature of scientific evidence.

My focus is on tech that connects us to ourselves and each other, rather than disconnecting us. In low-risk pregnancies, human continuity of care is just as important as good tech. In the contraceptive space, I believe we need more nonhormonal choices. When it comes to sexual pleasure, I have no interest in sex robots.

The rise of femtech is accompanied by large seismic shifts.

In the medical world, there is a reconfiguration of who holds power in the examination room between the patient and doctor, as more people than ever can access information—and misinformation—about health online. With increased information and opportunities for patients to get involved, it's more important than ever that we learn about our bodies, so that we can advocate for ourselves.

We are at an unusual juncture, as people's trust in businesses is at an all-time high, while trust in governments continues to spiral, according to the Edelman Trust Barometer. Businesses are seen as competent, and business leaders are seen as unifiers in a polarized world. Almost seven in ten employees chose their workplace based on shared values and expect their CEO to take a stand on societal issues. What we buy and where we work are conscious decisions, and businesses play a role, for better or worse. Technology can be a great force for good, but in the wrong hands, and without ethics and regulatory oversight, it can be a tool of exploitation.

In the business world, there's a shift from "shareholder capitalism" to "stakeholder capitalism." This means moving on from Milton Friedman's doctrine that the utmost priority of companies is to return money to their shareholders by maximizing profits while ignoring wealth inequalities. Instead, businesses need to consider all stakeholders—employees, customers, and the well-being of society and the planet at large. We have an opportunity to create new types of businesses.

As I work on this book, it often feels like the universe rearranges itself. At the pub, strangers tell me about their contraceptive preferences. Meetings turn into conversations about

UTIs. The minute I sit down at a café on a Sunday to finally relax, two women start to loudly talk about their period migraines. At first, I think it's confirmation bias. But over time, it becomes clear to me that the conversations around women's health are getting louder. As I listen intently to understand the experiences of friends and acquaintances, I think of Maya Angelou, who said, "I come as one, but I stand as ten thousand."

PART I

SOMETHING NEW UNDER THE SUN

1

LAUNCH

WHO ARE WE TO INTERFERE WITH MOTHER NATURE?

Any day could be the day now. My friend Daniella usually races down the roads of London like a bullet train, but over the last three months she's had to slow down. The final trimester of her pregnancy has made her feel much heavier. As we sit down for tea and banana bread on a sunny spring day, she airlifts herself into the seat.

She tells me she has prepared a birth plan, but she's keeping an open mind about how the day might go, because it's impossible to predict what happens during labor. What she knows for sure is that her priority is for the baby to be born alive and safely and that she wants her own experience to be as painless as possible.

In the prenatal classes she attended with her husband, she has noticed a preference among the group for everything natural. "It's an overcorrection," says Daniella. Birth has long been medicalized at the expense of women's own preferences, and now some people feel suspicious about any form of intervention. "Despite the fact that everything you do up to that point is enabled by technology, all of the tests and scans," she adds.

Commenting on her birth plan, she says, "It's a pretty medical affair." It includes a TENS machine, medication, and an epidural—in other words, electric currents, drugs, and anesthetics.

A bit later, I talk to my friend Emma, who is also about to give birth. She can barely keep her eyes open, says she is eating like a horse, and has five naps a day. "I am very excited about meeting my baby," she says. To prepare for the birth, she has been watching hypnobirthing videos by the Positive Birth Company. The message is that "birth doesn't have to be painful. It is a natural process, and if you understand the process and keep calm, your body will do what it's designed to do." One of her affirmations is "I can do anything for one minute," as that's how long a contraction tends to last before there's a break.

For the time she will be in labor, she plans to inhale gas and air, ideally in a birthing pool at the hospital. She wants the birth to be "as natural as possible, with minimal medical intervention, using hypnobirthing techniques." She wants to experience what birth feels like.

From where I stand, each friend's choice is fully valid for her. As I explore the world of femtech, I keep that in mind. It's always her choice.

Something new under the sun

I have been keeping an eye on a medical device developed by the California-based start-up Materna Medical. For any new medical device or drug to be sold on the U.S. market, it first has to pass several rounds of regulatory approval by the Food and Drug Administration, a federal agency of the Department of Health and Human Services—and rightly so. In this case, the device is classified as being on "de novo" pathway—in Latin that means "of new." It's the first of its kind.

If approved, this device could drastically change both the immediate experience and the long-term effects of giving birth. It can take medical devices over a decade to go from being invented to being available on the market. For femtech products, it can take even longer because the fundraising path is more likely to be rocky.

"Raising money in women's health has been hard," says Tracy MacNeal, the CEO of Materna, at the beginning of our conversation. Why is that the case? "I think the primary issue is that investors are pattern seekers," she says. Investors who analyze a company will look for examples of previous companies that have made money in the same space.

But in this case, identifying a pattern is not straightforward for a reason that is truly mind-boggling. "The last real innovation in the fundamental standard of care in childbirth was the epidural in the 1950s," says MacNeal.

The first videotape recorder was invented in the 1950s. The first commercial computer was released then too—it was the size of a room and weighed 29,000 lb. The first floppy disk would only be invented two decades later. We don't think of these inventions from the 1950s as state-of-the-art anymore—but when it comes to childbirth, we do. And by the way, the speculum with its duck beak, which is used for pap smears, hasn't changed much since the 1870s. If this was the automotive industry, we'd still be riding in a horse-drawn carriage, wearing a fetching bonnet.

Welcome to being a woman

With her flowing red hair and silver earrings made of intricate circles, I can't help thinking that MacNeal would have been considered a witch in medieval Europe, where women were persecuted for acting as midwives, for teaching the secrets of sex, birth control, and abortion. Trying to improve birth has always been a dangerous business. In the sixteenth century, a Scottish woman called Eufame Macalyne was burned at the stake for asking a witch-midwife for pain relief during labor. But I digress.

MacNeal specializes in the commercialization of medical devices. Her previous companies have focused on orthopedics and endoscopy. "Somewhat more polite conversation," she says laughing. This is her first role focused on women's health. "And it's interesting, because previously, I was never asked, 'Who are we to interfere with Mother Nature?' When people get an artificial hip, nobody's asking that!"

An engineer by training, MacNeal worked in the pharma industry before setting up her own company, "because I wanted to have children on my own terms and not have to work a big corporate job and pretend I wasn't a mom." After selling her start-up, she worked for midsize companies before rejoining the world of start-ups as CEO of Materna. "Start-ups are a hassle," she laughs. "The highs are high; the lows are low. They're relatively high risk."

At first, she was taken aback by the shape of Materna's device: it looks like a dildo. Throughout my research, I have observed that this is a common reaction. People will look at a femtech device and exclaim, "It looks like a sex toy!" when in fact, that's just the internal shape of a vagina. As MacNeal points out, "They look like sex toys because our society thinks anything going into the vagina must be for sex."

Becoming the CEO of Materna was a breakaway moment for MacNeal. "I had been worried about what my network would think if I took this job." Would she dare to become the CEO of Vagina? "I had spent my entire career pretending I wasn't a woman," she says. "And then, all of a sudden, there was just no way to keep doing that. On the contrary, I had to embrace being a woman as a strength and bring other women along."

Seeing the early results of their initial clinical trials convinced her to take on the role. "We're all on the edge of our seats," she says. "What if we could totally transform one of the highest volume procedures in healthcare? And one of the biggest transitions in most families' lives? And to think that I might have blocked myself from the opportunity to make that kind of contribution simply because I was embarrassed? That would have been awful."

Childbirth is the number one reason for hospitalization worldwide. Most hospitals have a building just for births. "I do think that women are conditioned to be a bit fatalistic about it," she says. "Well, you know, 'Welcome to being a woman! This is going to hurt.'"

I admit that growing up, I assumed that by the time I was ready to give birth, all the world's technology would stand by to support me. Instead, I listen to my friends with some astonishment as they recount giving birth with the help of technology best described as "salad forks" and "toilet plungers," also known as forceps and vacuum delivery. The forceps, by the way, were invented in the late seventeenth century.

Why is now the time to bring more innovation to childbirth? "First of all, women are having babies later," says MacNeal. What's more, babies are born larger thanks to improved prenatal nutrition. "Babies could routinely be eight to ten pounds, but mums are not getting bigger. On the contrary, our pelvises are getting smaller." The combination of these factors means it's time to reimagine vaginal delivery.

Reimagining birth

The vagina is a muscular tunnel that stretches from the vulva—which you can see externally—to the cervix, which is the bottom of the uterus, like the knot of a balloon. The cervix looks like a tiny pink doughnut, and it mainly opens to let in sperm, or let out menstrual blood, mucus, or a baby. In a relaxed state, a vagina is like a deflated parachute with the ability to stretch.

So how exactly does the device called Materna Prep work? MacNeal shows me an illustration of a baby in a uterus. "A lot of people don't know what the cervix is or where it is, but it's the bottom of the uterus," she says.

In the early and first stage of labor, the cervix dilates and effaces. "For some women it's an hour, and for some women it's three days," she says. The device does not touch the cervix, which dilates to about 10 centimeters in its own time. What the device does is it pre-stretches the birth canal while the cervix dilates. "Muscles are viscoelastic—if you stretched them suddenly, they tear, right?

"For decades, we've known stretching before and after exercise is better for them," she says. "What we're doing is that rather than having those muscles go from zero to baby, we're slowly stretching those muscles before the baby comes through the birth canal."

The device looks like a mini purple flashlight with four arms on its sides, and that's the company's intellectual property. "It's super boring to watch, because it dilates a millimeter at a time," says MacNeal. A nurse applies the device, and it dilates automatically as its arms stretch slowly to about 8 centimeters. That's not as big as the baby's head, but almost. "You need to get pretty close to the baby's head size for efficacy is what we learned."

Materna Prep

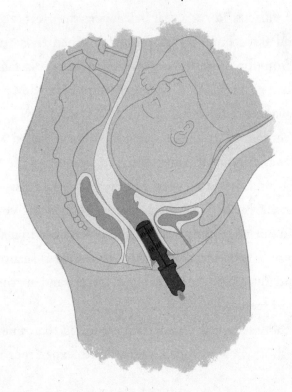

The speed at which it dilates, and the final diameter, is still being tested. Once it has dilated, the device is taken out, and the muscles in the birth canal stay stretchy for up to three hours. Once the cervix is fully dilated and the baby enters the birth canal, the second stage begins.

If approved, the Materna Prep device could shorten the time of pushing a baby through the birth canal. It could also protect the pelvic floor muscles, which support the vagina, bladder, and rectum. These muscles contract during orgasm, and they control the bladder and bowel. If these muscles weaken, it can lead to stress urinary incontinence or, worse, pelvic organ prolapse, which causes pain and discomfort and can require surgery.

What makes this device unusual is that it is preventative. The pelvic floor is "like a seat belt," explains MacNeal. The pelvic bone and muscles "form a seat belt where the urethra and the vagina and the rectum all go through." When those muscles separate from the bone, the organs they hold up can fall out of place. "I had never heard of prolapse before I joined Materna, if you can imagine; I didn't even know what it was."

The company has already created a dilator called Milli to help with vaginismus, the involuntary tightening of the vaginal muscles. It remains to be seen whether Materna's new dilator can help with birth. "The main reason I joined the company was that in our pilot study, we reduced pelvic floor injury by 60 percent, not to mention the potential to reduce C-section rates and potentially reduce the incidence of forceps and instrumental birth," says MacNeal.

What about vaginal tearing? It's estimated that nine in ten first-time mothers who have a vaginal birth experience tearing or a graze or an episiotomy. "We are collecting data on perineal lacerations," she says, using the medical term for tearing of the perineum. "Those are classified in four degrees, and we're collecting that as a secondary endpoint. Our primary endpoint is the pelvic musculature measured by ultrasound."

It has been shown that perineal massage, which aims to stretch the tissue between the vagina and anus in preparation for birth, can reduce the risk of tearing in birth.

It also decreases the need for episiotomies, which are cuts made at the vaginal opening by healthcare professionals to create more room as the baby's head appears. Episiotomies are a largely outdated medical practice. The American College of Obstetricians and Gynecologists (ACOG) issued a recommendation against the routine use of episiotomies. The persistent thought behind these cuts is that they're precise, but research suggests that natural tearing is preferable in most cases. When episiotomies are done as routine procedures, they do more harm than good: they can lead to postsurgical infection, deeper tears, long-term discomfort, and slower healing. It's an example of over-medicalization.

Not only new technology and new insights are needed but also greater education on what we already know: a supine birth position in the second stage of labor may be more convenient for healthcare professionals, but it increases the risk of birth injuries for mothers.

MacNeal has two children, who are teenagers now. "I was very much aligned to the idea that my body knew what to do. And I did not know that 50 percent of us will end up with incontinence or prolapse. And we're almost six times more likely to have those symptoms if we've had a vaginal delivery."

Women may feel too embarrassed to talk to their doctors about what's going on below the waist, "because we're taught from the time we are little girls that it doesn't even have a polite name," says the CEO of Vagina. "Part of what we're trying to do is normalize the conversation," she says and goes on to praise two other femtech companies, Elvie and Joylux, which are covered in this book.

"I think the media has been incredibly important in women's health, continuing to publish on issues of maternal mortality, racial disparities, and gender disparities, and not letting it go." As a result, investors are increasingly taking notice.

MacNeal says investors are beginning to wonder "Are we still on the bleeding edge? Are we on the leading edge of something? Am I going to get ten times my investment because I'm an early mover who sees an important trend? Will I be brilliant? Or will I be foolish?" She adds, "They're all trying to figure that out right now."

A challenging topic in a challenging place

From the beginning of life itself to near-death situations, femtech entrepreneurs blaze trails to help other women. Maria is a twenty-four-year-old Venezuelan mother of three struggling to make ends meet. Over the last three years, the price of a loaf of bread has gone up by 260 percent, as the country is engulfed in an economic and humanitarian crisis. Condoms cost half her daily wage. In her local area, hospitals are failing, and now, she needs an abortion.

In desperation, she consults someone, anyone. She is given a drink, and someone performs an abortion on her by using a hook. That night she wakes up in a pool of blood and wonders if this is how she's going to die. A story like this is not dissimilar from the stories of the women Dr. Roopan Gill has taken care of in northern Nigeria and Yemen, where she has worked as a field gynecologist. She is the cofounder of Toronto-based Vitala Global.

In Venezuela, abortions are illegal in almost all circumstances. In the absence of safe options, women turn to dangerous methods. "They go and do it with herbs or with coat hangers," Gill tells me, and I am speechless. "People are still dying from unsafe abortions, and the vast majority of the unsafe abortions happen in countries that are facing humanitarian crises," she says with both urgency and a sense of calm. Gill has the strong presence of one who is good at emergency situations, a woman who gets things done.

One in three women has an abortion in her lifetime worldwide. Each year, 111 million unintended pregnancies occur in low- and middle-income countries. They result in 35 million unsafe abortions, which can lead to complications and injuries, and an estimated 22,000 women and girls die from unsafe abortions.

There's a prevalent assumption that creating restrictive laws around abortions reduces their number, but that's a fallacy. Banning abortion only bans safe abortions.

"What ends up happening is that it increases the number of unsafe abortions," says Gill. Vitala's internal research shows that one in three women have an abortion in Venezuela, which is in line with places where abortions are legal. In other words, reducing access to abortion does not decrease the demand for abortions—it only makes them dangerous.

According to the Guttmacher Institute, unintended

pregnancy rates are the highest in countries that ban abortions
and lowest in countries where abortion is legal. In countries with
bans, the number of unintended pregnancies ending in abortion
has increased from 36 percent in 1990–1994 to 50 percent in
2015–2019.

Making abortion illegal drives up abortion rates.
Note: Rates are shown without China and India because the countries
have a large effect on the average due to the size of their populations.

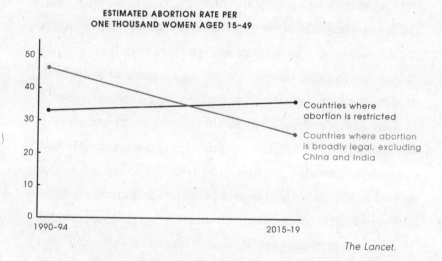

ESTIMATED ABORTION RATE PER
ONE THOUSAND WOMEN AGED 15-49

Countries where
abortion is restricted

Countries where abortion
is broadly legal, excluding
China and India

The Lancet.

Gill, who earns a living as a gynecologist in Canada, first
learned about the self-managed abortion movement when she
was working at the World Health Organization's unit dedicated
to preventing unsafe abortion. The introduction of safe and effective abortion medication—rather than only surgical abortion—
was a revolution in the space of abortion care. It was approved by
the FDA in 2000.

In 2019, Gill won a grant for innovators at the Grand

Challenges Canada, to fund abortion-related work in low- and middle-income countries. "That was my opportunity," she says. "I looked at it as seed funding."

The first app she designed, myPostCare, provided information on postsurgical abortion care for Canadian women in remote settings, focusing on diverse populations. Gill realized how powerful an app could be. "And I said, I want to do this in a humanitarian setting." This time around, her friend Dr. Genevieve Tam, also a trained obstetrician gynecologist, came on board as a cofounder. Together they set up Vitala Global as a nonprofit, "with the mindset that down the road, we want it to be more of a social business."

"Not only did we choose a very challenging topic, we chose a challenging country," says Gill. It's challenging because of the ban on abortions and the humanitarian crisis. Gill and Tam focused on Venezuela because they had connections with the nonprofits Fòs Feminista and PLAFAM, which advocate and deliver sexual and reproductive health services in the region. They also chose the country because of the population's high smartphone use. "We knew that if we wanted to do something that's related to tech and abortion, we needed to choose a place where there's a high chance that people are going to use it," says Gill.

An app for abortion

In countries where abortion is illegal, feminist groups operate underground. In Venezuela, they offer what is known as "harm reduction counseling" by providing information on what safe medical abortions entail. Could this idea of grassroots-based communication that saves women's lives work as an app?

First, Gill and her circle of local partners wanted to understand the full context. "We need to really understand what their legal and political situation is." How are women engaging with technology? What is the clandestine market like? "Everything we're building is not in a silo."

Why do the users of the app need an abortion? "It could be an older woman who already had babies, or a younger girl who's in school and whose contraceptive failed. It could be due to fetal anomalies," says Gill. There are many reasons—ultimately, the choice should be hers.

Creating their app, Aya Contigo, was an iterative process. They surveyed one thousand Latinas through social media, and the survey revealed that one-third of the respondents have had an abortion, in line with numbers in other countries, but crucially 15 percent of them have had an unsafe abortion. This was followed by qualitative interviews.

Gill knew she wanted a feminist supply chain that's local to the region. The user experience and interface designer they hired is from the Dominican Republic, their illustrator is from Colombia, and the developers are from AnnieCannons, a nonprofit that trains people who experienced gender-based violence to be software engineers. During the design process, they realized that app users want a person they can talk to behind the interface. "We've embedded a live chat support within the app and hired local staff."

On the app, users fill out a self-assessment checklist to find out whether they fit the criteria for a self-administered medical abortion. The WHO recommends medical abortions only for women who are fewer than twelve weeks pregnant.

All it takes to have a safe abortion are some pills that are inexpensive, easy to use at home, and reliable. The first pill, mifepristone, blocks the body's progesterone from supporting the pregnancy. The second, misoprostol, which is usually taken 24 to 48 hours later, causes the womb to contract and expel the pregnancy a few hours later.

Research has shown that misoprostol alone, taken in certain doses, can be used safely and effectively to end an early pregnancy in cases where both pills are not available. But the combination of mifepristone and misoprostol is the recommended regimen.

The process does not require any surgery or an anesthetic. It ends a pregnancy successfully in over 95 percent of cases, and the risk of severe, life-threatening complications is between zero and 1 percent.

The pills have been tested on a very large scale—they have been used by millions of people for over three decades—and they are not the innovation in this case. What's novel is that abortions can be made safe by providing information, access to pills, and a trusted partner to walk someone through the process on an app. It allows for privacy, confidentiality, and a measure of control over the process.

At the same time, the pills are not widely known about. The barriers to abortion tend to disproportionally impact those who are most vulnerable in society: people living in poverty, areas of conflict, or remote, rural areas.

Our hypothetical app user Maria finds out how medical abortion works. Then she is told how to get hold of the pills in her local area, without resorting to the black market, which can provide questionable medication at extortionate prices. Instead, there are organizations on the ground like Women Help Women and Women on Web that operate in a covert manner to provide the pills.

The app shows her what to look out for next. Fever lasting more than 24 hours could be a sign of a potential infection. The app shows pictures of the normal amount of bleeding to expect: the blood should not fill more than two large pads per hour for two consecutive hours. It informs her to look out for extensive pain that cannot be managed with ibuprofen and Tylenol.

If one of these complications arises, or if she wants additional peace of mind on whether the abortion is complete, the app gives her strategies on how to engage with the formal healthcare system—by saying she had a miscarriage and getting treatment that way.

In recent years, abortion rights have become more restrictive in some countries. The 1973 Supreme Court ruling *Roe v. Wade*—which made access to safe and legal abortion a constitutional right—was revoked in the United States in 2022. In Europe, Poland has introduced a near ban on abortion, and women are suffering the deadly consequences.

To find out how to access at-home abortion pills across states in the United States, visit the Plan C website. In the UK, the pills can be accessed through the NHS for up to ten weeks of gestation. In some European countries, the pills can be taken only at a clinic.

Would Gill consider expanding to new locations? "We would still want to do the human-centered design work to really understand what it is that's unique to that population," she says, "and then adapt the tool." One day, an app for abortion could be the norm.

More than a vessel

"You don't really wake up in the morning thinking, 'I'm going to talk about the things that nobody wants to talk about,'" says Dr. Tania Boler, the founder and CEO of Elvie, based in London. "My passion has not always just been around women; it's been about taboo health issues more broadly."

For Boler, the topic of taboos and their consequences is deeply personal. "My mum was adopted from Indonesia and spent her formative years in an orphanage there." It was a traumatic experience that had an impact on the rest of her life. "My childhood was dominated by quite highly stigmatized taboo issues about race, and also mental health and addiction problems. She couldn't really look after us, and then, unfortunately, she died when I was fifteen. And I think that's really impacted me," says Boler. "For me, it meant I became quite tough, I grew up far too quickly.

"But it did give me a drive, a purpose for what I wanted to do in my life," she says. As an adult, she reflected on her childhood. The stigma she felt about her mother and her upbringing, the shame she had internalized—the secrets that were a consequence—all appeared to her as what they are: socially constructed.

"It's for cultural and societal reasons that taboos exist," she says, but "fundamentally, these things are not immoral or wrong." By shining a light on taboos, we can prevent a lot of suffering. This has been the guiding principle of her career.

"I went to Oxford. I was lucky enough to go to university, and then immediately went to work in Mexico with street children." She did a PhD on whether cash grants can help to reduce the educational disadvantage of orphans in South Africa. Then, she got a job at the UN to work on access to safe abortion and HIV education—highly stigmatized issues. She says, "I think I learned a lot from working in abortion and HIV, which is relevant to Elvie."

The inspiration for Elvie's first product began at a Pilates class. "Like many women, I was very ambitious and driven," she says. When she got pregnant, suddenly everybody's focus was on the baby. "It's as if you're this vessel to carry the baby." So, when the Pilates instructor told her to do pelvic floor exercises to look after her own body, it resonated.

Once she researched pelvic floor health, "it just immediately struck something deep inside me," she says. "One in ten women needs to have this really barbaric operation post-menopause, because of pelvic organ prolapse, and all of this is preventable and treatable through exercise." Pelvic organ prolapse can have multiple causes: vaginal childbirth, hormonal changes in menopause, long-term pressure on the abdomen, aging, and genetic factors, according to the U.S. Office on Women's Health.

At first, Boler wanted to create a business based on the French government's model of providing all new mothers with pelvic floor rehabilitation sessions led by specialists. She thought of it as a service-based model and spent six months working on this idea. "I thought, 'Well, if France can do it, we can all do it too.'"

A potential business partner told her, "This isn't going to work commercially; it's going to be difficult to scale." It's an important moment to highlight. "Nobody realizes that often your first idea doesn't work out, and you have to pivot—and the pivot is a good thing." Boler speaks in a way that's confident and thoughtful.

Out of the ashes of her first idea, she decided to work on technology that can easily be used at home: Elvie's Kegel trainer.

Kegel exercises, or "Kegels," can help to strengthen the pelvic floor muscles. These exercises can be done with or without devices, which can help to gamify the process. Not all pelvic floors are equal, and it's therefore worth seeking individualized information or consulting a physiotherapist who specializes in pelvic floors.

In 2013, the idea for the Kegel trainer won her a £100,000 grant at Innovate UK. "I think it was the happiest day of my life," she says. "The crazy thing about the tech world is that as soon as you've launched, they're like, 'What's your next product?'"

Category creation

"We could have gone in different directions, right?" Boler realized just how many of the products focused on women's health are badly designed. In the end, though, the breast pump was crying out. "It's such a horrible product, and it's so intimate."

Traditional breast pumps were large, noisy, and cumbersome machines. They needed to be plugged into the wall and often required both hands. The engineers Boler hired for Elvie had previously worked at Dyson—this means they were experts at suction technology. Turning their attention from sucking dust out of a carpet, they landed on how to suck milk out of a breast.

"Often when you innovate, you choose one thing to really innovate on," she says. Confronted with the traditional breast pump's outdated design, the Elvie team made a bold move. "It's quite risky to do more than one thing at the same time in innovation. But we just felt, you know what, this product is so shitty, we need to start with a blank piece of paper." They decided to create a breast pump that is quiet, small, wireless, and controlled through an app. "Just pop it in your bra and let it go."

Elvie Stride Breast Pump

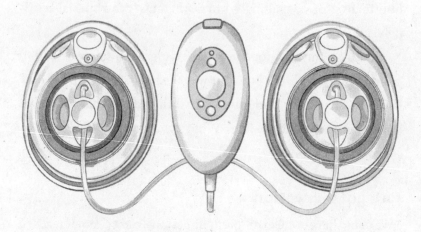

They started working on the "proof of concept"; that's a pilot study businesses conduct to determine whether a new idea can potentially work. "The key thing is to start doing a huge amount of testing with women," she says. "Breasts and vaginas are areas of the woman's body that are highly sensationalized, and there has been very little academic research."

Seven months into the design process, she attended the Consumer Electronics Show and encountered the start-up Willow, also working on a wearable in-bra breast pump. "That was like the day our heart stopped, to know that we had a serious competitor," she says. "I think it's normal with innovation; often there will be other groups around the world who've also identified a similar problem and come up with a similar vision."

What's more, because women's health has seen little

innovation, it makes sense to look at innovation in adjacent categories and transfer it to your category rather than reinventing the wheel. "Most breast pumps use a mechanical motor. We use this little, tiny thing called a piazza pump. It vibrates 10,000 times a second, and it'd been used in the medical space—and we applied that to the breast pump."

One feature of femtech is that it's difficult to sell a product to a market that doesn't know what it's missing. "We call it 'latent need,'" she says, "because women have powerful health problems, but they don't know about the problem. The solution is a bit of education before you are able to get adoption for your technology or what they call 'demand generation' in commercial terms."

What it means for femtech entrepreneurs is that they are creating new categories of products and services. "I had no idea how hard category creation is," says Boler. "It's very difficult to get the unit economics right in order to scale, because you're having to educate women about the issue. Then you need them to realize that the technologies or the cost of acquiring a customer is incredibly high."

"If you look at us as the business, it's the breast pump where our sales have gone through the roof. We're now at $100 million of annual revenue runway, which is massive." Elvie has a partnership with the National Health Service to provide pelvic floor trainers in the UK. In the United States, they designed a wearable pump at a lower price point, the Elvie Stride, which is available through health insurance. "There's always an economic case for the health systems to invest in preventative care for women."

The advice she always shares with femtech founders is "You've got to be careful about which investors you bring on board. In femtech, you need 'patient capital' [investors who work with longer time frames], because some of these things are going to take a long time. Whenever you've got category creation, it's not an overnight success."

A gradual cultural shift

Not all taboos are equal. "There are some issues within woman-hood that have been un-tabooed very quickly. One of them is menstruation. Again, it doesn't mean everyone is there yet; you always have that adoption curve," says Boler.

It would be flippant to say that all taboos in women's health can be reframed in positive terms. "Having to terminate an unintended pregnancy is incredibly hard," she says. So is having a miscarriage. Pelvic floor health is still in the shadows. "Right now, what we're beginning to see is an opening up around menopause as well. It's a gradual cultural shift, right?" Boler is an optimist because she's an entrepreneur.

For me, femtech is where business and culture meet. Boler agrees. "It still surprises me when people are like, 'Oh, why is women's health stigmatized?' Notice that we need to under-stand the oppression of the female gender and our sexuality over centuries. And it surprises me how little people understand that historical context," she says. "We still have female genital mutila-tion, a clear modern-day sign of the ongoing oppression."

"We're made to feel dirty and ashamed of the fact that we menstruate or really any touch point to do with our sexual-ity." When it comes to vaginas, sexuality and motherhood are two sides of the same coin. "I think that's why men and society struggle with the vagina: it's the source of your sexual power, but also the source of motherhood," she says.

The three ventures in this chapter encapsulate how I see femtech: it can be a novel medical device, a digital app that provides access to healthcare, or a tech company that reimagines how to address our health needs. An engineer, a gynecologist, and a social scientist are here to interfere with mother nature. Driven by taboos, they are blazing a trail for all of us.

I admit that my interest in these ventures is not purely journalistic. Rather, I want to know: What can they offer us? When I began to delve deeper, I knew I would learn more about innovation. What I did not expect was to learn a lot about my own body.

Innovations that make birth less painful, safe abortion more accessible, and breastfeeding more convenient don't exist in a vacuum: they expose the very fabric of the society we live in. I knew I needed to find out what it is that stands in the way of such ventures and what can be done.

2

MONEY

WE NEED TO TALK ABOUT INVESTORS' PROBLEM WITH VAGINAS

Financial journalists are a curious breed. Just like people consult the weather forecast, financial journalists take the temperature of the FTSE 100 or the S&P 500. They interpret the sentiments that drive demand and supply: when the price of gold goes up, it's because people might be worried about the economy. The stock market reacts to political events—it is depressed, and it rallies—so much so that journalists personify it: the market is "vibrant" or "sluggish." Sometimes, "uncertainty is weighing heavily on the market," like it might weigh on an old lady who is waiting to see if her lost cat returns. Observing the stock market means observing people's emotions about the world.

Any financial journalist meets up with sources over coffee, and then, there are press dinners. It's common to be the only woman in a room, as the vast majority of business leaders and investors are men. We'd be sitting at a place like the Hotel Café Royale in London's Soho, surrounded by gilded walls and cherubs on the ceiling. Below the chandeliers is a decidedly different sight:

a group of bedraggled journalists from all the major newspapers, with bookish tote bags and unkempt hair, loudly munching our way through three courses, while an investment fund manager stands at the front talking about the economy, accompanied by the clinking and clanking of our forks.

What exactly is investment for? Companies raise investment in order to grow. Imagine you're running a café in your neighborhood. It's going well and you're making a profit. If you want to open two more branches in other parts of town but you don't have the capital, you can ask a bank or involve another type of investor, who will give you the capital and, in return, have a stake in your company.

There are different types of investors. The managers of large investment funds, those who invite journalists to press dinners, tend to focus on large corporations that are publicly listed on the stock market, like Meta and Tesla. They're the ones who invest on behalf of pension funds, insurance companies, and banks, whereas venture capital (VC) investors tend to focus on start-ups, which have the potential to scale and create breakthrough technology.

A start-up is a company "designed to create a new product or service under conditions of extreme uncertainty," according to Eric Ries, the author of *The Lean Startup*. Banks don't tend to give loans to extremely risky ventures. That's where different types of investors come in. The first investors in a start-up business are often so-called angel investors—the term originated on Broadway, where wealthy theatergoers, who lived uptown, descended downtown like angelic beings to provide money for high-risk theater productions, saving the day for many a play.

Angel investors have the disposable income to take big risks and invest in ventures that don't take off in most cases. There's only so much money a start-up can borrow from a bank or that a founder—who isn't from a wealthy background—can put into an early-stage business, and that's where other investors come in.

Money is raised in funding rounds. As a rule of thumb, the "pre-seed" or "seed" round is the riskiest, as that's when companies are funded based on the strength of their idea, their team, and a prototype, also known as "proof of concept" or "minimum viable product." After that, the rounds are named with letters. At the Series A round, a company is likely to have some happy customers and initial revenue in what's known as "product market fit." Series B and C are for start-ups that are growing rapidly. Later rounds are for large, established start-ups that continue to scale.

After a stint as a staff writer at *Money Observer*, I made the risky decision to leave my staff job to become a freelance journalist in 2018. As a freelancer, I am my own boss, and I'm the business. I began to understand entrepreneurship on a deeper level. I write for multiple publications, and my sources and stories transcend borders, just like innovation and investment do.

The reason I'm interested in start-ups is because that's where innovation tends to happen. It doesn't happen at large, bureaucratic legacy institutions but within small and flexible teams with big ideas. Once start-ups gain traction, they are often bought by or collaborate with large companies or governmental institutions. Think of BioNTech: before 2020, it was a little-known start-up, run by a Turkish-born couple of scientists in Germany.

At conferences, the softly spoken scientists insisted that the novel mRNA technology they helped to develop could bring about a medical revolution. They were met with a room full of raised eyebrows from the scientific community. Once the COVID-19 pandemic hit, everything changed. Launching "Project Lightspeed," they received €375 million from the German government and collaborated with Pfizer to produce the world's first COVID-19 vaccine.

How does innovation get funded? There is this pervasive assumption that business is rational, that we make our financial decisions as informed and rational actors. It was only when the Nobel Prize for Economics in 2002 was awarded to two Israeli psychologists, Daniel Kahneman and Amos Tversky, that we began to realize quite how emotional and whimsical we are when it comes to finance. In their work on "Prospect Theory," they showed that people aren't always rational when it comes to money. The same people who would drive across town to save $5 on a $15 calculator, for example, are unlikely to take a drive to save $5 on a $125 jacket—even though the difference in savings is the same. Their work launched the field of behavioral economics.

While investors use a wide range of data-based metrics, they are not immune from the whims of preference and emotional attachment. They favor sectors they understand and products they want to use themselves. I recall a press dinner where the fund manager next to me extolled the virtues of a dog food company he had just invested in: it was growing, and even if the economy tanked, people would still buy food for their precious pets. When he got up from the table, his colleague turned to me and said, "You know, ever since he bought a puppy, he has been banging on about this dog food company."

Without investment, there would be no innovation. So, what happens to vagina innovation when almost 90 percent of venture capitalists are men?

The vagina pitch

To answer that question, I speak to Colette Courtion, a Seattle-based entrepreneur with a previous career at PepsiCo and Starbucks and single mother to her five-year-old son, Coleman. I ask her to tell me about the time she pitched her company to a group of investors.

"I walk into this room, and there were about thirty men, all white hair," she says. "And I said, 'I'm here to talk about vaginal health'—the looks on their faces! They turned red. They started shuffling their papers. It was a complete disaster, and I received no funding from them."

Her company is called Joylux, and its flagship product is a consumer technology device that uses light and vibration with the aim to restore vaginal tissue and strengthen pelvic floors after birth and menopause. Annoyed by the blank faces she kept encountering, Courtion made a decision. "I did something...it's sad that we had to come to this, but I had to hire a white male that looks like them."

I pull up the company's website and see the headshot of a man who is the chief financial officer. He is in his early sixties with kind eyes and a salt-and-pepper beard—the golden ticket. "That's what turned the ship for us," Courtion says. "It changed the way that these male investors perceived me because it was as if one of their own was endorsing the company." It occurs to me that Courtion literally hired herself a beard.

"I'm a very dynamic speaker. I captivate a room," she says, and I can picture it. She speaks with the efficiency of an arrow, while her hands gesture calmly, as if to soften her words in the air. But after every pitch, investors would address questions to her CFO. To them, every business plan needed the insight of another man.

Some investors would say, "Let me talk to my wife," and depending on how the conversation went, they would dive deeper. "So, they come back and go, 'Wow, my wife has this problem. I never knew. This is interesting. Tell me more.'"

Since launching her company in 2014, Courtion has raised a total of $16 million, and she has ten employees—but so far, all of the money has come from angel investors rather than bigger VC investors. "We can't get the attention of any major VCs," she says. "It's so disappointing to me, because from an investor perspective, it's such a massive market opportunity, and these men just can't pull their head out of their ass, because the word 'vagina' scares them."

Courtion talks about a range of interconnected issues from bladder function to vaginal dryness and pain during sex. But some investors have turned her down because sexual function is part of the equation. "Their concern was that it would be perceived as sexual. It was so infuriating to me that a VC would turn us down because of sexual function, when it's part of just how women function," she says with the determination of a lion; her hair makes me think of a mane.

While the proportion of start-ups founded by women world-wide has doubled to 20 percent from 2009 to 2019, the investment they receive is staggeringly low. Venture capital investors are overwhelmingly male—about 90 percent in the UK and United States. Just how difficult is it for female founders to raise money for their ventures?

What determines if entrepreneurs raise money?

I decide to contact Maya Ackerman, a professor at Santa Clara University in Silicon Valley, who conducted the world's most comprehensive study on why start-up founders successfully raise money. As we speak online, there are eight hours of time difference between us. It's close to midnight for me, so I chug two mugs of black coffee, while the Californian sun brightly paces the sky behind Ackerman.

"Most people are not born to wealth, and the fact that there are investors who are willing to believe in you and your idea is wonderful, right?" she says. "Because it gives an opportunity for people to run a business."

Venture capital determines which start-ups fail and which succeed, and therefore, it determines who gets to take a product to the market, who gets to shape our economy.

In 2021, Ackerman led a team that analyzed 48,000 companies and their founders from three continents across twenty industries.

What factors determine whether start-up founders successfully raise money? Is it because they went to a top university? Is it because they have previously run a business? Is it because they sold said business successfully, which is known as an "exit," therefore returning money to their investors? No, it turned out to be something else entirely.

The most important requirement to raising money turned out to be having a Y chromosome. "Whether or not a company is led by a guy seems to be more important than whether or not the founder went to a top school and whether or not the team had prior exits—it's crazy," says Ackerman. She is a professor who doesn't mince her words. I think the students must love her.

"We're brought up with this idea, that there's only a bit of sexism left in our society. In reality, most people don't even realize how deeply sexism runs," she says.

I bring up a common refrain from investors: there aren't enough female entrepreneurs. Ackerman agrees that investors blame it on a pipeline problem, so her team decided to analyze the average amounts that were raised.

Mixed-gender teams with a male CEO raise the most: $35 million on average. They are followed by male-only teams, which raise $22 million on average. Mixed-gender teams with a female CEO raise around $11 million, and female-only teams raise the least, with an average of $8 to $9 million. It's an international pattern.

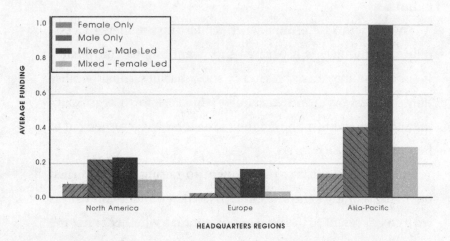

**Mixed teams can have an advantage
as long as the CEO is a dude.**

Ackerman et al., 2021.

It's not just male investors who can be sexist; women are susceptible to the same behavior. "It's about how society views gender roles," says Ackerman. "It would be incongruent with how humans work to imagine that women would magically overcome all the social influences, that only men are somehow magically susceptible to becoming sexist," she says. We all grow up in the same world. "We are constantly taught what men and women are and how we should be treating each."

Supporting this point, a 2018 study led by Professor Dana Kanze found that when talking to male founders about their start-up, VC investors tend to pose encouraging questions like: What is your aspiration? Where do you want to get to if everything is fine? Can you tell us a bit about yourself? What does success look like?

In contrast, female entrepreneurs are more likely to be asked skeptical questions like: How do you prevent people from gaming your game? What safeguards do you have against that? How long will it take you to break even? Can you talk a little bit about the competitive environment?

In other words, VCs were more likely to ask men promotion-oriented questions while asking women prevention-based questions. Of course, your business is cast in a more positive light when you get to talk about your vision and potential for success, as opposed to talking about your potential pitfalls.

This tendency does not just apply to male investors—it's equally true for female investors. Anybody can be sexist. Women are not inherently better or more moral than men. Instead, I'd say it all comes down to the culture we live in and the gender norms we choose to uphold.

The attitude toward female entrepreneurs goes some way to explain why start-ups founded by women got only 2.1 percent of VC money invested in the United States in 2023, according to PitchBook, even though it is estimated that at least 20 percent of start-ups are launched by women. It's even harder to get funding for a venture that requires investors to talk about vaginas on a Monday morning.

The bias we find in the VC world extends to more traditional forms of funding. When applying for a bank loan, female founders are more likely to be rejected. What's more, women's health innovation is not only underfunded in the world of investment but everywhere—from academic grants to government-sponsored medical research.

What can be done? "I guess my advice is not for female founders," says Ackerman. "My advice is for the investors: stop the discrimination."

Bootstrapping: When the CEO is on the customer service phone line

Crystal Etienne knew from a young age that she is an entrepreneur. There was a large apple tree next to the apartment block where she grew up. "The apples used to be all over the grass," she says. "And I thought, 'Oh, that could get cleaned up much faster if I bag them up and sell them—then people will take them away.'" Today, she sees this action of her six-year-old self as her first foray into entrepreneurship.

After a career as a business operations manager setting up four mall-based lingerie stores in New York, the idea for her current company came to her when she was lying in bed. Looking down, she noticed the wings of her period pad sticking out between her legs.

"I didn't like how it felt," she says. After drawing a picture of underwear that would keep the pad in place, she went to the Garment District in Manhattan to explore a range of materials for the pad. She decided to use multilayered material that has the capacity to absorb the same amount of period blood as two to three tampons. "I figured out a solution that would make it more comfortable for myself," says Etienne. Today, her company, Ruby Love, sells period underwear and swimwear—and no wings are sticking out.

When she launched her company in 2016, she used her savings and bootstrapped for the first three years. A self-described Type-A perfectionist, Etienne ran the business by herself for the first six months, taking on all business functions, from being the CEO to picking up the phone when people called customer service. "The company started making money immediately, so I reinvested those funds back into the company," she says.

In the first year, her company made $300,000. In the second year, it made over a million. In the third year, her company made over $10 million. "I was able to bring period swimwear to the market," she says.

Companies usually raise funds in order to scale. "I surpassed that pace, and then I needed more funds in order to keep it up," she says. After three years, Etienne decided it was time to raise money from investors. In 2019, she raised $15 million for her company, the fourth largest investment round ever raised by a company founded by a Black woman in the United States.

I ask Etienne if anything surprised her along the way.
"Nothing surprised me," she counters with a smile, "besides the
fact that the company grew so quickly." I make a mental note to
emulate her confidence next time I'm giving a talk.

I tell Etienne that I have mixed feelings about how female
founders should engage with the data we have on fundraising. On
the one hand, I think it's crucial for us to analyze data to disman-
tle the structural barriers that exist in society. On the other hand,
emphasizing this kind of data can discourage people from trying
to succeed. (I'm glad I never cared about my statistical chances of
becoming a journalist in London.) Entrepreneurs need optimism.

Etienne echoes this sentiment. "The data needs to be there
because it is troubling, and at the same time, if you pay attention
to that, some people don't have strong personalities, and it will
bring them down, like, 'Oh, I can never do it. Or I'm not going
to get it.' And I just think that that's a bad way of thinking. So, I
would say: ignore the data."

What does she think needs to happen so that more women,
and women of color in particular, can set up their own companies? "I don't think it has anything to do with color," she says. "I
think it just is women or people in general. You just need to think
of a problem and a solution. And if you go into it with the right
mind and the right heart, when you realize that it can scale—
that's when you have a big vision."

As we speak, I realize just how important it is for founders to
have a large dose of confidence and faith in themselves and their
idea. To launch a business, they need to believe—and convey
to those around them—that what they have in mind is not only
possible but worth it.

There are two views: the systemic and the individual. The way I think of it is as having two contrasting notes in my pockets: the first note represents the data discrepancies that reveal societal sexism and racism. The second note shows me the success stories, the solutions—it represents optimism and confidence—and it's this note that energizes me. It's optimism that propels entrepreneurs forward.

Etienne successfully bootstrapped her start-up, and by the time she was raising money, her business was hugely profitable, so she had her pick of investors. In conversations with femtech founders, I have come across two more strategies founders have used to successfully raise money for vagina-centric businesses:

- **LEAN ON DATA:** Founders move their business case away from personal experiences to data-driven pitches. Afton Vechery, cofounder of San Francisco–based Modern Fertility, paid for surveys before fundraising, to be able to show investors that there is a need for her venture. Kate Ryder, the founder and CEO of New York–based Maven Clinic, conducted focus groups.

- **LEAN IN TO TALKING ABOUT VAGINAS:** Lora Haddock DiCarlo, who founded an Oregon-based sex toy company, makes sure to say the word "vagina" as much as possible. "My best advice is to absolutely dig your heels in and know that what you are doing is amazing." And what if it makes investors blush? "The purpose of my company is literally to destigmatize sexuality and masturbation, particularly for women. So, if you don't like the word 'vagina,' then you're not going to be very comfortable for the rest of your life, because this is the direction society is going in."

Researchers at the Kauffman Foundation found that women-led teams generate a 35 percent higher return on investment. Researchers at the University of California, San Diego, and the California Institute of Technology found that female-led start-ups were more likely to go public and about 7 percent less likely to fail. There is a strong business case for investing in female-led start-ups. What it takes is for us to reimagine our ideas about entrepreneurs.

Records on spikes

It may seem as if the business world has long been "a man's world," which is now, slowly, opening up to women. But is that actually the case? My knowledge of art history tells me that artists like Berthe Morisot—who was one of the founders of Impressionism and hugely acclaimed and financially successful in her time—were subsequently written out of history. I wonder if the same has happened to women in the world of business.

I join a group of female historians at the Economic History Society, who have sat in wood-paneled libraries, gingerly looking through old business records. To uncover the history of women in the business world, researchers look for documents at archives that have thus far been overlooked. Some of these records are still speared on spikes; other records are presented on large parchments, rolled up like giant sausages, covered in ashes and soot from World War II.

As I listen to these historians, I realize that they address the same questions I'm exploring now: How did women get capital? How and why did they run their businesses against the odds? I'm not sure if this is amazing or depressing. The history of women in business doesn't exactly replicate itself, but it continues to rhyme.

While many women historically ran smaller fashion, textile, beauty, or laundry businesses, there are examples of women at the top of unexpected fields in the decades beginning with 1820: Madame Saget in Paris was an engineer whose company was given a government contract to set up oil-powered streetlights across Paris. Julia Ridgeway in Albany, New York, ran the biggest plumbing business in the region, proudly featuring her name as the "Proprietress" in bold letters on advertisements. Elizabeth Gold, who ran a large plumbing and glazing business, was in charge of getting the pipes of Sydney, Australia, fixed. Rebecca Lukens headed up a steel manufacturer in Pennsylvania that became the nation's leading producer of boilerplates under her leadership.

Over the last few years, the history of women in business has experienced a renaissance. In groundbreaking research, historians at Cambridge University found that in the nineteenth century, some 30 percent of British businesses were run by women. The actual figure might be even higher.

Not much was known about female investors in the eighteenth and nineteenth centuries until a group of historians led by Professors Janette Rutterford, Josephine Maltby, David

Greene, and Alastair Owens unearthed British shareholder regis-
ters from the last three centuries.

What they found was astonishing. Despite being excluded
from male business networks, when Britain became "a nation
of shareholders" in the eighteenth century, women were active
investors right from the start. The proportion of female shareholders was 15 percent in 1870 and tripled to 45 percent by
1935.

Looking at company records of that time, I'm struck by
the fact that businesses proudly proclaimed their investors
were women. In the United States, the American Telephone
and Telegraph Corporation boasted that most of its shareholders were women by 1920. The chairman of a London-based
dog biscuit manufacturer stated at the firm's annual general
meeting in 1903 that out of 1,482 shareholders, there were "585
ladies," who were serious "investors and who were therefore,
as a rule, preferable to those who bought the shares merely as
speculation."

I remembered the investor I met at a press dinner who
invested in dog food after buying a puppy. Were these Victorian
women, whose socioeconomic circumstances allowed them to
invest in a dog biscuit company, also likely to have a dog? I put
this question to Professor Jane Hamlett, who does research on
animals in Victorian Britain. "Yes, it's likely that these women
might have been dog owners—dog ownership was fairly
common in this period. People from all social groups owned and
were attached to dogs, but wealthier people with more resources
did have more capacity to keep dogs, as they could be expensive
and needed space."

Does that mean Victorian women were more likely to invest in products they wanted to use? "Oh yes," Rutterford says. "It was the age of conspicuous consumption, so they liked brand names and things they understood." They had a preference for companies with a local presence. They invested in Lipton tea and the drugstore Boots. I'm certain they would have liked to invest in femtech too.

While women have always invested in companies, two discourses have been used against us. The first emerged in the eighteenth century, claiming that women were speculative and emotional investors. After all, Fortune, the fickle goddess of commerce, is a woman.

By the twentieth century, the discourse turned to framing women as cautious investors, due to our "nesting instinct." This view still prevails today. Financial commentators claim that women are risk-averse, as if that's inherent. It's encapsulated by the idea that Lehman Brothers would never have collapsed during the financial crisis had it been run by Lehman sisters.

In reality, women are not inherently risk-averse when it comes to investing. If men were paid less for doing the same work, held fewer positions of power, and had a "second shift" of domestic work with childcare and elderly care, they'd be more risk-averse too. The surprising history of female investors shows us that women have always been keenly involved in the world of business. It's worth remembering this, so that women can become confident investors once again.

The rise of femtech funds

Over the last decade, a small group of pioneering women have set up novel investment firms. In 2013, Trish Costello set up Portfolia, a network of angel investors, in Silicon Valley to bring more women and more diverse investors to the market. Her motto is simple: "If women want specific companies in the world that address their needs, the only way to do that is for women to become the investors." In 2018, the network launched the world's first femtech fund.

Since then, more femtech funds have emerged. Alice Zheng is a VC investor at RH Capital in San Francisco, a fund that focuses on tech innovation in reproductive and maternal health. "It is fun being at the forefront," she says. "It's such a nascent field." Zheng is a trained doctor with an MBA, but what I find equally revealing is that for three years in college, she performed in *The Vagina Monologues*, the groundbreaking play written by Eve Ensler in 1996.

At RH Capital, she invests in early-stage femtech start-ups she describes as "digitally enabled and consumer focused." It is an impact VC fund, which means they look for companies that can help underserved groups while being profitable businesses. RH Capital has a sister nonprofit providing programs for start-ups on how to, for example, work with Medicaid, the U.S. government program that provides health coverage to people with low incomes.

Funds that invest in women's health innovation specifically include Steel Sky Ventures, Amboy Street Ventures, Avestria Ventures, and Coyote Ventures, as well as the philanthropic investment portfolio The Case for Her. These funds are pioneers because they have the expertise and enthusiasm to invest in companies that can then attract venture from more general, bigger funds and institutions.

Combined, such femtech funds have invested hundreds of millions of dollars. It's an encouraging development. But the figure is dwarfed by the billions invested by crypto-focused funds. Given the numbers—and given it might take 268 years to close the economic gender gap worldwide—we cannot wait for femtech investors to power the industry or for female investors to reach parity. We need to get everybody on board.

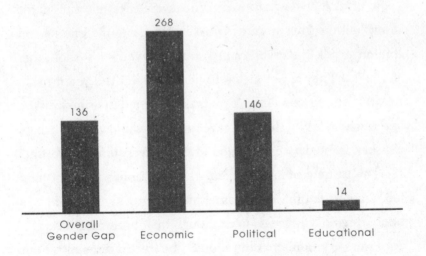

Our great-great-great-grandchildren might close the gender gap in 136 years, according to current trends.

World Economic Forum.

To bring innovation to vaginas, women who are in male-dominated VC firms, and men who lead funds, need to turn their attention to female well-being. I set out to find them.

From "one of the guys" to a
woman who represents women

Lizzy Goldman is a charismatic young woman who began her
career as an equity trader at Morgan Stanley on Times Square.
"On the trading floor, there were some women, but there was
still this feeling that you're constantly surrounded by men," she
says. "So, when you are the only woman, how are you supposed
to behave?

"In some ways, I think I did this incorrectly at first, because
I was more junior and new to having a career. My response was
'Okay, try to be one of the guys'—but at some point, you feel so
not like yourself, it feels inauthentic to who you are.

"I know it's a silly example, but I'm a big vodka soda girl. I
could drink it all day," she says. Whenever her team went out for
drinks, all the guys ordered whiskey. "If you're the one person
drinking vodka, everybody makes fun of you—it's 'shoot-the-
shit jokes.' They're not meant to be offensive." And yet, it made
her feel like she stood out. "Eventually, I started to drink whiskey
and thought, 'Why should I have to drink whiskey? I really hate
whiskey.' I would have to *inhale* and *exhale* every time I took a sip."

The turning point occurred when she applied for her next
job. "I got a job offer at the same time as a guy I know, and I was
offered significantly less," even though their professional experience was very similar. "Why should I be treated differently? I'm
the same as everyone," she thought. "I tried to justify it in all
these different ways. I really didn't want it to be because I am a
woman that I was being offered less. But deep down something
was saying I can't ignore it, even if I don't want it to be the case."
It took her two years to come to terms with what happened.

She accepted a different job offer and now works for Olive Tree Ventures in Tel Aviv, which focuses on digital health and invests in companies in the United States, Europe, the Middle East, and Asia. How does she see being a female investor in a male-dominated field now? "I think there are two ways to handle it, and I've gone through both ways. One way is to say, 'I'm just like everybody else. Why do people expect me to behave differently? I don't want to represent 50 percent of the population. Why do I always have to fight for something?' and I think until this year, that was more of my approach.

"And now, I view it as empowering to say, 'Wait a second, I can represent, and I can fight to create some form of change.' I love finance and I love investing, but it's not an altruistic profession, right? It's something you do to make money either for yourself or for your investors. I've always viewed it as something that would allow me to give back in different ways." She exudes a combination of warmth and natural authority.

Over the last few months, Goldman has been researching the femtech space to look for investment opportunities, and she says, "There could be a diamond in the rough." I can hear the excitement in her voice.

She doesn't think femtech will be dominated by one player, like Amazon, which dominates book sales. Healthcare, in general, is moving toward personalization. She says there could be multiple companies with "significant market share because women need such different things at different times in their lives, depending on the type of woman you are and what your demographic is.

"Women just have embarrassing things happen to us, and

health conditions we didn't know existed. You don't want to put it into Google, or you have to go on a private browser." She observes that there are many community-based companies in the space. "We really need a place to talk.

"Anecdotally, I discuss this all the time with my fiancé. He eavesdrops on me and my girlfriends talking, and when they leave, he's like, 'Why do you care so much about each other's lives?' Then, I eavesdrop on him and his guy friends talking—they don't need to talk about periods or sex, because it's all so obvious to them, everything just works in one way—even headaches!

"Whereas women might have chin hairs growing in, because you put an IUD in, and you don't know why that's happening. Or you might have really big boobs, so that seatbelts are uncomfortable, or you're a runner and don't know what sports bra to wear. There are so many options here." Then she says, laughing, "I'm mostly surprised that they don't care more about each other's lives—I think we do it right."

When I first speak to Goldman, she has identified a femtech company she is interested in as a potential investment, but she hasn't told her bosses yet. We brainstorm how to broach the topic of vaginas. I recount the two strategies: lean in to saying "vagina," and present data-based arguments.

The next time we speak, she says, "I did it yesterday—I finally brought it up!" Her two bosses are men in their fifties. "They have kids and wives, which I think makes it easier," she says. "As I was talking about a vaginal insert, I was looking everywhere but my bosses' eyes.

"Based off our last conversation where you gave me ideas as

to how different women approach talking about vaginas, I just leaned into it, and I think, if I can get over it and talk about it more, my bosses will also get used to it. I don't think I created the problem, but I can help to normalize the words around the sexual wellness field.

"And I also think, as there are more sexual wellness-specific companies, or LGBTQ+ companies, mental health companies, anything that would have historically been stigmatized— everything is becoming destigmatized together."

We end the chat by both saying, "I hope so." I leave the conversation feeling encouraged. Given that women are still a minority in the investment world, it's paramount for male investors to put their weight behind the topic of female well-being. I decide to speak to those who are leading the way.

Bros who invest in femtech

In 2020, the company Ohne, which produces eco-friendly period products, caught the attention of Antonio Miguel, a young man who is the managing partner of Maze, a European social impact venture capital fund based in Lisbon.

Miguel has researched the femtech space and says, "There is a lot of unfulfilled market potential, when 50 percent of the population is not served according to their needs. There's a very strong business rationale."

He recognized the extent of the taboo around fertility, periods, and menopause. "To me that was a realization. I thought I live in a nice bubble, where people talk about everything, and very quickly, I realized: I knew nothing. And if I'm privileged—I have a great education, I have a job—and I know nothing, can you imagine the long tail of people who have no idea?"

In addition to reading up on the taboo around menstruation, Miguel decided to conduct a small experiment in WhatsApp groups of friends and acquaintances. He put together a paragraph describing his professional interest in eco-friendly tampons and posted it in a group of men. "It's crazy, because when I shared it in male groups, they were like, 'Let's not talk about this. Let's talk about football or something'—a cliché!" he laughs, his hands flying up momentarily.

Then, he shared it in groups with men and women, saying, "I'm thinking about investing in eco-friendly tampons. What do you think?" A female friend would say, "Oh, that's super nice." And then men would pipe up and say, "Come on, Antonio. Why are you looking at that? There are so many more prominent problems to resolve. Why are we even talking about it?"

Then, he'd share it in a group with female friends. "What happened was that the engagement was huge, and sometimes the women in those groups who were not very vocal started sending me direct messages about it. 'Oh, this is super cool. You should also look at this' or 'A friend of mine has endometriosis' or 'Oh, I follow this Instagram page,'" he says. "If I were a woman, I would better understand it from the get-go. But you know, that's been an interesting test."

This combination of an overlooked market, taboos, and engaged consumers means "you actually have the opportunity to create disruptive models and disruptive brands," he says. "And I have to confess, I love the thesis of investing in businesses that I hope make life better for my daughter."

Given that the entrepreneurial system is skewed against female founders, Miguel and his team have come up with a way of being more inclusive. "At the partnership level, we're three white males, which is something that needs to change, but we also need to better our approach," he says. "We've done some work internally to understand how we can be better."

- **TRACK INTERACTIONS WITH FEMALE FOUNDERS:** Every investment fund has a list of companies they are reviewing, the pipeline. Maze tracks whether the companies they have conversations with have a female founder.

- **FIND NEW NETWORKS:** They deliberately reach out to networks beyond their organic range to broaden the top of the funnel. They are aware that three white males would otherwise attract "a pipeline of other white males, who are part of circles of males."

- **MAKE PITCHING ENJOYABLE:** They have researched what an ideal pitching scenario is for female entrepreneurs, and it includes having other women in the room. The pandemic has shown that pitching a business online, rather than in person, is also seen as a positive development, because female founders feel under less pressure to think about what they're wearing.

- **DON'T SAY YOU'LL ASK YOUR WIFE:** The investors at Maze avoid the attitude that female entrepreneurs have so often described to me as "The *When Harry Met Sally* moment"—where investors say, "I asked my wife, and she doesn't have this problem." Even if we assume the wife is telling the truth, investors do not normally use one person as a benchmark for a whole market—so that shouldn't be the case for femtech either.

- **VALUE CONFIDENT WOMEN:** They are aware that people tend to be biased against women who are confident and assertive—which is seen as an important quality in a business leader—so they actively counteract this bias.

What's the result? The first nine companies Maze invested in only had one female founder, whereas the next ten companies they invested in had six female founders. Now, they invest in female-led companies in everything from software to femtech. Miguel says, "It speaks to the exercises that we've been doing internally to make sure that we broaden the scope."

It's time for the majority of investors to stop cockblocking the space.

A change in Silicon Valley

In conversations with start-up founders who talk about their trips to Silicon Valley, I learn that the office buildings are set back from the main road, seemingly unattainable, that the architecture of VC firms is meant to make you feel small. Founders are put through a series of challenges, and it sounds like Dante's *Inferno*. I picture the door to Peter Thiel's Founders Fund as Auguste Rodin's monumental bronze sculpture *The Gates of Hell*.

With that image in mind, I arrive at Palo Alto in the heart of Silicon Valley. This is the place where groundbreaking tech companies are famously launched out of garages, ever since Bill Hewlett and David Packard founded HP in a garage in 1939. The garage lore of the Valley was solidified by Steve Jobs, Steve Wozniak, and Ronald Wayne of Apple as well as Larry Page and Sergey Brin, who launched Google out of Susan Wojcicki's garage.

Throughout the ages, enigmatic cities have vied to be the centers of innovation and commerce. From Venice in the Middle Ages and Amsterdam's Golden Age to Calcutta during the Bengali Renaissance to today's global cities. Places where new ideas are born have dazzled visitors with their urban architecture and cosmopolitan crowds.

Venice is "the most triumphant city I have ever seen," wrote the diplomat Philippe de Commynes in 1495. On the Rialto Bridge, he could see people from everywhere in the world, each dressed in their own way. Amsterdam was an "inventory of the possible," said the philosopher René Descartes in 1631, a place where he found "all the commodities and all the curiosities one could wish for."

Driving through Silicon Valley with my friend Jess, we stop at an intersection, and I excitedly point at a sign for Sand Hill Road. It's the central artery of the investment universe. Sand Hill Road is to the world of start-ups what Wall Street is to bankers, Broadway to musical actors. Jess says, "I don't see anything."

And really, there is not much to see. Sand Hill Road is a multilane road with block buildings hiding behind hedges and palm trees. It's a suburban sprawl. We spot exactly one pedestrian. This is when I realize why Google and Apple were founded in a garage: there is not much else here.

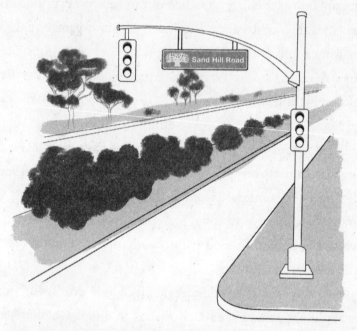

A few days later, I have a meeting in the lion's den, a VC firm in Silicon Valley. There is no good option for me to get there on public transport, so I order the most basic Uber. Within a few minutes, a Tesla glides silently toward me. It drops me off outside of a Spanish-revival-style mansion housing multiple firms. I make my way to Lux Capital. I expect to enter through The Gates of Hell, but all I find is a heavy office door.

I'm asked to wait inside the front lobby. The coffee table is decked out with quaint objects, a troupe of toy robots, a silver plane model. On the wall, there are vintage posters envisioning the future of NASA travel with a grand tour of Jupiter, Saturn, Uranus, and Neptune. I am pleased to see a large collection of books on inventions, physics, science, and one called *Getting Smart*.

Change is afoot. Silicon Valley has indeed been getting smarter. While I am working on this book, a small group of women have joined the world's most powerful venture capital firms, and they have begun to channel unprecedented amounts of money into women's health innovation.

In 2021, Maven Clinic, which offers virtual care focused on women and families, raised $110 million in its Series D round—the largest deal on record in the space—making it a unicorn. The mythical creature has come to stand for privately held start-ups that are valued at over $1 billion. I want to know more about this generation of female investors who are driving the change.

I'm here to meet the investor who co-led the $110 million deal. Deena Shakir, who is the only female general partner at Lux Capital, comes out of her office to meet me. She is easily the most stylish person I have met all year. We walk out into a court-yard, where we sit at a round table in the shade of a coast live oak tree and talk as brown acorns occasionally drop around us, like echoes of Newton's apple.

Healthcare is not a sector Shakir expected to specialize in, although she does come from a family of physicians. It was during her time at Google that she first encountered innovation in the healthcare space. "I started meeting amazing entrepreneurs who were building these companies with bootstrapped funds that were doing more than my team of 750 people," she says. "It hit me that real innovation in this space was unlikely to come from within big tech, although it might happen in partnership with big tech.

"During this period of working and exploration, I had two children of my own and two very complicated pregnancies and deliveries." She almost died in childbirth twice. "And I was in the heart of privilege, having access to the best healthcare and resources," she says. It led her down a rabbit hole of research on how dysfunctional the maternal health system is, "the Black maternal health crisis and the disaster that is women's health more broadly.

"I recognized how unbelievably underfunded it was, not only within the context of venture capital, but even within research and development in clinical trials. It was just incredibly unfair, and it was illogical. And from a business perspective, it made no sense. Not only do women represent half the population, but also 80 percent of the decisions and dollars that are made in healthcare."

Some might wrongly assume that the total addressable market for IVF is small, given that only a small percentage of people have IVF treatments. But, as Shakir points out, "It's not because a small percentage of people are suffering from infertility. It's because there are so few places to get access. There's a misperception that it's a 1 percent problem, whereas it affects families of color more in some cases."

What Maven Clinic provides is a comprehensive range of healthcare services online. When Shakir first met Kate Ryder, the founder of Maven Clinic, she says, "We bonded over our labor experiences." But while her personal experience helps her win deals, Shakir makes a distinction between that and making the case for a women's health company to her investment partners. To show that there's an urgent unmet need, she actively nourishes a network of large employers, insurance companies, and pharma companies. "This is clearly something they are asking for," she says.

For femtech to become more mainstream in the eyes of traditional VC investors, the category still has to prove itself. "We're still betting on a future that hasn't happened yet," she says. "We need to see those big public offerings, those big M&A [mergers and acquisitions], these really valuable generational companies that can pave the way for future ones to come." Investors often say more "exits"—companies being acquired or going public—will bolster the case that femtech companies are a category worth investing in.

Investor expectations

As a writer, I can cover whichever company I find interesting. If I were a VC investor, my choices would be much more limited.

When investors put money into a business, the returns they expect to make vary by fund and are typically not made public. As a rule of thumb, VC investors who write checks at the pre-seed stage expect more of these companies to fail. Let's say if one in ten companies succeeds, then that winning company needs to return a very high multiple, ideally 100 times, on its investment to cover all the potential failures. For investors involved in later stages, businesses become less risky, but the return potential of a "home run" also decreases. Series A investors might be looking for a 10 to 15 times return, and later stage investors might aim for 3 to 5 times.

For that reason, only a few companies are potential candidates for VCs—given how prominent venture capital is, it is astonishing to know that only 0.25 percent of companies receive venture funding. Yet these companies have an outsize impact on the American economy: since 1974, 42 percent of companies to go public have been venture-backed, and according to some estimates, venture-backed companies account for 85 percent of research and development spending—the driving force behind innovation.

Investors only consider companies that have the potential to grow exponentially. For this reason, they are attracted by markets that already have unicorns in them.

"We have Maven and Kindbody, who have proven that it is a real investment space," says Leslie Schrock, who is an angel investor, advisor, and the author of *Fertility Rules*. Commenting on what makes companies promising for investors, she says, "They're building platforms, they're not building point solutions. If a company is only focused on one tiny thing—and there's no plan to expand horizontally within a big enough market—that's not a good investment."

What needs to happen for more funding to flow into women's health innovation? "We need even more success stories," says Halle Tecco, an entrepreneur and angel investor, who cofounded Rock Health, a seed fund focused on digital health. "We're already starting to see great value coming from companies in this space. The more these companies grow and succeed, the easier it will be for everyone else to fundraise. We also need investors to realize that women's health is a ginormous opportunity. It is simply not a niche!"

In 2023, women's health companies received 4.3 percent of the total venture capital invested in health-focused companies, according to PitchBook. It's a small percentage, but a 59 percent increase from the previous year.

It's clear that the sector needs more VC funding, but given the specific return expectations and time frames that come with this money, we need to go beyond funding models that rely on VC, including more government funding and philanthropic grants, depending on the start-up.

Femtech has half the global population as target customers. It has a market potential of $1 trillion, according to FemHealth Insights. This makes women's health innovation a trillion-dollar taboo. But what is undeniable is that change is slowly underway.

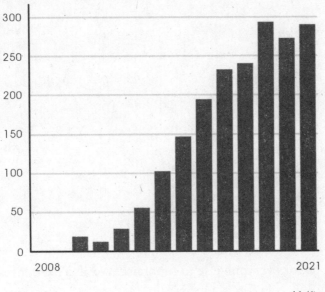

Number of FemTech Deals

McKinsey.

Commenting on the femtech movement, Alice Zheng says, "I think that the movement has really elevated the conversation in general for women's health." As funding is slowly catching up with reality, I find out how research can do the same.

3

RESEARCH

COULD A BRA SAVE YOUR LIFE?

It's a crisp October morning in Chicago as Professor Nicole Woitowich steps out of a busy commuter train. Even in the morning, Michigan Avenue is a high street bustling with people, but she doesn't mind cutting through the crowds as she makes her way to what she knows is going to be a lecture that changes the course of how science is done. Coffee in hand, she marvels at the fact that not too long ago, she was a graduate student and now she is the professor.

Northwestern University's Feinberg School of Medicine is just a stone's throw away from Lake Michigan in a modern building with a curved glass exterior, next to the Gothic home of the law school. A cold wind blows over from the lake as she enters the building. Woitowich begins the lecture by asking her students to design an experiment. "You are the research team who is tasked with creating the COVID-19 vaccine," she tells her group of fifty graduate students. Who's going to be in the study? And which variables will make a difference?

"It matters how old they are," one student responds. "Their sex and gender," says another. "Race and ethnicity." Many of the students work with animals and cells, so "their weight and size" comes up soon. "Do they have a history of illness?" "Are they allergic to anything?"

"All of these things matter," says Woitowich, nodding with encouragement.

But once she presents the next slide, the room echoes with a collective gasp. It shows a list of the major Covid vaccines, and their Phase I and II trials, which determine a drug's effectiveness, safety, dosage, and side effects—and none of the major vaccine trials analyzed their data by sex.

"They're surprised because they're thinking, 'Oh, these are things I would do!'" Sex is an obvious variable the graduate students would analyze if it were their task to design the research. "Guess what! That's not what's happening here," says Woitowich, who is direct and down-to-earth.

Why does this matter? "When we think about sex differences, we think of breast cancer versus testicular cancer," says Woitowich. But men and women experience many diseases differently, including COVID-19. "Biological sex influences our immune system," she says, as men are more susceptible to infection because women can mount a greater immune response. It's an evolutionary underpinning of female biology. "We have a stronger immune system during childbearing ages to protect the survival of the species," she says. "But on the flip side, because of that higher level of immune protection, women are upwards of three times more likely to develop autoimmune conditions."

There's more. "I see scientists confuse the words 'sex' and

'gender'," she says. Sex, she explains, refers to "biological attributes associated with physical and physiological features including chromosomes, gene expression, hormones, and anatomy, usually characterized as male or female." Meanwhile, she continues, gender is "a social construct that associates certain behaviors, roles, expectations, identities, and values with being a girl, boy, man, woman, or a gender diverse person. It is not a binary, and it is not static." Therefore, sex is biologically defined, while gender is socially constructed. She emphasizes, "It's important to use these correctly, and most students tend to know this."

However, she has noticed that older generations of scientists prefer to say "gender" because they consider "sex" to be a bad word. I have observed the same tendency. We say "gender-neutral bathrooms" when we mean "sex-neutral bathrooms." We ask, "What's the baby's gender?" when we mean the baby's genitals. In the world of science, the distinction is ever more important, because like race, ethnicity, and socioeconomic background, sex and gender can each lead to different health disparities.

Just like sex, gender also influences our health. Noise-induced hearing loss is more common in men, because they are more likely to work on construction sites. In cultures where women cook over woodburning stoves, they tend to have more lung damage than men. "Women are traditionally the caregivers," she says. "And if you're taking care of a lot of people in your family, you may deprioritize yourself and put others first."

At the end of the lecture, Woitowich wants her students to use the terms "sex" and "gender" correctly, to always report the sex of their cells or animals, to justify any single-sex studies, and to analyze and report the sex differences in their data.

Afterward, students email her saying, "My lab doesn't do this. How do I talk to my boss about starting to do this?" There is hope that the next generation of scientists is better informed than the current one. But why is something most graduate students consider common sense not the norm to begin with?

Protecting women from rather than with research

Clinical trials, as we know them today, are relatively new. The core idea traces back to 1747, when the Scottish physician James Lind set out to cure scurvy in sailors. He divided twelve sailors into two groups—a "treatment group" and a "control group"— and gave lemon juice to only the treatment group. It proved to be an effective remedy.

The idea of clinical trials gained ground in the twentieth century. In 1928, in London, Alexander Fleming discovered the bacteria-fighting power of mold. He named it penicillin. Ernst Chain, Howard Florey, and Margaret Jennings found a way of purifying it so that it could be used to treat bacterial infections. But the British industry did not have the capacity to commercialize penicillin, so scientists took it to the United States, the world leader in medical innovation. The development of penicillin was accompanied by clinical trials, and in the 1960s, the FDA actively promoted its use.

It was a series of tragedies that led to the categorical exclusion of women from clinical trials. In the 1950s, the German drug thalidomide was widely used to treat nausea and morning sickness in pregnant women across Europe. Scientists did not realize that a drug could pass through the placenta to reach the fetus, and in the case of thalidomide, no tests were done on pregnant women. It's estimated that the drug led to severe birth defects in over 10,000 babies. In the United States, there was a parallel tragedy of diethylstilbestrol, which caused harm to pregnant women and their babies.

It's understandable that regulators wanted to protect women and children. In 1977, the FDA's *General Considerations for the Clinical Evaluation of Drugs* stated: "Women of child-bearing potential should be excluded from the earliest dose ranging studies." However, the guidelines also said women could be included if there was "adequate information on efficacy and relative safety" in earlier studies—but this second part was ignored by the research community. The decision to protect women *from* research came at the cost of protecting women *with* research.

The guidelines were "widely misinterpreted to mean exclusion of all women from all clinical trials and undoubtedly contributed to their inadequate representation or exclusion in many clinical trials conducted thereafter," according to Ameeta Parekh, a senior adviser at the FDA.

But I wonder whether it was "misinterpreted" or whether it was simply an interpretation of convenience. Women were thought of as more complex trial participants. Our fluctuating hormones could "mess up" otherwise neat results. Including only male participants in trials saved costs and increased a drug's probability to succeed. Rather than requiring drug developers to pay more up front to run equitable research, women continue to pay for the consequences down the line.

In 1993, the FDA decided to reverse its guidance for three reasons. Scientists and health professionals became aware that drugs affect different populations differently. The "bikini version" of medicine, which assumed that women are simply smaller versions of men—apart from our breasts and reproductive organs—and that our hearts, bones, lungs, and pain physiology are the same, began to crumble.

But to this day, the consequences of the fact that drugs were created for the average man continue to be felt. Out of ten prescription drugs withdrawn from the U.S. market between 1997 and 2001, eight posed greater health risks for women. According to a 2020 study, women are nearly twice as likely to experience severe side effects from drugs.

A second reason the FDA reversed its guidance was that more women had joined the medical profession. "When female physicians join female patients in asking about such common concerns as the effects of aspirin in preventing heart attacks or the long-term safety of hormone replacement therapy during menopause, the male monopoly in the design of clinical trials is bound to crumble," said Dr. Ruth Merkatz at a conference on the inclusion of women and minorities in 1993.

And finally, the skyrocketing cost of healthcare and the gaps in coverage have brought consumerism to healthcare. The customer had become queen, expecting better and more choices in healthcare given they had to pay for some of it. Over three decades later, these trends continue to magnify.

When the FDA reversed its decision in 1993, Dr. Merkatz said, "I believe that women, like men, wish to be included because modern twentieth-century medicine offers examples of such stunning successes that hope for even greater medical advances is always an enticing possibility."

Then, she quoted Simone de Beauvoir, who wrote in 1970, "Representation of the world, like the world itself, is the work of men; they describe it from their own point of view, which they confuse with the absolute truth."

When I look at medical history, it's clear to me that anyone who innovates for women's health today—whether they know it or not—stands on the shoulders of those feminists who paved the way before us.

Bad science

Thanks to the advocacy of hundreds of researchers and patients, guidelines were established for women and minorities to be included in clinical trials funded by the National Institutes of Health (NIH) with the NIH Revitalization Act of 1993. In 2016, the NIH announced its Sex as a Biological Variable policy, requiring research to balance male and female cells and animals in preclinical studies. At the same time, the U.S. FDA Office on Women's Health launched the "Diverse Women in Clinical Trials Initiative" to include a greater range of women in trials. In 2013, Canada updated its guidance on the inclusion of sex in drug safety and efficacy research. The EU clinical trial regulation required participants in trials to be representative of those who will eventually receive the treatment. Does that mean the problem has been solved?

Every five years, a group of researchers led by Stacie Geller at the University of Illinois at Chicago analyzes hundreds of

NIH-funded clinical trials. They show that even in studies where women have reached parity, there is a glaring problem.

Studies don't tend to disaggregate their findings by sex. So even if women are included in clinical trials, the differences researchers might encounter are not actually analyzed. Out of 142 NIH-funded studies Geller and her colleagues monitored, only 26 percent analyzed their findings by sex and only 13 percent by race or ethnicity.

This bias sets in early in the research process. Woitowich analyzed 720 studies conducted on mice and rats and found that the majority—58 percent of studies, which included both sexes—failed to analyze their findings by sex. "That's just bad science," she says. If sex is not reported as a variable, researchers waste taxpayer-funded money when studies can't be replicated fully—a hallmark of productive research.

Those researchers who failed to include female mice are, however, good at coming up with creative excuses. "We observed difficulties when dealing with female mice," one team of research-ers wrote. Why? Because their cages were harder to clean. "I'm not even making this up!" exclaims Woitowich, as she sees my incredulous face. "This is literally pulled from articles." It's an excuse. Not unlike saying no to vaginas on Monday morning.

"To avoid the influence of hormonal changes, only male rats were included," wrote another team. "Using male mice reduced gender-dependent variability," wrote others, to which Woitowich hollers, "Mice cannot have a gender! They're not getting the terminology right."

Besides, a 2023 study on mice led by Dana Rubi Levy at Harvard Medical School has shown that despite long-held

perceptions about female mice, it's actually male mice who exhibit
more erratic behavior. The researchers placed thirty-two mice in
a giant bucket. Observing how male and female mice explore the
bucket, they found that female mice had more reliable patterns
in how they explored the bucket, regardless of their hormonal
states. "Individual males, on the other hand, were more likely to
change their behavior from day to day," says Professor Rebecca
Shanksy, one of the study's researchers.

Out of the 720 academic journal articles in Woitowich's
study, only 30 provided a rationale for having a single-sex study
or a lack of sex-based analysis. If we exclude female mice from
early research, that means certain drugs never make it through the
pipeline. "They didn't work on male mice, so they're thrown away,"
she says. "We don't know how they could've worked on women."
This is not just a problem for women; it's a problem for all.

"By studying both sexes, you can develop treatments and
therapies that are more effective for everyone," says Woitowich.
"A lot of people have this misconception that sex differences are
just about hormones and reproductive organs." But sex differences matter in every area. In one case, researchers studying treatments for glioblastoma analyzed their data by sex and realized
that women responded better to treatment than men. It allowed
them to design a treatment that could help men just as well.

It should be mandatory to include women, and female
mice—and to disaggregate studies by sex—but for now, that's
not the norm. Yet there is hope. Studies have found that there is
a certain group of scientists who are more likely to analyze their
research by sex. Can you guess who this group consists of? Yes,
the answer is female researchers.

A team led by Cassidy Sugimoto found that if the first author and the last author—in other words, the two most important authors—of a study are female, the chances of it being analyzed by sex are higher. Just how much more likely is it, you ask? The answer is: *26 times more likely.*

Closing the gender data gap

The more I learn about women's health, the more I realize that everything is interconnected. Our hormones can interact with every aspect of our health—from heart health to diabetes and acne. Our body size, fat distribution, and organs influence how we metabolize drugs. The way we feel pain differs. How we communicate that pain differs. And the way it's heard by medical professionals differs.

The idea that women's health is defined by conditions that affect women "solely, differently, or disproportionately" makes less sense, I realize—because that includes everything. When it comes to women's health, nothing is generic.

Since 2022, *Nature*, the holy grail of scientific publishing, has prompted researchers to provide details on how sex and gender were considered in their study. The European Association of Science Editors created the SAGER guidelines to encourage the reporting of sex. "It's a really low bar," says Katie Schubert, president and CEO of the Society for Women's Health Research (SWHR), a nonprofit based in Washington, DC.

"All it really means is that you just have to say, 'Yeah, I thought about this, and here's the reason why I'm not going to do that,'" says Schubert. Most of these research guidelines are still in their early implementation phase. Besides, having to "consider" sex doesn't necessarily translate into analysis.

The more serious approach would be to ask: How are they measuring implementation? And how are they measuring progress? SWHR has found that it's hard to figure out which journals follow the guidelines. "My biggest question to them and to other publishers is really: What are the consequences? If you don't follow these guidelines, what happens then? Because without some meaningful accountability, it's difficult to determine whether it's helpful or not," Schubert adds.

Unlike Woitowich's students, many researchers weren't trained to analyze their data by sex and gender, or to even use the correct terms for the two. "It's really hard to shift that culture, particularly after the FDA excluded women from trials, and then came back and said, 'Oh wait, that probably wasn't the way to go,'" says Schubert. We are now backfilling sex-specific data into existing models. Schubert adds, "Wouldn't it be amazing to have this incorporated into science classes for younger folks?"

Closing the gender data gap means redesigning how clinical trials are run. The SWHR has been talking to the FDA on how to remove barriers to clinical trials for women. "Do you need to think about the time of day or days of the week? Transportation issues? Can you get someone childcare?" asks Schubert. The barriers are well known. But there needs to be a concerted effort to create systemic change.

"You need to not only make sure that your research population is reflective of whatever the broader population is, but you also need those same folks at the table, having these conversations," she says. As ever, it comes down to funding.

For now, we need to mind the gender data gaps. At the FemTechnology Summit, Dr. Marjorie Jenkins put it like this: "When a doctor gives you a drug prescription, it's okay to ask, 'Has this been studied in women like me?' I think that we have to be our own champions for now, while working through these broken systems." She continued, "Start being in a position of power, start sitting at the table, because when you're at the table, you have authority and influence to create change."

No to the status quo

The upshot of the disparities in how we conduct health research affects women in two ways. First, our understanding of conditions that are seen as "general," such as heart health, migraines, or diabetes, is mainly based on data derived from male bodies.

It took several women to be involved in car accidents—because they were still drowsy in the morning after taking sleep medication—for the dose of Ambien to officially be halved for women. Many other drugs would benefit from a sex-specific dose adjustment, so that women no longer suffer from disproportionate side effects.

According to the WHAM Report, investing $300 million in women's health research in the United States across three diseases—cardiovascular disease as well as Alzheimer's and rheumatoid arthritis, which affect women predominantly—would yield a return of $13 billion to the economy, as women would have fewer years of dependence on others and more healthy years of life.

And second, our understanding of female issues, such as

endometriosis and adenomyosis, is woefully inadequate. In the UK, childbirth and reproductive health are the focus of less than 2.5 percent of publicly funded research. There are five times more studies into erectile dysfunction (ED) than into premenstrual syndrome (PMS)—despite the fact only 19 percent of men have ED, while over 90 percent of women report symptoms of PMS.

Femtech entrepreneurs often tell me that investors look at their creation and then proceed to ask: Why has nobody done that before? They are looking for past patterns to recognize the potential for future success. As we have seen, the answer has multiple prongs: Women's health is shrouded in taboos. It is underfunded. It is underresearched. There are many existing inequities.

It's also a matter of who gets to innovate. In a large-scale study of all U.S. biomedical patents filed from 1976 through 2010, researchers led by Rembrand Koning at Harvard Business School found that patents with all-female inventor teams are 35 percent more likely than those with all-male teams to focus on women's health. "Our findings suggest that who benefits from innovation depends on who gets to invent," they concluded. Once again, it's about skin in the game.

Female pain has been ignored and normalized for centuries. Studies find that both men and women underestimate the pain of female patients compared to that of male patients. At emergency departments, women with acute abdominal pain are 13 percent to 25 percent less likely to receive strong "opioid" pain medication, and women with chest pain wait longer to be seen by a healthcare professional than men.

The Women's Health Strategy England was launched on the basis of evidence from 100,000 women across the country,

84 percent of whom felt they weren't listened to by healthcare professionals. That is how entrenched the societal attitude of "just suck it up" and "welcome to being a woman" is. And that's in a country that cares enough to investigate these inequities, never mind places that haven't even realized there's a problem yet. Healthcare professionals need to learn to listen, and women need to keep insisting on getting heard, so that medical gaslighting— "it's all in your head"—is no longer acceptable.

What astounds me as I look at the status quo is that women are both over-medicalized, with routine episiotomies for example, and under-medicalized, when we're told to "take deep breaths and journal" to counter serious menopause symptoms—it's not the kind of advice a man with erectile dysfunction would be given.

Is it surprising that women, who are forever taught to "be nice," are less likely to complain about symptoms and side effects? But just because something is normalized that doesn't mean it should be normal.

One of the biggest obstacles that femtech faces echoes an obstacle feminism has always faced: most people are so used to the status quo, so used to conventional thinking, so used to "this is how it's always done," that they don't even see the problem.

A life-saving bra

It was a bra that first attracted me to women's health innovation. Over the years, I have covered a broad range of stories, from the birth of a baby giraffe to the future of AI, female philosophers, the qualities of top CEOs, female Impressionists, cybersecurity in banking, and considerations on whether to invest in gold,

whether to invest in biotech, and whether supplements for eye
health work. I covered Brexit. I uncovered weapons in a "social
impact" fund. I reviewed books and plays, including a critique of
our financial system sung by drag kings.

As a jack-of-all-trades, I attended a conference on healthcare
innovation at King's College London organized in conjunction
with the Massachusetts Institute of Technology (MIT). From
my seat on the balcony, my ears pricked up when Alicia Chong
Rodriguez entered the stage to talk about heart attacks.

When people are asked to picture a person having a heart
attack, most of us imagine an old man. When we are asked about
typical symptoms, we tend to think chest pain that radiates down
the left arm and pressure on the chest. Those symptoms are
typical for men, but not for women.

Heart disease is the number one killer of women in the
United States and the developed world. Yet only one-third of
participants in clinical trials are female. We know much less
about how to detect heart health issues in women. While the
symptoms of men are considered "typical," the other half of the
population has symptoms that are considered "atypical."

That's why women wait longer to call an ambulance after
initial heart attack symptoms and have a 50 percent higher chance
than men of receiving the wrong initial diagnosis following a heart
attack. For women, it is not only harder to recognize, diagnose,
and treat, but given the risk of misdiagnosis and treatment delay
after a heart attack, women also face higher mortality rates.

"The reason there is a lot of latent bias is because we have
insufficient data," says Chong Rodriguez, founder and CEO of
the start-up Bloomer Tech, based in Cambridge, Massachusetts.

"We're unaware about the differences of women's symptoms, and there are adverse treatment outcomes."

She says, "As an engineer who has been the only woman on teams in the tech industry throughout my life, I really wanted to solve this using technology." With her cofounders, Aceil Halaby and Monica Abarca, she embedded medical sensors in "smart bras" to collect data on cardiovascular health.

Not only did I learn that women have different symptoms before heart attacks, but there are people who are actively working on solutions. I knew it was a story I had to write. In the conference break, I jumped up from my seat, ran down the stairs, and asked for Chong Rodriguez's business card.

Then, I messaged a newspaper editor who always likes my stories. No response. I messaged another friendly editor. Tumbleweed. There was no interest. They thought the story was too niche. A smart bra? For what?

For a while, I focused on other stories. And yet, this story held on to me. Whenever I sat down to write, I had an uncanny feeling that the business card was following me around. There it was, lying on the printer. There it was again, gazing at me from the bookshelf. I will try again, I thought, nodding at the business card, when the time is right.

Then, the COVID-19 pandemic hit and the world observed that men and women reacted to the virus differently. Sex differences in health were thrown into the spotlight—perhaps, one could say caustically, because men initially exhibited worse symptoms than women—*Invisible Women* had brought the gender data gap into public conversation, and I finally managed to write about the smart bra for *The Guardian*.

Bloomer Tech named their start-up after Amelia Bloomer, the nineteenth-century American women's rights activist, who campaigned against restrictive corsets and pioneered more comfortable clothes for women, which became known as bloomers. "Medical devices can be cumbersome and annoying," says Alicia. The team decided to transform a medical device into an everyday garment that sits more comfortably around breast tissue and can provide medical-grade data and "that women will actually want to wear."

When I first spoke to the Bloomer team, they were working on embedding ECG (electrocardiogram) technology and sensors inside bras, but over time, they say, "we realized women would not agree on just one bra type." So instead, they created a band that can be attached to a bra of any type and size to make it "smart." It distributes several sensors around the torso that can track heart rhythm, pulse rate, breathing, temperature, posture, and movement. They use machine learning on that data to decode symptoms.

Their first goal is to close the gender data gap by enabling women's participation in clinical trials. The Bloomer bra "can get shipped to your home, and you can just be part of the trial remotely." It could help researchers uncover more sex differences in heart health, which would ensure that data used to train AI models on heart health is more representative in future.

In the long run, the company would like for any woman at risk to be able to monitor her heart health. "Monica and I have very intimate stories of family members experiencing this, telling us how they weren't able to either communicate or get an answer from their physicians," says Halaby.

The biases at play between male physicians and female patients are well documented. In one large-scale study, Professor Brad N. Greenwood and his colleagues analyzed heart attack patients admitted to hospitals in Florida over two decades. They found that women have higher odds of surviving a heart attack if their emergency department physician is also a woman.

But there is also a hopeful insight. Greenwood's team found that male physicians are more effective at treating female patients when they work with more female colleagues and when they have treated more female patients in the past.

If we fill the gender data gap that exists in heart health, physicians are more likely to identify female symptoms that are currently still considered "atypical."

No longer "atypical"

For now, much more needs to be done to research female heart health and explain what "atypical" means. "I used to be very shy, but these days, I have no time for that," Petronela Sandulache tells me. At an event for Swiss healthcare start-ups in Zurich, where she is based, she listened to a VC investor give a keynote speech. "He had a background in gynecology and looked like George Clooney," she notes. When he talked about his investments in the femtech space, he mentioned that one in eight women die of breast cancer. "I jumped off my chair and launched myself at the microphone," says Petronela, lurching forward with an outstretched arm.

"What about one in three women who die of heart disease? And that 50 percent of them are misdiagnosed with anxiety, depression, or heartburn?" she said. "There was silence from George Clooney and from the audience," she says.

It all began with a personal story, as it often does in femtech, when her mother was feeling unwell. Various doctors said it might be an intestinal flu. "They didn't do any checks, and they told her, 'Come tomorrow; we'll have a look.'" Then she says, "But there was no tomorrow." We pause. Through her grief after her mother's death, she realized, "I really needed to understand what happened."

She began to research women's health and the disparities in medical diagnoses for women. When she came across the book *Sex Matters* by Professor Alyson McGregor, Sandulache promptly asked her for a chat. Since then, Sandulache has galvanized a community of cardiologists and survivors around her start-up CorDiFio—and McGregor is now her advisor.

Sandulache's app provides women with a snapshot of the risk factors related to their heart health, including family history, blood pressure, and cholesterol. The goal is to collect the information digitally in one place. "We want to generate a personalized health report that women can take with them to doctor visits," she says. "If you're a doctor and you have a patient coming in with a folder of 200 pages, you might have a heart attack yourself."

Since 2020, she has been using her savings from previous roles in the corporate world to build this app, while her partner, a professional magician, pays their rent. The aim is to educate both patients and doctors about women-specific heart health risks—and, therefore, reduce the risk of misdiagnosis.

Older generations are less likely to question the authority of medical professionals. "They think of doctors as half-gods in

white coats," Sandulache says. An app can help younger generations support their parents, "because we're much more digitally
savvy and more used to finding our own information."

Why are women more likely to be misdiagnosed? And how
can we protect ourselves? I ask McGregor. She says, "Women
don't fit into a particular pattern recognition, and doctors are
taught pattern recognition." It reminds me of investors who look
for patterns too. "The unfortunate thing is doctors have been
taught male patterns of presenting with disease." They are more
likely to overlook heart health issues in women.

How do women's "atypical" symptoms present themselves?
"Women don't normally say it feels like an elephant sitting on
their chest," she says. That's a classic phrase for men.

Chest discomfort is a common symptom, but, as McGregor
says, "it doesn't necessarily either feel the same way in a female
body, or it's not communicated the same way because of gender
roles."

She says, "I find most women say 'discomfort'—they don't
want to say 'pain'. They'll say, 'It's just this uncomfortable
feeling', and it tends to have lasted for a few weeks." She says this
can indicate microvascular disease, which is more common in
women.

Compared to men, whose fat is often focused on their
abdomen, women have a body fat distribution that's more
dispersed. McGregor notes that the same applies to how fat is
stored in the arteries. "Men can have areas in their arteries that
get easily clogged, while women have fat more diffusely around
their arteries." Our current diagnostic methods detect clots, but
they do not assess diffuse fat in smaller arteries.

"Women are much more likely to have a heart attack that presents with shortness of breath, with fatigue for weeks, and some nausea than men."

Common candidates for misdiagnosis are depression or indigestion. Why is that the case? "I think that both psychiatric diagnoses and gastrointestinal are very easy to just assign because they're more subjective," she says. "Culturally, women are more invited to be emotional. Men, not so much. So, if a woman has to go see the doctor, and she's nervous because she's seeing a doctor and she doesn't feel well—that could be easily interpreted as anxiety."

One way to detect a heart attack is to do a blood test that measures troponin levels. Troponin is a type of protein in the heart muscle, which is sent into the bloodstream if the heart muscle isn't getting enough oxygen. But for a long time, the reference range of this test was too high for women. Once hospitals started using a lower reference range, "all these women got diagnosed with having a heart attack," she says. "Women have smaller blood vessels, smaller heart muscles, different ways of developing disease, mostly microvascular disease—we were not detecting their heart attacks, because the test's clinical trials were so skewed at the time."

It's important to know that some risk factors are higher for women than men and vice versa. "For women, smoking has a much higher risk of developing into a heart attack than if a man was the smoker," she says. In contrast, hypertension is a higher-weighted risk in men.

And then, there are sex-specific risk factors that only apply to women. "And that's been totally ignored," says McGregor. "There are specific conditions that occur in women that can then later lead to heart disease, like peripartum complications, gestational diabetes, hypertension in pregnancy, or preeclampsia," she says.

Meanwhile, trans people, who take hormones, can be at risk of disease patterns of both sexes. Trans women, who take estrogen, for example, have an increased risk of female-pattern coronary disease, as well as an increased risk of deep vein thrombosis, pulmonary embolism, and blood-clotting disorders, similar to the risks associated with hormonal contraception.

It's important to understand those individual risk factors, so that when "a doctor's trying to assess the risk of a heart attack in a patient, they're not just looking at them through the lens of a male."

From Mars to mastitis

All of female health requires innovation—from heart health to period pain. Compared to the obsessive interest our most powerful entrepreneurs show in space travel, an egg traveling down the fallopian tube here on Earth commands little attention.

I'm often reminded of a story my grandfather told me. Whenever we go for a walk, my grandfather cannot walk by a scrap heap without swiftly pulling out a plank, a set of screws or a pole, that I will soon thereafter recognize in the form of a new chair. He was a successful inventor in the Soviet Union, despite the fact he was continuously discriminated against based on his ethnicity, and I grew up on stories of inventions.

I learned that new technology is often met with derision or panic. "People will soon get tired of staring at a plywood box," they said at the invention of the television. "Women's bodies were not designed to go at fifty miles an hour," they said at the construction of the railways—our uteri might fly out of our bodies.

One day, my grandfather was out for a walk on the streets of Kyiv with my mother, a toddler sitting in her buggy, squinting in the sun. None of the buggies he saw on the streets had sunshields, so he drew a design and sent it off to the patent office. His application was rejected. A similar design existed already, invented decades ago. It was beautifully drawn, showing a lavish buggy with a sunshield. But it hadn't been commercialized. "The country was too focused on the space race," he says.

This obsession with space, once again, determines what we invent and what we commercialize. Wouldn't it be great if Elon Musk were less obsessed with Mars and more interested in mastitis?

I'm particularly interested in practical, nonhormonal, preventative, and noninvasive innovation that has the potential to be groundbreaking. I decide to pay a visit to a world-leading center for medical innovation to find out what it takes for our grandchildren to see the innovation we all need.

4

UNMET NEEDS

WHY IT PAYS TO LOOK FOR PROBLEMS

Medical innovation has often happened through chance discovery: X-rays were discovered by accidental observation, and happenstance brought us penicillin and the pap smear. But there is a pioneering academic center that takes another approach. They argue that medical innovation can be taught.

I've come to the Stanford Byers Center for Biodesign to find out how they teach innovation. The medical part of Stanford University consists of a row of imposing glass buildings flanked by palm trees. If there's a place on campus where students stumble home from a party, I get a sense it's not here, where people in scrubs energetically stride past me like Sim characters. Stanford University is seen as a central ingredient to Silicon Valley's success.

Stopping at a small student café, I go to the counter and order a berry scone, only to be told that I need to order it through an iPad by the entrance. Scone in hand, I observe a group of nerds, and I feel an affinity. I too am no longer a Luddite but the kind of futuristic person who orders pastries on an iPad. Then,

I unwittingly crumble the scone all over myself, and with it crumbles my smugness.

Arriving at the Biodesign center, I lurk by the entrance and overhear graduates talking about clinical trials. Then, Professor Josh Makower comes toward me, welcoming me by lifting his arms cheerfully like he's an Italian chef and I'm his favorite customer.

We walk into the open-plan office, where Biodesign fellows smile at me from framed group photographs. Since 2000, their alumni have been named on issued patents 1,391 times, and their technologies have been used to care for over 7.6 million patients.

"At Biodesign, we try to give them a reproducible, stepwise process they can use in their future careers," says Makower, who heads up the center. They call this process the "Biodesign innovation process." It is a form of user research and product development created for clinical settings, and it has been adopted by medical institutions around the world.

It starts with "need finding." The first step of the Biodesign process begins with an ethnography. Just like an anthropologist in a faraway land who learns about a tribe by immersing herself in their culture, Biodesign fellows roam the corridors of a hospital observing the behavior of the following peculiar tribes: physicians, healthcare providers, hospital staff, and patients.

The fellows observe people wherever healthcare happens. They may follow them through a pharmacy as they shop. Or they may observe people at home to see where they keep their medicine and how exactly they remember to take it.

I ask what it is they're looking for. "We're looking for problems," says Makower. At the time of their immersion, the fellows are not allowed to think of solutions yet, which is not an easy feat for engineers. If they can't help it, they can write down some ideas and put them away. But their sole focus is on discovering as many problems as possible.

"It forces you to dwell on the problem before you start solving it," he says. This may seem logical. "But it's amazing how often it doesn't happen, because people will come up with an idea, and they'll fall in love with it, and then they spend all their time figuring out a way to justify why it's the right solution rather than having done their homework up front."

Start-ups have a very high failure rate. Makower argues that is because the problem they think they have identified is not a real problem. Instead of putting the "unmet need" first, they get caught up thinking: Where can I apply this laser? What can I do with this balloon?

"This is why there are a lot of medical solutions that either aren't successful, don't work as well, or can't be paid for," he says. "I have some great ideas that have not made it to market because they just couldn't exist in a commercial frame.

"What we're trying to do is improve the probability of success, given that advancing things in medicine is so tremendously difficult." That's why it pays to spend some time looking for problems that are actual unmet needs. "If you get the problem right at the beginning, after all the battles are over—you win."

A better way

"We're looking for problems, but we're also looking for emotion and stress," says Makower. "If the surgeon starts to sweat in the middle of an operation and you ask, 'Is everything okay?' they might say, 'Yes, everything's fine.' They're not going to say, 'I'm worried this person is going to bleed out.' They'd say, 'Oh, no, that's what we're trained to do—look away.'" But regardless of what they say, you have observed their emotions.

Makower first developed the Biodesign process when he was working on an ob-gyn project at Pfizer decades ago. "We saw all these hysterectomies and the patients were young." He asked why this operation was necessary and was told the women had fibroids that caused bleeding. "So, we're taking out the whole uterus for a fibroid? It was mind-blowing." It was obvious to him that this was not an acceptable way to address a benign growth that can be treated in another way.

"Obviously, it's partially because men have dominated a lot of these domains. They're not necessarily in the heads of the stakeholders as much. But even women in that environment, they get trained 'this is just how you treat it,'" says Makower, who trained as a physician as well as an engineer and holds over 300 patents and patent applications.

"When you're a physician, there's no latitude for creativity," he says. "They don't want you to go into a patient's room saying, 'For you, I'm going to do something special,'" he says, once again with the gusto of an Italian chef.

"We send people who are smart and from different backgrounds into some of these environments and they go, 'Why are they doing that?'" In contrast to physicians, the Biodesign fellows don't have a direct responsibility for the patient. Their mission is to find problems and ask themselves: Could there be a better way?

Once a team has identified a set of unmet needs they want

to focus on, they then go on to consider all the stakeholders: patients, those who treat patients, the healthcare provider
system, and the economics involved.

Makower explains just how difficult it is to get a medical
device off the ground. "You have to have the idea and it has to
work." Then it must be validated through clinical trials. At the
same time, the start-up has to figure out how to get paid. Then it
has to build a sales team and create awareness. "And you're fighting all along the way," he says, "all sorts of regulatory bodies and established academic points of view."

"There must be a better way" is the guiding motto of innovation. But that doesn't mean that everything new is necessarily better than what came before.

"What we teach people here at Stanford Biodesign is that if you really want to change the world, and really want to introduce a new medical therapy, you have to conceive of it with a viable and attractive business model that returns money to investors."

Why are start-ups better at innovation than established companies? Big companies are

The three stages of medical device innovation.

IDENTIFY

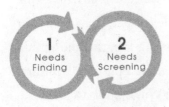

INVENT

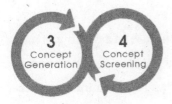

IMPLEMENT

*Stanford Byers Center
for Biodesign.*

"not that great at going into completely new spaces, because it's generally highly risky—and they're pretty risk-averse." Besides, I add, established companies are invested in the status quo.

Inventing the future

As we walk through the open-plan office, we look at rows of glass cases along the walls. The displays are lit up and exhibit what the center is most proud of: prototypes of the medical devices that were created here.

Materna, the vaginal birth dilator, was created here. I look out for more devices that have been developed specifically for women. In one of the displays, there is a long needle with a white-and-yellow tube attachment. It's the Epiphany Epidural System created by James Wall and Ken Wu. Epidural anesthesia is commonly used for childbirth, and this device was created to provide "a safer, more accurate way to introduce the needle," says Makower.

On the other side of the corridor, there is an assembly of flat, rounded cases in white, blue, black, and gray. It's Emme, a contraceptive pill case that's connected to an app and reminds users to take their birth control, founded by Amanda French and Janene Fuerch. "This company was recently acquired," says Makower with pride. Then there is Pelvalon's Eclipse, a nonsurgical, vaginal insert for women experiencing loss of bowel control.

We walk past the Prototype Room, where cables burst from their stands. There's a microscope and small shelves neatly labeled "motors" and "connectors." A model baby lies atop a stack of multicolored trays. In the corridor, a spine is hanging

from the wall, next to an oversize eye, hand, and foot. I realize it's
an adult playroom.

And then there's the Brainstorming Room, which is lined
with whiteboards across all walls filled with scribbles. A small
group of fellows is having a heated discussion. "These will be
our founders of the future!" says Makower. The founders are too
engrossed to notice us, so we move on.

Makower's office is lined with books and the devices he
invented. I spot Willow, the wearable breast pump he cofounded,
led by CEO Laura Chambers. And then, there is Nuelle, a sexual
arousal device for women. It's a tale of two femtech devices.
Willow has become a success, but Nuelle failed to excite. I'm glad
both are on display.

I ask about Nuelle. "We've faced barriers at every turn,
because somewhere along the way, somebody got squeamish."
He describes the social dynamic "where you have people who
are saying, 'We shouldn't be talking about this. This shouldn't be
a topic anyone wants to hear about,' and then others are saying,
'No, no, no, we got to educate people, because some people don't
even know what their own body parts are.'"

Nuelle launched in 2012, about a decade before "sexual
wellness" became a shelf at Bloomingdales and Sephora. I wonder
if it was too early. "It's a really complicated space. It was one of the
hardest projects I've ever worked on," he says. "Willow's different
obviously; women are embracing that. I mean, there's no contro-
versy about being able to pump anywhere." I come away feeling
that the difference in how these two devices have been received
is as old as the Madonna-whore complex.

Those who innovate in female technology face hurdles of

stigma, a lack of knowledge among everyone, and reluctant investors, policymakers, and researchers. What is the joy of innovating in a space that is this difficult?

"I like going into spaces that have not been solved, that don't have good solutions," he says. "That's what I do. I am not a follower. I want to go fix things. I want to make it better, and so," he says with a hearty laugh, "I look for problems!"

Applying the Biodesign process

I talk to a founder who has used the Biodesign process to launch her company. "I'm the daughter of two feminists" is the first thing Holly Rockweiler, the CEO and cofounder of Madorra, says when I ask about her background. "My dad's an engineer, my mum's a social worker, and from a young age I was interested in how engineering can be applied to help people—so I think it's a nice blend of who they are that became me."

Rockweiler studied biomedical engineering at Washington University in St. Louis and went on to work for Boston Scientific, a large medical device company. After a few years, she realized she wanted to be closer to the experiences of patients. She enrolled in the Stanford Biodesign fellowship. "I wanted to go out and learn firsthand what the problems were, and then figure out ideas and then put those prototypes in front of people and see how they work rather than innovating just in my cubicle."

Wearing a lab coat, she walked the corridors of the teaching hospital in the ethnography phase. A tag around her neck identified her as a researcher. As part of a small team of engineers and physicians, who observed what was going on around them, she carried a notebook to capture her observations. "Nurse tripped over cord during consultation," could be one, or "patient complains about gastroenteritis."

Over several weeks, each team of Biodesign fellows shadows physicians and patients, who have given their consent. They go for lunch with the physicians and listen to what they're talking about. Then, they go back to their own team of researchers and compare notes: What did you see?

Rockweiler and her team compiled a long list of about 500 problems they narrowed down to 16. For each problem they created a "need statement," which has the following structure: a way to solve a specific <insert problem> in a well-characterized <insert affected population> to achieve a measurable <insert outcome>.

If the problem you focus on is nurses tripping over cords in the operating room, your outcome might be to reduce the number of sprained ankles. The open-ended nature of the need statement allows researchers to think more broadly than just saying they need wireless power. Could the nurses wear special socks? Could they levitate? Even if it's impossible, it opens people's imagination to creative solutions.

"Besides observing, we did a lot of follow-up interviews with the physicians and nurses and patients," says Rockweiler. They looked at existing research. They analyzed the market size and the current landscape of solutions for each unmet need on their shortlist. They filled the whiteboards of the Brainstorming Room again and again.

Their final shortlist of unmet needs included an idea on men's sexual health, addressing Peyronie's disease. Another unmet need they included was vaginal atrophy, a condition that affects 50 percent to 70 percent of all postmenopausal women. When Rockweiler and her team spoke to the patients for each unmet need, they noticed a marked difference.

You care about this?

"We found that the patient population for vaginal atrophy was just so grateful that we were working on it, and so intrigued and supportive. As opposed to the men we talked to, who were closed off and very defensive and there was a constant assumption that we were out to profit off them, the women we talked to were like, 'Are you kidding? You care about this? Wow.'"

The team decided, "We could be fighting uphill, or we could be working with patients who are very interested."

What is vaginal atrophy? "When the estrogen in the body declines, either naturally because of menopause, or artificially because of cancer treatments, the vaginal tissue becomes thin, dry, and inelastic," she explains. "That leads to symptoms of vaginal dryness, pain with intercourse or dyspareunia, and all kinds of day-to-day problems—not just losing out on intimacy but also pain with walking, wiping, wearing jeans, or riding a bike."

She says current treatments fall into two categories: lubricants and moisturizers or hormone replacement therapy. "It's like, 'Oh, it's dry? Here, put some lotion on it. Oh, you've lost your estrogen? Here, have some more.'" But that doesn't necessarily work. "We met so many women who said that they were uncomfortable using hormones, or they were not able to use hormones based on their health history."

Initially the main patient population they identified were menopausal women. Then, they identified additional populations who may not want to use hormonal solutions for vaginal atrophy. This includes cancer patients, women with cardiovascular risk factors, and transgender men.

"If they're undergoing a transition from female to male, they will often go on hormone therapy, and that can lead to vaginal atrophy and dryness for them at any age. And the treatments are estrogen therapy," she says.

But a transgender man might say, "No, I'm on testosterone and I want to drop my estrogen levels. Why would I want to use estrogen?" says Rockweiler. "There is a lot of unmet need in the transgender community."

Listening to what the patient wants

The Madorra team created a list of features that are must-haves and nice-to-haves based on their research. Rockweiler says, "We heard very loudly from our patients that they wanted something that didn't require insertion.

"What we learned is they wanted something they could use themselves and be in full control of," she says. "If we take a parallel from the birth control space—they don't want an IUD; they'd want a NuvaRing or something they could insert and take out themselves." It couldn't be an implant that has to be administered by a physician.

"What we've developed is an ultrasound-based solution that's home-use, totally external to the body, and is able to re-create the body's natural lubricating mechanism, thereby treating the atrophy and dryness," says Rockweiler. It's possible to use it in concert with hormones.

Madorra

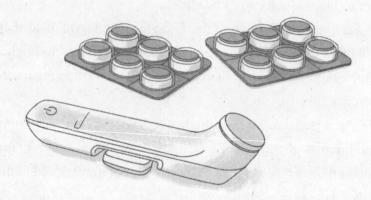

What compelled her was that "what we had was not a rocket-science-level solution. We had a pretty simple solution but felt really shocked that no one was paying attention to this area," she says. "So, we felt like we could make a really big impact with a low-risk product.

"Women deserve options, and we provide them with another option that's medically backed." They are going through the FDA's regulatory process. "We're on the de novo path," she says. A new category is being born.

The FDA's regulatory process for new medical devices can involve providing clinical evidence to demonstrate that the device is both effective and safe. Depending on the device's degree of novelty and level of risk, the bar differs. "Since we're the first of our kind, we've had to work closely with them to define what that bar should be," says Rockweiler. This is followed by clinical trials.

"If we had had all the money we needed on day one, it would have been going a lot faster," she says. "It's a process of moving the ball forward as much as you can, while you then go out and get more funding." It has been six years so far.

The best femtech companies address unmet needs on a large scale. But I notice that many of these unmet needs are stigmatized to an extent where they are not only unmet but also unknown.

How can femtech entrepreneurs make their solutions known? "The internet has enabled a lot of ways to educate people," Rockweiler notes. The physicians they have spoken to said "they don't like talking about this problem, because they don't have good solutions—hormones are their only option." If they know their patient can't use a hormonal solution, they're less likely to address the issue.

"I think the fact that we exist, in and of itself, is a way of advocating for women's needs and providing a platform for a dialogue. We want to elevate the dialogue on women's sexual health needs, and I think that femtech, in general, is doing that," she says. This conversation has arrived.

Femtech start-ups and failures

Given the high-risk nature of start-ups, it's ever more important for founders to identify the most pressing unmet needs at the beginning of their journey to increase their chances of success. Because most start-ups fail.

If a company shuts down for financial reasons, there are several possibilities. Did they fail to identify an actual unmet need? Was their solution unpopular? Did they spend money on fruitless parts of the business? Was theirs the wrong business model? Did they run out of money because they were too ahead of the curve? It's hard to tell.

Years before the current wave of smart breast pumps, California-based Naya Health was founded in 2013. It raised around $5 million and brought a new breast pump to the market, but five years later the company went dark. It no longer replied to customers whose $1,000 pumps stopped working. According to CNBC, it shut down because it struggled to raise funds to keep going. Moxxly is another breast pump that went out of business. These pumps have, nonetheless, paved the way for newcomers. Early business failures can be a fertilizer in that they can create the preconditions of social acceptance for a new category.

Some companies fail because they can't scale. Seattle-based Poppy was an on-demand childcare platform that put families in touch with a range of local caregivers who included recent graduate students and professional dancers. The company raised $2 million and was well received among thousands of families, but it didn't find a business model that allowed it to make a sufficient profit to keep going.

The Cusp, a menopause-focused telemedicine start-up founded in 2018, shut down after two years, stating it had failed to secure more funding. Trellis, a New York–based boutique egg-freezing clinic, shut down after a year, also stating financial reasons.

Sometimes acquisitions can go south. Houston-based FemTec Health acquired a range of companies, including femtech company Ava Women, which produced the multisensor menstrual cycle tracking bracelet. In 2022, allegations emerged that FemTec Health misrepresented its financial status and the number of its customers, as well as failed to pay several vendors, according to an investigative report by Erin Brodwin of Axios. Brodwin also revealed that the $38 million raised by FemTec Health came from an investment vehicle run by the founder himself. It shut down in 2023.

With acquisitions there's a risk that an established company could acquire an innovative start-up only to shelve the product.

Then, there are companies that fail because of what they are. A Dutch company, founded by two guys, tried to move into the sextech space with an app called LegalFling in 2018. The idea was to use blockchain-based contracts to "verify explicit consent before having sex." But that's not how consent works. This app failed because it was based on a fundamental misunderstanding of the nature of sexual consent, which can be revoked at any moment.

Some companies fail by a lack of robust research. In 2014, Boston-based biotech company OvaScience claimed to have identified "egg precursor cells" on the outer layer of women's ovaries. "These immature egg cells have the ability to grow into fresh, young healthy eggs," the company said. They claimed these cells could improve existing fertility treatments and reverse the biological clock. The company was valued at $1.8 billion. By 2016, it had raised and spent $228 million. But other scientists were not able to replicate the research. In the end, the company was sold for parts.

In the case of many early stage femtech companies, it's simply too soon to tell whether they are promising or not. The underlying research, if it exists, on many women's health issues is nascent, and many products are still in the development phase. With new forms of contraception, we don't know what their side effects might be yet.

Those who want to revolutionize women's health need to solve a real problem with a real solution. They need to do so at the right time, with robust research, with a viable business model, a strong team—and with a healthy dose of luck.

Putting the market on the map

I talk to the woman who is at the forefront of defining the femtech market. Dr. Brittany Barreto lives in Raleigh, North Carolina, with three cats, three dogs, a turtle, and a guinea pig. A trained scientist, she previously launched a dating app and then joined the Capital Factory fund in Texas. "I started to mentor founders," she says. Every time she was introduced to a women's health company, she found herself canceling the rest of her day's plans to focus on that company. "I found them to be working on the most important problems and solutions."

One founder she met was Dr. Julie Hakim, a pediatric gynecologist and inventor of a vaginal stent. Hakim does reconstructive vaginal surgery on girls who have birth defects or experienced trauma. She told Barreto that she had to use makeshift vaginal stents made of medical gloves stuffed with gauze. "I was like, wait, and you work at one of the top children's hospitals in the world. I just couldn't believe that," Barreto said. "And then she told me that during radiation treatment for cervical or ovarian cancer, many women's vaginas actually melt shut, because there's no stent to stay there to maintain its walls," she says. "That was the moment that I was like, that's it. I can't contribute my efforts to anything else."

Barreto couldn't find a list of companies working in the femtech space, so she started to collect them in a Google sheet in March 2020. "I started to realize, huh, that's why we have twenty organic-cotton tampon companies," she says. "They didn't know each other existed." The sheet she created was for external awareness, to show investors and large companies who's in the space, but also for internal awareness, "so that we stop replicating the same shit and actually work on things that women really need."

She launched her consulting firm FemTech Health to advise companies on their women's health strategy and acquisitions, as well as FemTech Focus, her podcast cofounded with Hakim. In 2021, they released their first report called the FemTech Landscape. They quantified the women's health industry as a $1.2 trillion market.

To get this figure, the report looked at the market size of 103 health conditions across 22 subsections of health, including menstruation, menopause, and maternal health. In cases where an issue affects everybody, like cardiovascular health, brain health, and bone health, they divided the market value by 50 percent to account for women. But we know that women are disproportionately affected by some of those issues, so the estimate is likely to be conservative.

Barreto was shocked to discover there is no market research on certain areas of women's health like PMS. "How come no one's quantified how much women spend every month for their PMS symptoms? That's insane. That speaks to the disparities and what people are studying in terms of value in markets." In some cases, it's impossible to put a figure on the market size, because the solution is still in development, like the use of tampons as diagnostic tools.

Estimates about the femtech market can read like wine labels: not always telling. What are notes of green berries and a hint of brioche supposed to mean? What complicates market size estimates is that analysts have differing definitions of femtech.

One of the first figures about femtech, put out by Frost & Sullivan, was a $50 billion market by 2025. *Precedence Research* says it's $103 billion by 2030. Elsewhere, the global menstrual market alone is estimated to surpass $62 billion by 2033, and the menopause market is said to be a $600 billion opportunity. Perhaps the actual market size exceeds anyone's current imagination.

In this book, I focus on companies that are consumer-facing. I primarily look at wearable consumer tech, medical devices, and apps. Some companies in this book already have "product market fit," which means they have customers, while others are still in clinical trials and may never make it to the market. Any idea that's discussed here should be seen as a starting point for further research rather than the complete picture. Some products are completely new, while others have been created by many companies at this point, so it's a good idea to read reviews to figure out which one might be best for you.

None of this is medical advice. I am not a medical doctor. And each person is different. It would also not be possible to cover all of women's health innovation in one book; for that I would need to write a library. Besides, this is not an encyclopedia of ailments; it's a feminist business book.

Start-ups fail. CEOs can get ousted. Regulation can change. Data can leak. Business models can change. Companies can pivot to psychedelic drugs. Anything can be "disrupted." But I believe the underlying issues I uncover here remain an integral part of our everyday reality for as long as women have bodies.

PART II

WOMEN-CENTRIC DESIGN

5

PERIOD APPS, THE OG

WHAT IT TAKES TO TRACK AN EGG

In 2016, Ida Tin, who founded the period app Clue, suggested that "femtech" should become the term to encompass technology addressing female health needs. She argued the portmanteau might help investors, who would no longer have to say they funded a company that helps women not pee their pants. Ever since then, the term femtech has galvanized and energized the community of tech innovators.

In my research, I was amazed to find that this was not the first time a period-focused company has used the term. Deep in the archives of Harvard Business School, there is a case study about a tampon business called "Tambrands Inc.: The Femtech Soviet Joint Venture." It begins with the following words: "In mid-June 1988, Edwin Shutt, chairman, CEO, and president of Tambrands Inc., flew to Kyiv for the signing of a joint venture agreement." I am spooked. It's the time and place of my birth. The purpose of his trip was for Tambrands, then a Fortune 500 company, to manufacture and distribute Tampax tampons in Soviet Ukraine. The materials for the tampons were sourced from the UK.

"Femtech found itself in the enviable position of being 'the only game in town' as the sole producer of tampons in the USSR," notes the case study. In the first year of operating, the deliveries of Tampax tampons to Ukrainian pharmacies sold out in less than two hours.

The case study states that the Femtech Soviet Joint Venture avoided explicit product advertising. Tony Butterworth, Tambrands' director of international product development, said, "Quite frankly, Soviet consumers don't believe advertising, because history has said that when the government advertises something, it is stuck with inferior, shoddy merchandise that it is trying to move out." News about tampons spread by word of mouth.

In the last century, tampons were well received, providing a sense of comfort and convenience. In this century, there is no doubt that the period app—the mother of a new generation of femtech products—has changed the conversation about periods once again. It has externalized an internal process. There are calls for periods to be treated as a vital sign for health, just like our pulse or body temperature, though we are still far from the body-swap fantasy Gloria Steinem envisaged, where periods are a boast-worthy event.

The idea that we can track our periods digitally has spawned a generation of over 300 apps. What began as "period tracking" has moved on to "fertility tracking" and "digital contraception": from when to expect our next period to when to increase the chances of conception to when to avoid pregnancy—each claim stronger and riskier than the previous.

The OG of period apps is Berlin-based Clue by BioWink, founded by Ida Tin and three male cofounders in 2012. They raised $55.5 million, according to Crunchbase, and have 11 million users. In femtech circles, Clue is praised for its wealth of educational content.

The most downloaded period app is London-based Flo Health, with 200 million users, according to Statista. It was founded by four dudes in 2016, who raised $75.5 million— more than any other period app. Even in the case of period apps, a group of four men has raised the most.

The first app to be cleared by the FDA as a digital contraceptive in 2018 was Stockholm-based Natural Cycles. The app's foray into digital contraception caused a media storm when a spate of unwanted pregnancies emerged among women who had used the app in Sweden. After an investigation, the Swedish Medical Products Agency found that the unwanted pregnancy rates are within their range of effectiveness.

The effectiveness of any contraceptive depends on whether it's used correctly. To assess this, clinical trials use the "Pearl Index" to describe the number of pregnancies occurring per 100 women over one year with "perfect use" and "typical use" of a contraceptive. Condoms, for example, are 98 percent effective with perfect use. As with any contraceptive, the failure rate tends be higher during the first year of use.

Natural Cycles is 98 percent effective with "perfect use" and 93 percent effective with "typical use." It's worth noting that according to a study led by the company itself, fewer than 10 percent of cycles recorded on their app are "perfect use" cycles, which means the vast majority are 93 percent effective with "typical use."

The British advertising regulator, however, decided that Natural Cycles' ads on social media—which billed the app as "highly accurate"—were misleading. As Olivia Sudjic, who wrote about needing an abortion after using Natural Cycles, has pointed out, the CEO and cofounder Elina Berglund has previously described her ideal user as a woman who is planning to have children at some point and who would like a break from hormonal contraception before trying.

It's noticeable that the company's marketing materials have become much more nuanced since then, explaining who it is and isn't for and how effective it is. As more digital contraceptives emerge, there will, no doubt, be echoes of this cautionary tale.

Delete your period apps?

In the aftermath of the U.S. Supreme Court's decision to overturn *Roe v. Wade* and revoke the constitutional right to abortion, several tweets implored: "Delete your period apps." Period apps generate bigger data sets about menstrual health than anything we have ever seen before. The research potential of these data sets is tremendous—but, if they end up in the wrong hands, so are the risks.

I talk to Laura Shipp, a PhD researcher specializing in period apps and cybersecurity at Royal Holloway, to find out more. Shipp began her PhD research in an interdisciplinary cybersecurity program. One evening, she dropped by the home of a friend who had just started using Natural Cycles. Has anyone researched the cybersecurity of such apps, she wondered? But when she spoke to academic colleagues, she found, "There was just no interest in it."

"People told me that I should focus on more widely applicable apps," she says. "That it was too niche to focus on." Undeterred by the lack of interest among her colleagues, Shipp decided to pursue her PhD on period apps and has become a pioneering researcher quoted on Bloomberg and Hannah Witton's YouTube channel.

Not all period apps are created by companies we would define as chiefly femtech. "There are games developers, utility companies, big companies that generate random apps, that now have a period tracker, because it's a place to put advertising and another way of generating revenue," says Shipp.

What are the red flags to look out for when picking an app? "Look at if they have a privacy policy, because a few apps don't have a privacy policy at all." She says it's a red flag when apps ask for camera access or microphone access. It's a good idea to google the app you're looking at and follow recent news stories.

In Shipp's 2020 study on the data security of thirty period apps, Clue is mentioned as an app demonstrating that, "when spending the necessary resources and effort, companies can provide reasonably good privacy policies." Shipp says, "I really recommend the privacy-first apps as well, which don't collect your data, particularly in Roe versus Wade terms." She mentions the apps Read Your Body and Drip.

I was encouraged that her period-app study found "the industry follows slightly better practices than the general app ecosystem." But the study also concluded that none of the privacy policies are easy to understand. What's more, apps could make consent more granular. Shipp says they could give people the ability to consent to whether they only want their data to be part of academic research, or also new product development.

Regulations about data privacy and targeted advertising keep evolving. Femtech companies can raise the bar in several ways, says Lucy Purdon, senior tech policy fellow at Mozilla

Foundation. "Not selling user data should be the bare minimum," she says. She also recommends avoiding Meta Pixel, a piece of code developers embed to track user activity and target them with advertising on Facebook. Companies should look into their analytics tools and software development kits to check what data is shared, with whom, and for what purpose. And, finally, she recommends seeking help from regulators. In the UK, the Information Commissioner's Office (ICO) offers a regulatory sandbox, which helps innovative companies that use personal data for their products embed privacy by design.

After the overturn of *Roe v. Wade*, one concern is that law enforcement in states that criminalize abortion could subpoena tech companies to gain access to people's period data, to try to glean whether someone had an abortion. Whether to delete your period app ultimately depends on the politics of where you live and on how you balance privacy and convenience. According to the Electronic Frontiers Foundation, the most common scenario for those who get prosecuted for having an abortion is when a family member, partner, or hospital staff turns them in to law enforcement. The evidence used to build a case can include messages, emails, browser history, GPS data, or purchasing history.

Overall, period app data is not the most revealing kind of data. On an app, some missing period data is common, and it's not conclusive proof for anything. Besides, it's very easy to enter false data into a period app.

Companies that have been fined by the U.S. Federal Trade Commission (FTC) for sharing user health data with third parties include the period app Flo Health but also mental health app BetterHelp and telemedicine platform GoodRx.

It's worth pointing out that any organization that holds health data, whether it's a start-up, a hospital, a charity, or a governmental organization, could expose this data unintentionally by being hacked or by using the wrong digital tools. In 2023, an investigation by *The Observer* revealed that several trusts at England's National Health Service were unwittingly sending patient data to Facebook, because they were using Meta Pixel. An investigation by *The Markup* revealed that several top hospitals in the United States did the same. Who holds more of your health data, your doctor or your period app? Traditional healthcare providers, who hold vast troves of our health data, are in many cases less tech-savvy than the makers of period apps.

The myth of the 28-day cycle

As part of my research, I conduct a self-experiment. I track my cycle on Clue, Natural Cycles, and Flo Health for six months. I am amazed to discover that each app predicts a different ovulation date for me: day 14, 15, and 16, respectively. I also notice that each time I travel across the Atlantic, my cycle extends. Can my body ever work like clockwork?

In most textbooks and charts, a "normal" menstrual cycle is represented as having 28 days. In this textbook version, the cycle begins with the first day of menstruation and is shown as having two equal halves of 14 days each: In the first half, the follicular phase, the egg matures and is released during ovulation, which is smack-dab in the middle of the cycle on day 14. In the second half, the luteal phase, the womb prepares for a potential implantation of the fertilized egg. Except it isn't quite so. Only 13 percent of women have a 28-day cycle.

In a collaboration between University College London and Natural Cycles, a study led by Professor Joyce Harper analyzed 600,000 menstrual cycles. They found that the average cycle length is 29.3 days. Some 65 percent of women had cycles that lasted between 25 and 30 days. Then, the length of each cycle tends to vary month by month. The average follicular phase lasted 16.9 days, and the average luteal phase was 12.4 days long. This means ovulation doesn't consistently occur in the middle of the cycle or on day 14.

Medical professionals typically base the due dates of births on calculations assuming a 28-day cycle, which makes them less accurate. (In addition to the fact that due dates can naturally vary by weeks.) Apps that predict ovulation on day 14 for their users, regardless of previous history, assume a 28-day cycle, which, once again, makes them less accurate. The rigid idea of a 28-day cycle gives a false sense of "normal" and "abnormal." So, it's time to stop considering the 28-day cycle "the norm."

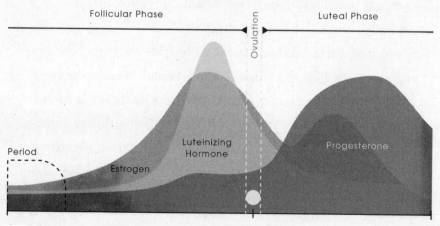

A more accurate menstrual cycle

I ask Shipp why each app is predicting a different ovulation date for me. "Those apps give you predictions based on each of their proprietary algorithms," Shipp says. "Part of their value as an organization is how they generate their predictions.

"I think what the apps do is give you a window, more than anything else," she adds. One central challenge is that cycle length and regularity vary widely. "Stress and other environmental factors have a much bigger impact than maybe some of the apps account for," says Shipp. Alcohol, weight loss, stress— and, as I have learned, travel—can all have a knock-on effect on our cycles.

"Apps give people a place where they can record information about what's going on in their body and give an idea of when you're going to ovulate," says Shipp. They help to track pre-period symptoms. "The more data you have, I imagine the more accurate the prediction will be, but you can also do that prediction work yourself," says Shipp. She is referring to more traditional fertility awareness-based methods (FABM).

Fertility awareness-based methods go digital

Historically, these methods have been known as "natural family planning." The World Health Organization defines them as "methods for planning or avoiding pregnancies by observation of the natural signs and symptoms of the fertile and infertile phases of the menstrual cycle."

This typically involves tracking calendar dates, body basal temperature, and cervical mucus. Or as one woman I met during my research told me, she can detect ovulation by touching her cervix to see if it feels like the tip of her nose, or softer like a lip.

Only 3 percent of women in the United States use traditional FABMs, and their effectiveness varies wildly depending on the method, the way it's been taught, and the precision with which it's implemented. Tracking your cycle is not a new idea—it's the digitalization that's new.

Pregnancy rates are highest if you have sex on the day of ovulation, which is when one of the ovaries releases the egg. Once the egg is released, it can fuse with sperm for 12 to 24 hours as it travels down the fallopian tube. For a long time, scientists thought that sperm compete against each other in a survival-of-the-fittest race where the strongest swimmer wins. More recently, researchers have discovered that's not the case.

It's the egg that makes the decision. Far from passively waiting for her prince in the fallopian tower, the egg evaluates its candidates. Then it sends chemical signals, so-called chemo-attractants, to its chosen sperm—it's the law of attraction. When the egg and sperm fuse, a flood of zinc is released, and sparks can be seen under the microscope.

By the way, the sperm is the smallest cell in the human body, while the egg is the largest and can even be seen without a microscope.

The second-highest chance for conception is the day before ovulation, followed by the second day leading up to ovulation. That's because sperm can live for multiple days.

One established and effective method, for those who want to get pregnant, is to detect the day of ovulation by using pee sticks that measure the level of the luteinizing hormone (LH), which peaks before ovulation. One study of the Clearblue Easy Fertility Monitor—which relies on LH pee sticks—found that 22.7 percent of women who used the device got pregnant within two cycles, compared to 14.4 percent of those who didn't. A surge in LH can very effectively predict ovulation a few days in advance. Some strips are more sensitive than others, just as some pregnancy tests are more sensitive than others. It's worth noting that the LH strips don't tend to work for those with PCOS, because their LH levels can peak several times, and the strips have a higher price tag than an app.

When it comes to period apps, I've often heard critics say, "Oh, they're only right 21 percent of the time." I've come to think of the study they're referencing as the "21 percent study." In 2018, researchers asked 949 volunteers to collect urine samples for one entire menstrual cycle and analyzed the LH to detect their ovulation day. They then looked at 55 period apps, which predicted an ovulation date and compared it to their data. Their findings? "Most calendar apps attempted to provide users with their day of ovulation, but maximal probability of this being correct was 21 percent."

I notice that the researchers are affiliated with Clearblue, the maker of LH strips, a competitor of period apps. This is interesting, because it highlights the fact that competitors do research on each other, but it doesn't make the study less valid. Taking a closer look at the study, I find that what it says is, if an app pinpoints ovulation at day 16, this is about 21 percent accurate.

The study also found that if an app presents a ten-day fertile window (on days 10 through 19), it is 98 percent likely to capture the ovulation date, and if an app presents a six-day fertile window (on days 12 through 17), the probability is 81 percent. Just as with a nice living room, it's having a large window that matters.

Treat women like grown-ups

I talk to Carrie Walter and Audrey Tsang, the CEO duo of Clue. When Clue made its transition from consumer technology app to a regulated medical device company in 2021—from periods to conception and contraception—Tsang and Walter took over the baton from Ida Tin.

In the business world, CEO duos are relatively rare. Investors ask: But who makes the decision? "Our answer is always 'Well, actually, both of us!'" says Tsang. "If you tell one of us something, trust that the other is going to know within the next day or so." Throughout the interview, I can see the two complement each other in a dynamic that's a laid-back waltz rather than a dramatic tango.

"My background is in consumer tech products," says Tsang. "Nobody ever talks about healthcare as fun. Like, 'Oh, can't wait to go take my pill.'" For her, technology gives us the opportunity to provide people with valuable information and make healthcare more engaging.

"I've got a background in regulatory law. I spent about a decade in big corporate contexts and reputation-sensitive industries from nuclear to med tech," says Walter. She has two children; one was born in Britain and the other in Germany, and Walter was astonished by how wildly different each experience was. "How can the healthcare experience be so different?" she asks. "These are not even radically different countries. They're next to each other; they're both rich, Western, allegedly science-based systems."

Commenting on her pregnancies, she says, "It's just extremely difficult to find evidence-based, grown-up content on this very predictable life stage." What was considered dangerous during pregnancy in one country, like going to the sauna, was common in another. "Why on earth is it so hard to demand as a woman that you're going to be treated like a grown-up when you go through that phase?"

Walter's second pregnancy was difficult. "I was very, very sick, very depressed," she says. "It was incredibly hard to turn that internal experience into something my healthcare provider could interact with." She wanted a way to analyze her experience. "I was feeling very sick, but not equally sick all the time. I was desperate to start feeling better, but I couldn't really tell because it was all a blur.

"I think this is so often what the female reproductive experience is," she says. Whether it's the symptoms we experience throughout our cycle, whether it's pregnancy, postpartum or perimenopause, the key indicators are internal. "It's not like you're standing there with a broken arm. What you're saying is 'I'm so sick that I want to jump off a bridge, and if I didn't already have a two-year-old, I probably would.' And that is extremely hard to externalize."

For Walter, Clue is about general health literacy and about our ability to turn our experience into data—both to understand our own bodies better and to be able to communicate those insights with healthcare professionals.

Throughout my research, I've met women who track their

period data meticulously on an app to be able to make a case to their doctors and get better care.

Chocolate cravings and doomsday feelings

I want to know how most people use Clue. "The far most common use case is that they track their period and know when their next period is coming," says Tsang. In business the term "use case" refers to how, why, and when a customer might use a product or service.

"The second most common is understanding patterns in their cycle. That can be anything from, like, 'Oh, I get a chocolate craving around the end of my cycle' to, for me, I tracked migraines around the middle of my cycle, around ovulation." The most popular categories tracked on the app are, in order, pain, emotions, sleep, energy, and sex.

I mention that many people I've spoken to use Clue to have a rough idea as to when their next period is coming. Walters says, "They are partially looking at 'Well, when do I need to have tampons with me?'" She looks at the app whenever she gets a sense of "'Oh, I just responded really emotionally to that.' I wonder if maybe it's that time when I tend to feel a little bit doomsday. That's where I find it very helpful. And for that, it just needs to give me a bracket."

"Because of Clue, I recognize that it's really hard for me to fall asleep the day before I get my period," says Tsang. "I don't know why. It always seems to happen. That self-knowledge is more empowering, and it's a better fit for the use case, than 'Oh, on October 4, you're going to start your period.'"

"Very few people actually have a completely predictable cycle, and so anything that is fundamentally algorithm-based predictive can't predict the fact that you've just changed time zone and had a stressful week," says Walter.

"Women don't appreciate how individual those symptoms are. I was speaking to someone recently who told me that they and all of the female people in their family get knee pain two days before [their period]. Would any healthcare provider have told them that? No. Maybe they're the only people in the world who have this. Maybe they're not."

Conception versus contraception

Clue Birth Control was the second app, after Natural Cycles, to receive FDA clearance as a digital contraceptive. "There's always going to be a portion of our user base trying to get pregnant, trying not to get pregnant, and understanding that has really informed our product development," says Tsang.

For Clue's FDA clearance, researchers at the Institute for Reproductive Health at Georgetown University conducted a study with 718 women in 2019. They found the app is 97 percent effective at preventing pregnancy with "perfect use" and 92 percent effective with "typical use."

"It's so important for anybody who does fertility awareness-based birth control, which is what our birth control method is, to understand why having a really smart statistical buffer in there is so important," says Walter. "People usually underestimate and don't understand how big that window needs to be." That window depends on how variable your cycle is.

Clue Birth Control is not for everyone. "It's fundamentally not for women and girls who are too close to adolescence. And that's because your cycle has to stabilize over time, so you've got to be at least eighteen," says Walter. "Your cycle length has to be between 20 and 40 days, and your cycle variation has to be nine days or below. That covers probably 80 percent of the currently cycling population. And if you're not in that group, the chances are you're heading into perimenopause, or you're adolescent or you've got some condition."

The algorithm behind Clue Birth Control uses Bayesian statistics trained on a large set of fertility data. It estimates the percentage likelihood that you would get pregnant if you had unprotected sex on any given day. The app starts with a 16-day high-risk window, and depending on your cycle, it can narrow down to an 11-day minimum. Those with a more variable cycle are shown a longer buffer. A buffer is always needed; even though the egg lives for only about a day, sperm can survive for multiple days.

Does any additional input—such as temperature or mucus— make the algorithm more precise? "No," says Walter, "and this was a very conscious choice." Clue's standpoint is that temperature or mucus data introduces more noise than helpful information.

"It's hard to tell, like, is it egg white? Or is it creamy?" comments Tsang on cervical mucus. As for temperature, Walter says, "A late night, a slight infection, whatever it is, can mess with that." That's why the only input they require are period dates.

"Is this the right method for everyone? No, of course not," says Walter. "Women really need to understand the choices, the tradeoffs, and the fact that no method of contraception is actually 100 percent."

"If I were somebody who needed to do a lot of time zone travel and knew that I had a pretty irregular cycle, I'd probably opt for a different method," she says. "I've had times in my life where I absolutely would not have wanted to be pregnant and then other times, in between my pregnancies, or two years before my first pregnancy, where I didn't want to be pregnant, but if it had happened, it wouldn't have been the worst thing either. And I definitely didn't want to be on hormones," says Walter. It's about "choosing what's right for you in the context of your life."

Data privacy post Roe v. Wade

One of the reasons I have chosen to interview the CEOs of Clue is that the app's terms and conditions are transparent. We talk about the political climate following the overturning of *Roe v. Wade*. What do they make of people on Twitter saying, "Delete your period apps"?

"I think there's a little bit of healthy paranoia there," says Walter. She notes there are period apps that are not regulated and don't disclose their business model. "Regardless of the reproductive rights situation in my country, I wouldn't be giving my intimate data to the vast majority of players out there."

"We're GDPR regulated," says Walter. GDPR is the European Union's General Data Protection Regulation, which came into effect in 2018. It regulates how companies gather, process, and store the personal data of EU citizens, and it's considered to be the strongest privacy and security law in the world.

"We don't sell data, we never have," Walter continues. The data they store is anonymized. "Part of the worry, I think, in the

U.S. is that there's going to be some kind of sweeping reproductive surveillance by the state—how realistic that is, is hard to tell."

The risk is that cycle tracking companies might be subpoenaed by governments. Walter says, "We will never respond to any request by law enforcement." What's more, they have never received such a request before. "We have users in every country in the world—many of which are not great on reproductive rights—and no government has ever tried." Besides, she says GDPR would make it illegal for Clue to disclose any of its user data.

"In European countries, part of the philosophical background of GDPR is really providing a bulwark for citizens against the fascism that Europe experienced in the twentieth century," she says. "We live in Germany, and Germany is particularly data paranoid. Because right here where I'm sitting, two different regimes used people's private data against them." She is referring to the Nazis, who murdered six million Jews, and the Stasi, who ran a totalitarian regime. "That memory sits deep," she says. "And the idea that German authorities would facilitate or even let us help another country's government prosecute its citizens based on health data? I mean, it's absurd!"

Whether our data is safe with a company partly depends on a company's business model. Clue is a freemium app—the majority of users have the free app, while some pay for Clue's conception and contraception premium version. What percentage of their users would have to pay for the app for it to be a sustainable business?

"We're a digital business at the end of the day. Our margins are strong, and our cost to produce something is relatively low, given we're not shipping anything or manufacturing anything," says Tsang. "So, it's a surprisingly small percent, and I think it's very achievable for us in the very near future."

Pee, spit, mucus, and breath

There are many ways to track our cycles by measuring rising hormone levels, as well as changes in our mucus and even in our breath. Each menstrual cycle, estrogen levels rise after the period. At its peak level, estrogen triggers ovulation. After ovulation, estrogen falls and progesterone rises. Progesterone stimulates the endometrium, the lining of the uterus, to prepare for pregnancy. If no pregnancy occurs, progesterone falls back to its baseline, the endometrium is shed through the period, and the cycle starts all over again. The rise and fall of these hormones impacts everything from our immune system to PMS.

An emerging number of start-ups are finding new ways to pinpoint our cycles. "I invented Proov in my basement in 2016, after my battle with infertility and miscarriage," says Dr. Amy Beckley, CEO of Proov. "I have a PhD in pharmacology, and I got married and tried to get pregnant, and it just didn't come easy to us. I was labeled 'unexplained infertile.'" She had her first child through IVF but didn't want to do IVF again for her second.

She thought, "I'm going to figure it out, because I have a scientific background." She talked to her reproductive endocrinologist and looked at the research. "The theory was, I was ovulating—making eggs—they were getting fertilized, but my body wasn't making enough progesterone to support the pregnancy, so I kept having miscarriages." It's called a luteal phase deficiency. Instead of going through another round of IVF, she asked for medication

to support her progesterone levels, after "timed intercourse"—
the technical term for having sex in time for ovulation. "Within
two cycles, I was pregnant, and I stayed pregnant—and she's
nine," she says with a beaming smile.

"Ovulation is not yes or no" is how Beckley puts it. In addition
to releasing an egg, the ovary has to produce enough progesterone to support the pregnancy. "We designed a urine-based test
that measures progesterone metabolites, and we measure them
across the implantation window."

Implantation happens in the luteal phase of the cycle.
"Typically, what happens is your egg gets released, if you timed
intercourse correctly—sperm fertilizes egg—it's gotta go from
the ovary all the way through the fallopian tube down to the
uterus and implant—that journey takes about seven to ten days.
It's really important that your progesterone remains high enough,
so that when it gets to the uterus, it can implant." The test is
FDA-cleared, and Proov has an active Facebook community.

Proov

She has raised $14 million from investors and another $2 million in non-dilutive grants from the National Science Foundation, the State of Colorado, and the U.S. Air Force. Why is the Air Force funding a fertility start-up? "Infertility rates are three times higher in the Air Force—in the military in general—than the general public," says Dr. Beckley. That's because people could be exposed to radiation, toxic chemicals, or poor water quality depending on their roles. Once again, an entrepreneur has solved an issue she encountered herself.

Spit

The answer to what your cycle is up to, could also be at the tip of your tongue. Over in Berlin, I talk to Eirini Rapti, the CEO of Inne. "I was always on the Pill or on the IUD," she says. "And in my early thirties, I started questioning it. The biggest rupture for me was getting divorced." She moved back to Europe from Malaysia and enjoyed being single. "I didn't want to be hormonally treated," she says. "I was experiencing a rebirth of my own body. I could actually—to put it bluntly—I could feel when I was aroused for the first time in a very long time, and you know, it's one of these things, arousal, that when you tune in, you feel it more and more and more, right?"

Once she was in a new relationship, she talked to her gynecologist back in Greece to find out which contraceptive method to try next. "How about we go natural?" The gynecologist taught her how to identify her ovulation and fertile window by charting her periods and temperature. "I remember thinking she was crazy," says Rapti. "I called my boyfriend, and he was like, 'Let's freaking do this. Let's just try. We both learn.' Long story short, I fell in love with the practice." It became an obsession of wanting to learn more about her body—and inspired her company, Inne, which has developed a saliva test, the inne minilab, that can track progesterone and cortisol levels.

"We establish your baseline, which can be different from mine, and different from cycle to cycle, and then once this baseline is established, we can start looking for a rise," she says. They don't just look for one rise in progesterone but three to confirm ovulation.

inne minilab

Unlike an LH test, she says, the inne can also identify anovulation, which is when an egg was not released from the ovary. It can identify a luteal phase deficiency. By analyzing cortisol, it can analyze the impact of stress on your reproductive health. "There's more and more research on how cortisol impacts whether you ovulate, whether you sustain a pregnancy, how bad your menopausal symptoms are," she says. But more research is—as always—needed.

Mucus

Cervical mucus is another fertile ground for cycle analysis. I speak to Kristina Cahojova, who is heavily pregnant and apologizes for eating a clementine while we talk. She always had very irregular periods. "It could be, like, 21 days to 70, completely random," she says. When her husband was transferred to Google's headquarters in Mountain View, she had "nothing to do. No friends. I didn't know a single person." So, she decided to focus on something she never had time for before: investigating her irregular cycles.

Making the most of Google's health insurance, she went to a reproductive endocrinologist, who told her to track her cervical mucus to understand the patterns of her cycle in a diary. "I was like, What the fuck? Do we track blood by how we see it or how we taste it? No! We have tests for everything and hardcore data!" Men aren't told to analyze their sperm by journaling. She decided to take matters into her own hands.

In her research, Cahojova came across "electrical imped-ance," which is typically used to understand the cycles of dairy cows, by analyzing their cervical mucus. (Yes, even cows get more innovation.) Within a menstrual cycle, the shift from estro-gen to progesterone dominance changes the electrolyte levels of the cervical mucus.

Her company's device, kegg looks like an oversize white grape drooping from a branch, with two golden circles at the bottom— they're the sensors that analyze the electrolyte levels of mucus. It's an FDA-registered Class I medical device. As well as being a cycle tracker, kegg is a two-in-one device that doubles as a pelvic floor trainer.

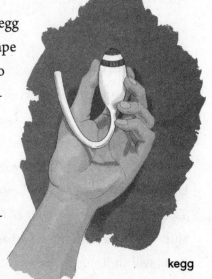

kegg

Breath

Most people don't know that it's possible to track our cycles through our breathing. Ovulation literally takes our breath away.

"CO_2 correlates with the estradiol, so it's going down before ovulation," says Lisa Krapinger-Rüther, co-CEO of Vienna-based breathe ilo. She compares the changes in our breath to hyperventilation.

In clinical settings, the method of tracking a cycle through our breath has been used for decades, but this is the first at-home device. The breathe ilo device measures the CO_2 levels in your breath to analyze your cycle on an app. It requires sixty seconds of breathing per day. She recommends not drinking sodas or going for a run right beforehand, as that interferes with your breathing.

breathe ilo

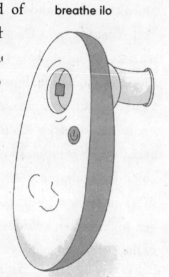

Cycle biohacking

Krapinger-Rüther has observed a fascinating shift in their device's user base. When the device launched, 90 percent of users were trying to conceive, and 10 percent used it for biohacking, which means observing aspects of your body and making incremental changes to improve your health, well-being, or performance. Two years later, 60 percent of their users are trying to conceive and 40 percent use it for biohacking, and she predicts that this trend will continue. "They want to know much more about their menstrual cycle. They want to understand why they have low energy sometimes, high energy other times.

"People have lower energy in the second half of the cycle," she says. "After ovulation, we can see that a lot of people have a dip in their mood." On the topic of fitness, she says, "You're more likely to build muscle in the follicular phase." That's the phase between menstruation and ovulation. She recommends higher-intensity sports in the follicular phase and slowing down, perhaps with yoga, in the luteal phase.

New apps have emerged to cater to those who want to improve their fitness by understanding their cycle better. Wild AI has created an app for women who do sports to train and recover based on their menstrual cycle. Jennis, created by the British athlete Jessica Ennis-Hill, is a wellness app for women to create an exercise regime based on their menstrual cycle.

If we count meditation or intermittent fasting as biohacking, then it's an idea that has been around for a long time. Wearable devices give us new ways to track our bodies—including our cycles—if we choose to. At this point, the research on how our cycle phases impact performance is still nascent and at times contradictory—and there is a lot of individual variation—so countercheck any biohacking advice with your own observations.

It is yet to be seen whether period dates, temperature, spit, pee, breath, or mucus wins the race to decode our menstrual cycles in the long run. There is currently no research on how these new devices compare. Each method partly depends on how accurately the device is used. It's possible that one method proves to be more reliable or more user friendly than the rest. It is also possible that one method has the better marketing strategy. Whether we prefer to pee on a stick or lick a stick could also be culturally dependent.

There is no Pearl Index for these devices yet. But it's only a matter of time for them to move into the contraceptive space. One day it might be possible to track an egg as it emerges from the ovary with an EggTrack app. But even if we could track an egg, that would not be enough to prevent pregnancy—that would need to be complemented with a SpermTrack device.

Understanding our bodies and our cycles can be empowering, because they have been shrouded by taboos far too long. The same is true for female sexual pleasure. I go on a search of those who demystify it.

6

SEXTECH

DEMYSTIFYING THE FEMALE ORGASM

In her early twenties, Berkeley-educated Anna Lee had a job as a mechanical engineer at Amazon in the Bay Area. In that role, she created novel ways for people to turn a page in a Kindle book. "It would feel like a button without a button actually being there," she says. A force sensor, sensitive to the push of a finger, turns the page and it's the same type of sensor that makes the door handles of a Tesla pop open. There is no way Lee could have known how she might use these sensors one day.

"I felt like I had a lot to prove as an engineer," says Lee. On a team of sixteen engineers, she was the only woman. "I dress a little more girly," she says. "You just never forget that you're different when you're a woman in engineering." The event that stood out was when her team 3D-printed a prototype for a wristwatch. It was supposed to be unisex. As she tried it on her wrist, she remembers saying, "I don't think this fits most women's wrists!" The face of the wristwatch was larger than her wrist. "They had this look of, 'Oh my gosh, we never thought of that.'"

Attending a tech conference, she met the founder of a sex toy company. From a product design perspective, Lee knew what Kindles have to endure to pass the testing phase: they are grabbed with sunscreen fingers, attacked with spills from Coke cans, and abandoned on a car dashboard in the sweltering desert sun. She asked the founder: How are sex toys tested? This is when she learned about an established industry standard: sex toys are tested on the tip of your nose, and that supposedly equals the sensitivity of a clitoris.

"I grew up in a conservative Korean family, so I was always scared of my own body," she says. But now she felt she had a superpower most engineers lack: she could design female-centric products. The not-so-unisex wristwatch and the nose-tested toy had illuminated the way.

Together with Liz Klinger and James Wang, she cofounded the sex toy company Lioness based in Berkeley, California. What interested Lee about sex toys was their organic shape—and she certainly wouldn't test them on her nose. Their idea was to create an AI vibrator that would adjust to your body's preferences. But a major hurdle scuttled this plan: There wasn't enough data on female orgasms to train such a toy. They would have to start with research.

The Ocean Wave

The Lioness team raised over $130,000 on Indiegogo, more than twice their original goal of $50,000, to launch their Lioness Smart Vibrator, which can measure and visualize female orgasms on an app. Lee spent three years building prototypes by hand

and 3D-printing them—from clay to foam, she created over one hundred iterations.

There are many ways of measuring a female orgasm. Our pupils dilate. Our heart rate goes up, and our breath shortens. The Lioness measures pelvic floor contractions, and what better way to do that than by using force sensors—which can detect really fine changes in pressure—as Lee already knew from her work on Kindles.

A Lioness vibrator has two force sensors on each side. It illustrates the pattern of an orgasm on an app in real time. The team has collected an unprecedented number of 100,000 sessions, all of which are anonymized. As Lee says, "My mum has a Lioness. I would never want to know her data or when she used it!" There are three primary types of female orgasms—although it's likely other patterns exist—according to their data, as well as smaller academic studies that have been done before.

Female Orgasm Patterns

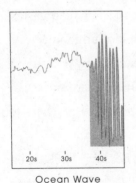
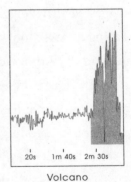

Ocean Wave   Avalanche   Volcano

Lioness.

They call the most common pattern the Ocean Wave. It is a rhythmic squeezing and relaxing of the pelvic floor muscles at a balanced level of force and relaxation. Its ripples are even. Almost three-quarters of orgasms fall into this pattern.

The second pattern, the Avalanche, has ripples that commence at a high force descending into a slope. The third pattern, the Volcano, has a pronounced spike that is followed by a dramatic drop. "It's what we consider a classic in the movies," says Lee. "It's how they would perform an orgasm." It is telling that most orgasms don't actually follow this Hollywood pattern.

"One of the most interesting things is right before the orgasm, we see what we call a quieting period," says Lee. "You see all these spikes, and then right before the orgasm you see this drop that's very steady." Something else the team discovered is that people don't seem to switch between patterns.

Orgasms can be the canary in the coal mine for a multitude of health issues. An athlete who uses the Lioness saw her orgasm flatline after she experienced a concussion. A dentist who researches sleep apnea and male erectile dysfunction has suggested analyzing the effect of sleep apnea on female orgasms. Taking a closer look at female orgasms could illuminate everything from cardiovascular health, as we already know that there's a parallel link between erectile dysfunction and cardiovascular health, to mental health. "We want to empower researchers to pioneer these studies," says Lee.

Lee herself shares her explorations with her large fan base on TikTok. Coffee enhances her orgasms, while alcohol and stress diminish their strength. "This has been a journey for me to be super comfortable." When she first joined the company, she never intended to become its public face. "I didn't want to talk about my own sexuality," she says. "I just wanted to be known as a good engineer! Obviously, this has changed quite a bit." We laugh.

Beyond the dildo

The term "sextech" was popularized by Cindy Gallop, who defined it as "technology, and technology-driven ventures, designed to enhance, innovate, and disrupt in every area of human sexuality and human sexual experience."

"We have not even begun to see what the landscape of sextech could be," Gallop told me. "The big problem at the moment is that when you say 'sextech,' people think one of two things: sex toys or sex robots. And there is so much more already, especially, being started by female founders beyond that." Besides, men are not typically the targets of sexual harassment and revenge porn, so they're less likely to put safeguards in place.

The non-profit Callisto, set up by Jessica Ladd, is creating a tech platform to make the reporting of sexual assault easier. Ohnut, designed by Emily Sauer, is a wearable set of silicon rings that serve as a buffer during penetrative sex for those who experience chronic pain. Emjoy, headed up by Andrea Oliver, is a collection of audio erotica.

Lorals is ultrathin latex underwear, created by Melanie Cristol, to protect from STIs during foreplay. VDom, an inflatable smart prosthetic penis, was developed by Denise Kinard-Moore, who wanted to have more spontaneous sex with her wife; she later discovered there is also demand from disabled people.

Nobody comes to the sextech industry through a degree in it. The closest you can get is by joining the Women of SexTech, led by Polly Rodriguez in New York, or attending the SexTech School, run online by Bryony Cole.

Working at Microsoft in New York, where Cole had moved from Melbourne, Australia, she hit a midcareer crisis in her thirties. Cole says, "I felt for so long, since I was a young girl, since I had gone through puberty, I'd been told to be small." It was time for a big change.

Inspired by the work of Esther Perel, she launched her Future of Sex podcast. "I had no idea what I was doing. I googled 'how to grow a podcast.'" The answer was to organize live events. Some Aussie friends had a café in Brooklyn, where she hosted the first event with a panel including Alexandra Fine, the CEO of Dame, and Polly Rodriguez, the CEO of Unbound. There were twenty-five people in the audience, and "twenty were my friends," she laughs. "But it grew from there very quickly over that summer." A few events later, there were one hundred people in the audience. "A journalist from the *New York Times* turned up, and that's when I realized, I'm on to something."

"I had a very average sex education and was just thirsty for knowledge," says Cole. Her podcast has been downloaded a million times. "And now six years down the track, I feel I've learned so much more personally than I anticipated." She has learned "how important my own pleasure and wellness are, and how important it is to communicate what you want, both in sex and relationships."

Sex research

Today, start-up entrepreneurs use tech to research and talk about sex. Originally, sex research emerged in academia, when Alfred Kinsey at Indiana University conducted a large-scale survey in the 1950s, showing that sexuality is a fluid continuum—called the Kinsey scale—in between heterosexual to homosexual, rather than two binary camps. He found that 80 percent of us are in the bisexual middle.

One decade later, William Masters and Virginia Johnson spent eleven years observing hundreds of volunteers—some with paper bags over their heads to preserve their anonymity—have more than 11,000 orgasms in soundproof laboratories. In studies that would no longer make it past an ethics committee today, Masters and Johnson charted the volunteers' breathing, heart rates, and perspiration, as they watched them masturbate and have sex with each other or with a camera dildo.

With their landmark study *Human Sexual Response*, published in 1966, they dispelled common myths of their time: masturbation does not lead to insanity, sex during pregnancy does not harm the fetus, women are not naturally "frigid" but can be multi-orgasmic. Masters and Johnson believed that all female orgasms were clitoral, because a vaginal orgasm still stimulates the clitoris—which is largely under the skin and hugs the vaginal canal like an octopus— from another angle.

As I'm writing this book, I have been asking friends to draw a clitoris. So far, nobody has come close to drawing it accurately. The clitoris, which is only visible at its peak, like the snow-covered top of a mountain, can be as big as 10 centimeters below the surface, and it has the shape of a wishbone with bulbs. It speaks volumes that most of us can't draw it.

Next time you find yourself wanting to draw a clitoris
in a public bathroom, here's a template.

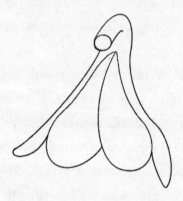

It's a reminder that female anatomy is overlooked. It goes some way to explain why heterosexual women orgasm during sex 65 percent of the time, while 95 percent of heterosexual men do, according to a 2018 study. Meanwhile, lesbian women orgasm 86 percent of the time.

Go Same

I'm early for my next interview at a French bakery in San Francisco. Sitting down at one of the tables on the sidewalk, I notice that the table wobbles. Like many things in central San Francisco, it stands on a steep hill, so I quickly stuff a pack of chewing gum under one of the legs, when Rob Perkins walks down the street with a wide smile and spiky blond hair. For most of our conversation, he positions himself on the chair cross-legged like he's sitting on a yoga mat.

I ask what it's like for him to be an expert at female sexual pleasure. At dinner parties, he encounters similar reactions to those of a sex therapist. When answering the ever-recurring "What do you do?" Perkins is met with what he imitates as nasal laughter: "'Ohh!'" He says, "The way a sex therapist silences that joke session is to talk about dysfunction or problems like, 'I work with people with spinal bifida.' 'Oh, okay.' There's this idea that talking about sexual function and pleasure for a population that needs medical attention is legitimate."

Conversely, talking about pleasure for the sake of pleasure— the idea of going from good to better—evokes discomfort. It evokes giggles. Pleasure for those who are already well, and flourishing, can feel frivolous. It is seen as selfish. The tentacles of this attitude extend far and wide. "It's the idea of someone just being gluttonous. In America, hard work and sacrifice are virtuous, whereas eating delicious food and running your toes through the grass, and masturbating, is frowned upon."

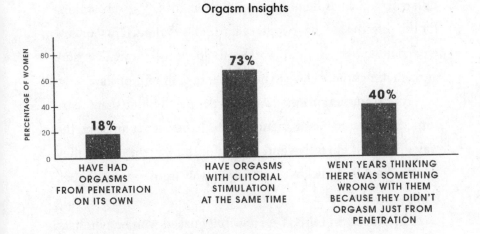

Orgasm Insights

OMGYes.com.

In college, Perkins shared a house with a group of friends. "Someone in the group realized that before orgasm, they need the motion to stay exactly the same," he says. "The expression in our group was just 'Go Same.'"

This idea inspired the name of their Burning Man camp. Years later, it would inspire their work, when Perkins partnered with his friend and cofounder, Lydia Daniller, a documentary filmmaker, whose life calling is to capture queer couples as fine art. Together, they interviewed a range of women to find out what they have discovered about their sexual pleasure. Their guiding question was: What do you wish you had known earlier? "Being in the room was so powerful," says Perkins. They documented these interviews on their platform, OMGYes.

Live-action vulvas

Partnering with researchers at Indiana University, they ran a large-scale, nationally representative study with 1000 respondents of different ethnicities, demographics, and incomes. "We were looking for the patterns in what people realize," says Perkins. They uncovered that women who can give details about their sexual pleasure are eight times more likely to be happier in their relationship.

"A really common email we get is people thinking that there's something wrong with them, because they don't orgasm the way they see it in Hollywood movies or the way they think they should," says Perkins. "We try to steer away from orgasm as goal, when possible."

The videos on OMGYes show fully naked women who talk about their pleasure. They show close-ups of live-action vulvas.

And yet, none of it feels pornographic. It's extraordinary. And they don't shy away from delving into sexual pleasure after trauma, trans pleasure, and pleasure in menopause.

The ongoing research now includes over 20,000 women. Their resulting videos introduce techniques, such as "edging"— delaying an orgasm to increase its intensity. Perkins says, "Some people get close to orgasm and just stop." He brings up his hands and draws rising circles in the air. "Some people get close to orgasm and then distract. And some people get close to orgasm and go all the way back to zero."

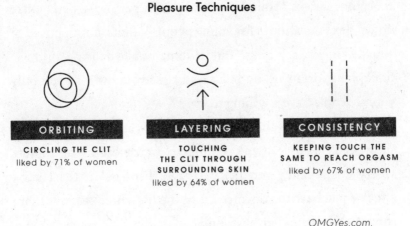

Pleasure Techniques

ORBITING
CIRCLING THE CLIT
liked by 71% of women

LAYERING
TOUCHING
THE CLIT THROUGH
SURROUNDING SKIN
liked by 64% of women

CONSISTENCY
KEEPING TOUCH THE
SAME TO REACH ORGASM
liked by 67% of women

OMGYes.com.

What does it take to understand your own pleasure? First, there's having hedonic insight, the idea of knowing what you like. "That is difficult right there for many," says Perkins. Then, it's knowing that what you like is legitimate. And finally, it's being able to communicate it.

"Partners can be really fragile about getting feedback, and there's fear that it's going to be hurtful," says Perkins. For many heterosexual men, it might be easier to hear "Look, there is this new research" rather than "Here's something you need to learn!"

OMGYes began with live-action vulvas, but now they are working on illustrations too. "We're finding that a non-explicit version with motion diagrams is actually more palatable." Many people come to OMGYes through the recommendation of their doctors or therapists, and Perkins believes a non-explicit version could accelerate that. Perhaps this version is more likely to be used in sex education, I wonder.

"There's a myth that we call the 'immaculate education,'" says Perkins, "that when you turn eighteen, you should just know everything about your body, and your partner's, and you're done." Sex education is for young people; adults are supposed to already know everything. "But in domains like dancing, or travel or cooking, or music, no one says I already know it all and only young people have anything to learn."

Since OMGYes first launched in 2015, attention spans have shortened. "People aren't willing to watch even four-minute videos the way they were five years ago," he says. "It's the TikTok effect—you have to convince me in the first three seconds that I should stick around until second ten."

Most start-ups in San Francisco, who raise VC money, aim for a growth curve that's as steep as the hill we are sitting on. They call it "hockey stick growth." Perkins prefers sustainable growth. The company has been cash flow positive since launch. A group of angel investors funded the company, getting back what they put in and additional amounts. OMGYes has over 100,000 subscribers and a team of ten, headquartered in Berkeley, California. It's available in twelve languages for a one-off payment.

The tendency I detected among VC investors to shut down the topic—no vaginas on a Monday morning—does not stop with investors. It also happens when young researchers want to study sex. It happens when academics submit articles on sex to prestigious journals. "The same way investors are shy about this, so are healthcare systems and governments," says Perkins. It's a reaction he has encountered at well-known institutions. It's easier to say no. It's easier to laugh it off.

In recent years, sexual well-being has received more attention. The World Health Organization has declared that good sexual health is "fundamental to the overall health and well-being of individuals, couples, and families and to the social and economic development of communities and countries." Research has found that sexual health programs are more successful if they don't focus only on preventing disease, as has traditionally been the case, but on promoting and acknowledging sexual pleasure as well.

Sexual pleasure is integral to our well-being. On OMGYes, "the touch techniques are the shiny thing to get people to go, 'Okay, I'll spend a Friday night doing that,'" says Perkins, "but the real effect is seeing a woman in her seventies say that she just discovered something that week about her pleasure, and realizing 'Wow, you do keep learning.'" It's seeing that pleasure "can expand and get better and better."

People just aren't designing in that space

When it comes to sexual well-being, the range of taboos is never-ending. I decide to look at a space that remains largely hidden.

"My younger brother, Andrew Gurza, is a disabled man, who lives with cerebral palsy, and he is also a disability activist," says Heather Morrison, the CEO and cofounder of Bump'n, which is based in Sydney. In 2017, Gurza appeared in a documentary called *Picture This*, where he spoke about his experiences of dating, relationships, and his sexuality. "A lot of people incorrectly assume the disabled community to be asexual or nonsexual," says Morrison.

"Disabled people are, at the end of the day, people like everybody else, and they have a whole realm of different sexual appetites and needs," she says. "In the documentary, he mentioned that he had lost the ability to masturbate. Even though we grew up together, I never think about how my brother masturbates—it's just not something I considered," she says, blushing, exactly like an older sister would.

After watching the documentary, she asked him why he doesn't use a sex toy. He explained, "They're both predicated on the ability to use fine motor skills and dexterity and have reach, to be able to sustain a motion for a long enough period of time. If I could use a sex toy, I would pretty much be able to use my hands unaided." Morrison realized that nothing in the sextech space had been designed for people with limited hand mobility. "I was really shocked, and I said to him, very naively, 'do you want to change that?'"

They decided to design the first sex toy for disabled people. What began as a case study of one led them to conduct a survey to find out whether this was a common problem. "We put it out into as many disability community subreddits online. We had about 150 responses all from people who are physically disabled." Over 56 percent of respondents did have difficulty self-pleasuring, and 92 percent of respondents, whether they had difficulty self-pleasuring or not, were seeking some device or toy that was designed with the disabled community in mind. Morrison says, "People just aren't designing in that space, full stop."

The most popular design

They partnered with a team of industrial designers, engineers, and occupational therapists at RMIT University to run a larger study, and they raised $15,000 (CAD) on GoFundMe to pay for it. Their initial ideas included a vibrating mini beanbag.

"We talked to about fifteen people with disabilities and fifteen occupational therapists around the world." The most popular design resulted in their Joystick. It looks like a long pillow with a large lobster claw. It's popular, "because it works across both sexes and has a lot of versatility," she says. "It was always meant to be something that you kind of hug into, and the middle component would have, like, a vibrator or a penis sleeve." They partnered with a commercial design firm to turn the prototype into a viable product.

Joystick

In the testing phase, they asked people to break the prototype, to find its weaknesses. They watched people assemble the product to make sure the packaging is as accessible to those with limited hand mobility. "It would be a terrible look to be, like, 'We're designing to make this accessible,' and then people being, like, 'Good one. I can't get it out of the box.'" For this reason, they've designed a large sticker with handles to open the box. "The idea is that you basically hook your hands into those loops," she says, and pulling the loops opens the whole box.

How many people have limited hand mobility? "When you look at developed countries around the world, we are looking at close to 500 million people, that takes into account people with disabilities that affect their hands, and then on top of that, people who have arthritis. That's likely to affect their hands as well." Clinicians have told them that patients who can use their hands but have low core stability could benefit from the device too.

"I did not realize how much it costs to make a physical product," says Morrison. No founder has ever told me their product cost less to develop than expected. It took three years to design the toy. Added to their GoFundMe money, they won awards in the disability space that came with funding, and they received some angel and institutional investment, adding up to $330,000 (CAD). The Joystick is available through a government-funded scheme in Australia, the National Disability Insurance Scheme, which covers different types of assistive technology.

"Everything we did is underpinned by this ethos: nothing for us without us. We always are in collaboration and consultation with the disabled community," says Morrison. "Andrew is the company's Chief Disability Officer"—a title they made up. "I don't think you can have a larger purpose without being guided by the people whom you're meant to be helping.

"A lot of people, both able-bodied and disabled-bodied, have a lot of questions around sex and disability, because from an able-bodied perspective, it's kind of taboo and we don't know how to address it," says Morrison. "And from a disabled perspective, because it's been so taboo for them, they haven't always felt they have a safe space to discuss it."

There are innovators who create new products, and then there are those who create access to existing products in places where people struggle to receive what they need.

Don't think about saving her soul—save her body

There have been several occasions when nurses mistook Morenike Fajemisin for a patient. Once, when working with the Nigerian government, she was asked to inspect the cold chain storage at a health center in Lagos. "But they didn't know that was why I was there," says Fajemisin, who is a trained pharmacist, looks younger than her age, wears cat eye glasses, and has heaps of charisma and a generous smile. There was a family planning day at the health center. The nurse jumped to the conclusion that Fajemisin was an unmarried, single girl looking for contraception. "'You don't need this! What you need to do is to stop sleeping with men!'—she gave me the full lecture."

"Here's a woman, who was in a facility that was offering contraception, whose job as a nurse is to make sure that those who are coming in, because they needed contraception, can get the care they need—she was chasing me out of the facility! Because she was personally concerned that I shouldn't be having sex in the first place," she says. "I remember being livid for hours after. That's exactly what she's going to do to the next younglooking woman that comes in."

On another occasion, she was working for DKT, a nonprofit she was a founding member of, providing contraceptive supplies to health centers. A nurse called her over and asked, "Are you a Christian?" She said yes. The nurse went on to criticize her for delivering contraceptives. Fajemisin retorted, "If the same girl that you've just refused contraception to shows up for an abortion, who are you going to blame?" The nurse said, "Her! Because she knows she should close her legs."

"And I said 'No, I would blame *you*. You are the one that made her have an unwanted pregnancy. She told you she doesn't want to close her legs, she told you she wants to get a contraceptive and you did not give it to her, so you are to blame.'" The nurse sat back and went quiet. Fajemisin's point sank in. Then, the nurse said she didn't know how to reconcile her duty as a nurse with her duty as a Christian mother. "At this time, it's your duty to first help her. Save her from the pregnancy. Don't think about saving her soul yet—save her body first!"

Abortion is legal in Nigeria only when it's performed to save the mother's life. And yet, the country has one of the highest abortion rates in the world, according to the Guttmacher Institute. Clandestine abortions by unskilled providers are a major contributor to the country's high levels of maternal death, ill health, and disability. Meanwhile, the use of modern contraceptives is very low, with only 12 percent of people using them, according to the latest Nigeria Demographic and Health Survey.

When Fajemisin joined DKT as a founding member, there was only one brand of condoms on the market. "I helped introduce over twenty different reproductive health products into

Nigeria by getting them registered at our own FDA, called NAFDAC." Prior to that, Fajemisin worked in HIV and tuberculosis management. After a decade of working in the sexual and reproductive health space in Nigeria, she felt "strictly working in family planning, or contraception or birth control as Americans call it, just wasn't closing all the gaps."

They only ever tell girls, not boys

I ask Fajemisin about sex education in Nigeria. "It doesn't exist at any level," she says. In the absence of any formal sex education, people turn to informal sources of information. "And they are also limited by the dividends of colonialism and the religions that are popular. Nigeria is mostly Christian in the south and mostly Muslim in the north," she says. Abstinence before marriage is a common expectation.

"What I find very interesting with the insistence on virginity is that they only ever tell girls—they don't tell the boys," she says. "It's even assumed that the boy will gain some experience." Who with? She quips, "Some fictional girl who is not your daughter?"

With no formal education, "it is not surprising that there are still some myths that will blow your mind." What are some of these myths? "If you have sex when you're on top, the sperm will flow down so you won't get pregnant." There are people who believe "if the person looks clean, you can't have an STI," she says.

It's one of the reasons she decided to pursue a sexual health educator certification in Canada. "It occurred to me that the best person to fix this is going to be someone like me," she says.

Even as a young pharmacy student, she was already sought out by her peers. Her thesis was on the healthcare-seeking behavior of young people who had STIs, and she surveyed her peers. "I had people pull me aside saying, 'thank you for letting me fill in that survey; I have some other questions.'" Or she would leave the room, and someone would corner her at the far end of the dormitory, asking her questions they obviously felt too embarrassed to ask their doctors. It was the first time of many when people would seek her advice, whispering, "I have a friend who..."

"How many are going to know me and feel bold enough to be able to ask me? But if I created a system, a business around solving this problem, then I could really reach more people," she says. "So that's when the dream for Whispa was born. I wanted to say to people: here's the right way to whisper."

The right way to whisper

At her company, Whispa Health, she says, "We're taking off the barrier young people might have around seeking access." Most of their clients are between eighteen and thirty-five years old. About 70 percent of their users are women. On the app, people can order products like condoms, at-home oral HIV tests, and emergency contraception. All products are delivered in plain, inconspicuous packaging.

People can chat with doctors anonymously by text on the Whispa app and book sexual health appointments. "It offers that shield of privacy our users want," she says. In the testing phase of Whispa, they discovered that anonymity was of paramount importance. "You're young, you're single, and you're in a society that believes you are virgins until marriage. You know you have to maintain some pious behavior on the outside, when your sex life is considered sinful," she says.

"You want privacy"; otherwise, "there's this slim chance that you're going to get recognized as that person that had HPV or genital warts last month." At clinics, Whispa users can simply say, "I have an appointment from Whispa," and their name will be on a list; nobody at the reception has to know more.

Fajemisin's team has identified health professionals, clinics, and laboratories that treat people in an open-minded way. "Lagos is the New York of Nigeria," she says. "It's the commercial epicenter. Lagos itself is, as we joke, a country. It's nearly 20 million people in one state, a good place to start before we began identifying partners across the country."

The Whispa app has been downloaded over 35,000 times. "That's the ecosystem I dreamt up," says Fajemisin. It has taken years to build it. "But I never gave up on that dream that the sexual reproductive health space was broader than family planning and that there needed to be a shame-free, judgment-free way for people to get the healthcare they need."

In 2019, Fajemisin won the 120 under 40 Ingenuity Fund. "Prior to that I'd been burning through my own savings, just building the product. It was a small grant, but it was exactly the leg up we needed to get the ball rolling," she says. Since then, Fajemisin has built a team of fifteen people.

"We can't remake the world overnight," she tells me at one point. But I feel that if anyone is remaking the world gradually, it is her. By providing access to contraception and STI testing, she is changing the conversation around sexual health. At the same time, the contraceptive space is changing rapidly. I want to find out what the future of contraception looks like.

7

THE FUTURE OF
CONTRACEPTION

I'VE SEEN THIS IN SCI-FI

Soon after my friend Amie stopped taking the contraceptive pill, she noticed an unexpected change. "It's super weird," she says. "All of a sudden, I'm attracted to types of men I have never fancied before." They are more alpha. It's a shift in attraction. And it's one of the lesser-known side effects of the Pill.

The Pill gave women unprecedented freedom when it was introduced in the 1960s. It also became a new form of pain medication. And yet, it remains somewhat of a mass experiment, as we are only beginning to research its many facets.

Women try an average of three to four different contraceptive methods in their lifetimes, according to research by the Kaiser Family Foundation. Reversible methods, like the Pill and male condoms, are more common in Europe and Africa, whereas permanent methods, including sterilization, implants, and the IUD, are more common in North America and Asia. But for 91 percent of us, there is no contraceptive method that has

all the features we find "extremely important," according to the
Guttmacher Institute.

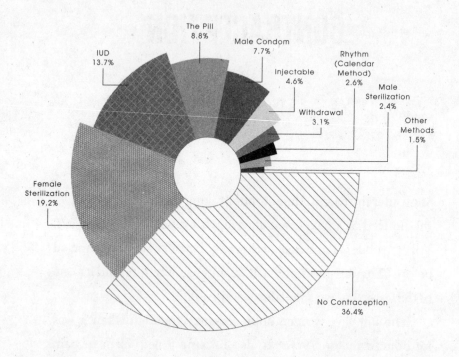

No contraception
is still the most common way of doing it globally.

United Nations, Contraceptive use worldwide.

A few weeks later, Amie returned to the Pill because its
benefits outweigh its downsides for her. The Pill is not only used
to prevent pregnancy. In fact, 58 percent of those who take it rely
on it, at least in part, for noncontraceptive purposes.

The combined Pill, which is the most prescribed type of Pill,
flattens our hormone curves and prevents ovulation. That's why
it can be used to manage pain, acne, mood swings, and headaches.

It can help to regulate the symptoms of endometriosis, fibroids, and PCOS. The Pill's impact is, however, highly individual. It can have the opposite effect and cause acne, headaches, and mood swings, among other side effects. It has also been linked to an increased risk of blood clots and pulmonary embolism.

One consequence that is often overlooked is ecological: the synthetic estrogen contained in the Pill passes through our urine, and it can contribute to the contamination of our rivers.

Before I interview the next CEO, I tell Amie about the company's product: liquid contraception. "You know, I've come across this before," she says thoughtfully, "but it was in science fiction!"

Liquid contraception

Saundra Pelletier is a blond firecracker with irrepressible energy. As the CEO of Evofem Biosciences, she runs one of the biggest companies in the femtech space. Evofem is listed on the NASDAQ, the American tech-heavy stock exchange. Since Pelletier became its CEO in 2015, she has hired 128 full-time employees, 63 percent of whom are women, and raised a staggering $501 million. In the business world of femtech, Pelletier is one of the leaders I think of as va-giants.

At a women's health conference, I heard somebody ask her: What do you do to relax? Without missing a beat, she exclaimed, "Martinis and voodoo dolls!"

This, I thought, is my kind of tech mogul.

Getting hold of Pelletier is not easy. Her chief of staff, Ellen Thomas, runs a tight ship. We arrange a time to speak, but

Pelletier has to catch a plane to meet the U.S. vice president, so I get bumped.

When we finally get to talk on Zoom, she holds up a photo of me. "I was given a lovely picture of you, Marina," she says. "Ellen thinks she's an FBI profiler; she just traced a drop of blood through your body. I know everything about you!" I sit back in my chair. "I'm just kidding!" But is she? There is no doubt that she is thoroughly well prepared. "I thought it was brave," she says about my *Wired* article, "and I think you have to be a little crazy!" I think it takes one to know one.

Her company's product, Phexxi, is a nonhormonal contraceptive gel developed by scientists at Rush University in Chicago. It comes in a prefilled applicator, shaped like a tampon, to be used within an hour before sex. Pelletier says, "A normal vaginal pH is 3.5 to 4.5. When semen enters, the pH goes up to 7 or 8, and a woman gets pregnant." To prevent pregnancy, Phexxi buffers a vagina's acidity, making it hard for sperm to move. "It helps the vagina maintain its normal pH," she says.

The product is 93 percent effective with perfect use in clinical trials reviewed by the FDA and 86 percent effective with typical use. The most common side effects of Phexxi are vaginal burning and itching. The company is currently in clinical trials to figure out if Phexxi's properties help to prevent gonorrhea and chlamydia.

It was initially called Amphora, but the FDA noted it might be confused with the MS drug Ampyra. "We had to come up with a new name," says Pelletier. They hired the Brand Institute, but the idea for their name came from an unexpected source. One of the company's accountants came up with combining "pH"—because the product helps women maintain their natural vaginal pH level—with "xx," female chromosomes, and wouldn't it be great if it rhymed with "sexy"? Phexxi!

The FDA regulates Phexxi as a drug. "Of all the drugs that are brought to market, only 10 percent of them actually get approved by the FDA," says Pelletier. "This is even after doing clinical studies, Phase I, Phase II, Phase III." She estimates it has cost $150 million to bring Phexxi to market.

Phexxi

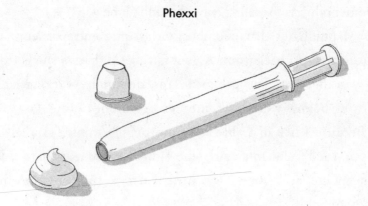

Are people ready for it? I tell her about my friend who said she came across liquid contraception in science fiction. Does Pelletier ever wonder whether it's too novel? "Yes, I do wonder that," she says. "But I don't think it's too novel for women. I think that women intuitively get it. It's like a contact lens. The first time you use it, it's a little awkward. Women are saying to us, 'Oh my god, I can't believe I was taking a pill every day. I was a slave to my contraception. I don't even have sex every week.'"

Not a Californian girl born
with a silver spoon

Pelletier grew up in Caribou, Maine, the easternmost state in the United States. "It's actually the furthest point that you fly to from where I live now, San Diego—that tells you how much I liked it there," she laughs. "Girls could only choose how many kids they had. None of them thought about going to college and being executives or having careers." Her parents worked on assembly lines at a food processing plant in Caribou. It was her mother, Pelletier's biggest supporter, who instilled in her that "if somebody has to be first, why shouldn't it be you?"

I point out that people often assume entrepreneurs are from well-off backgrounds. Is it fair to emphasize she is from a working-class background? "Yes, definitely, working class, if not below, you know, meager beginnings," says Pelletier. "Because I live in California now, people think I'm a silver-spoon-fed Californian girl, who didn't have to work hard a day in my life, and when I was little, I had to pick potatoes in a potato field!"

Her first experience of entrepreneurship was when Pelletier won the state championship for selling Girl Scout cookies. "I was relentless," she says. When I ask whether she remembers how many boxes she sold, Pelletier doesn't bat an eyelid. "I sold a thousand boxes."

Pelletier began her career as a sales representative and rose through the ranks to the executive level, at the pharma company G. D. Searle, which developed the contraceptive pill, now owned by Pfizer. She then launched a nonprofit called WomenCare Global. "When I transitioned from business to nonprofit, I actually believed that I was saving my soul, that I was an evil capitalist, that I wasn't doing enough."

But she felt alienated by other nonprofits. "They were wasteful and delusional. They confused emotion with action. They were holier than thou and thought the rest of the world are knuckle draggers. They were elitists," she says. "I hated the nonprofit world, and I hated the for-profit world. So, I decided, I'm going to make a place where I fit, because I'm going to be the boss."

At Evofem, she raised $25 million from Adjuvant Capital to lower the cost of Phexxi and provide it through nonprofit partnerships in Mexico, Ethiopia, and Ghana. She hopes the next generation of entrepreneurs "are much smarter than I am, and they try to build organizations that are hybrid—because that's really the answer."

Pelletier has a teenage son named Ford. "I've been a single parent since he was a year and a half old. I am hoping that I raised a gentleman and a feminist." How does she combine being a single parent with her high-pressure career? "As they say, it takes a village," she says. "If it weren't for the kindness and support of other women, I would be probably in the fetal position in the corner." She brings her son to work meetings and dinners, and she has a nanny. "My son's school says, 'Who's the mother? Is it Ellen? Is it Sarah? Is it Saundra?'"

What stands in the way?

"Welcome to my vagina" is the opening line of Phexxi's TV ad. "Young women love it. But we've had some older women say,

'I can't believe you say "vagina" on television'. And I say, 'It's a body part'. Is it okay to say 'If you have an erection for more than fourteen hours, call your doctor' because you're using Viagra? Is that okay? But we can't say 'vagina'?"

What stands in the way of female-centric innovation? "Prudish behavior and shame," says Pelletier. "Men, who haven't embraced equality." It also includes "behavior by women who are older, who grew up to be quiet and just suck it up. That mindset needs to change. Those women are not doing a service to the next generation."

The biggest obstacle is the lack of funding for women's health innovation. "People get upset when I say this. They're like, 'Saundra, that's old news—now that's changed.' I say, 'that's bullshit; it hasn't changed.' We're still not funding women's innovation. You know why? They say, 'Well, if it doesn't impact men, why do I have to fund it? It's not diabetes, it's not heart disease, it's not cancer. Why do I want to fund something that only helps women?' and I think, 'do you have a mother? Do you have a daughter? Do you have a wife? Probably not, because you're a jerk!'

"And yes, I did get funding. But it was the most torturous thing I've ever done." She estimates that she has pitched up to one thousand investors. It's not just the fundraising that has been difficult but running a public company comes with its own challenges. Retail investors attack her viciously on social media. "I hate it," she says.

Despite all of this, Pelletier has raised over half a billion dollars since taking over as CEO. What is her secret?

Playing dress-up

As a sales rep in the pharma industry, she was taught "It's the responsibility of the communicator to be the chameleon, to be the one who adapts, and how you present yourself is either going to be distracting or it's going to allow people to focus.

"And so, I have sections in my closet," she says. "Seriously!" There's the Barbara Bush section. "That is when I'm meeting with very conservative people. Their favorite flavor is vanilla, they *follow all the rules*, and they go to church on Sunday." For them, she wears a white blouse and a navy-blue suit. "It is very proper, and I wear pearls. *I actually wear pearls!*" she hollers. "When I put on the outfit, I laugh out loud! Oh, my goodness! And then I say to myself, 'If you have to wear this outfit, you have to deliver. If you're going to dress like this, you have to come back with a win.'

"I have a chauvinist misogynist section of my closet. I do, I really do. And those are the cool, edgy red tuxedo suit, with a camisole, jewelry. I never wear my hair like this." Her hair is tied back as we speak. "When I meet with a misogynist or chauvinist, I always wash my hair. It's always down, so you see that I have blond hair. I always have to be fluffy and pretty for the chauvinist misogynist."

Next up, she has a section for the "kind, good, decent men group." This style, she says, "is still proper, but it's just a regular suit and blouse—those outfits I like." And finally, she has a feminist section, which has everything from "faux fur jackets, feather shirts, red lips on my blouses." What is she wearing for our call? "One of my crazy skirts," she says. From the feminist section. "You don't care what I look like! You care about my brain and my heart and my ability to deliver. I could have worn a face mask!" I'm taken aback—for my interviews, I expect nothing less than a double strand of freshwater pearls.

"You are not evaluating me based on my physicality. I know that, and I love that. But that, unfortunately, is not the norm for me. That is the exception by a huge margin." On days when she doesn't have any site meetings or calls, she wears her feminist clothes. "My assistant knows when we're having outside meetings, because she's like, 'I see you're wearing the funeral outfit today.' 'I see you're Barbara Bush today.'

"I know that sounds weird. But I swear to you, that is one of the secrets of my success. It really is, because you need people to feel comfortable with who you are," she says. It occurs to me that her outfits serve as armor as well as nudges that remind her how to frame her argument. I also wonder if creating a degree of familiarity for the people she pitches could counteract the bias that confident women are perceived as less likable.

Pelletier says, "Why distract from my message? It doesn't serve me! I need them to do the right thing, which is give me money to support access for women."

Contraceptive candor

There is another liquid contraceptive that could be the stuff of sci-fi. I've come to Denmark to find out more. Men on bikes— with trailers full of toddlers—barrel past me as I walk down the street in Copenhagen's Nørrebro neighborhood. The country is known for its strong social institutions and family-friendly policies, including 52 weeks of paid shared parental leave and subsidized childcare. It's no surprise that it frequently ranks among the top countries on the World Happiness Index.

My destination is the BioInnovation Institute (BII), a nonprofit set up by Denmark's Novo Nordisk Foundation, which is the world's wealthiest charitable foundation, because it owns the eponymous pharma company. The BII was established to fund European researchers and support the burgeoning European start-up ecosystem. So far, European countries have lagged the United States in turning academic discoveries into successful life science start-ups.

Frederik Petursson Madsen, the CEO of Cirqle Biomedical, comes through the lobby of the BioInnovation Institute to shake my hand. When his company joined the first cohort of life-science start-ups to be accelerated at this institute, the building was so new, there were no chairs.

We walk past a series of open-plan laboratories where start-ups share equipment and table space with each other. We peek into a "town hall" meeting that is in full swing, held in English and focused on the current development of the building. The building is now bustling with people—and with chairs. Petursson Madsen is soft-spoken yet resolute, leading me directly to a preassigned couch in the lobby that has a professional kind of hygge. He is a guy with a plan. His posture is good.

"I started working on contraception about seven years ago," says Petursson Madsen. At the time, his girlfriend told him that she didn't want to take the contraceptive pill anymore, because of its side effects. "I think I, as many other men, wasn't very aware," he says. "But it didn't take long before I realized: I wouldn't use hormonal contraception!" I'm loving the candor.

Denmark has a long-standing tradition of sex education in the public school system. The number of teenage pregnancies is low, and the conversation about the Pill is changing. "I don't think it's a coincidence that, for instance, research on the side effects is coming out of Denmark and Sweden," he says. "There is a lot of frustration about the side effects and the lack of alternatives to hormonal contraception." Denmark and Sweden are at the forefront of finding alternatives to hormonal contraception, he says, "because there's more openness in terms of talking about these issues."

On hormonal contraception

Nordic countries are also unusual in that they collect longitudinal data from their population for medical databases. This allows researchers to conduct studies with vast sample sizes. A study from 2016, led by Professor Charlotte Wessel Skovlund in Denmark, analyzed the data of over one million women aged fifteen to thirty-four spanning over a decade. It found that teenage girls between fifteen and nineteen who were taking the Pill were more likely to be diagnosed with depression and prescribed antidepressants than those who did not take the Pill.

A second study led by Skovlund, published in 2018, found a link between taking the Pill and an increased risk of suicide. However, a large-scale Finnish study from 2022, led by Dr. Elena Toffol, found the exact opposite: suicide rates were lower among women who took the Pill. There is, therefore, no scientific consensus.

What complicates these large-scale studies is that they are "observational." They analyze large datasets that already exist to find correlations. But while both studies found a link between the Pill and suicide rates, that correlation does not necessarily mean causation.

The gold standard of scientific research is a double-blind, randomized, placebo-controlled trial. They allow researchers to, for example, compare one group of women taking the Pill to a "control group" of women who get a placebo pill but are similar to the first group in terms of their characteristics. "Double-blind" means neither the researchers nor the participants know who is getting the Pill and who is getting the placebo. One such Swedish study was led by Professor Niklas Zethraeus in 2017. It included 322 women, and it found that those who take the Pill have a reduced sense of well-being. What is clear is that many aspects of the Pill remain unknown.

If Petursson Madsen had to generalize, he says about 50 percent of those who use hormonal contraception don't experience any side effects, while the other 50 percent do—and would prefer a different method.

Cirqle Biomedical conducted a study with over 1500 women in the United States: 49 percent said nonhormonal contraception is very or extremely important to them, but only 14 percent use a nonhormonal method. It's not just a Danish issue. "It's a growing trend, so for me, there was good validation to dive further into it," he says.

Petursson Madsen knew there was an unmet need. "One of the theories is that often, the technologies to solve a problem already exist. It's just a matter of cobbling the two together," he says. Could there be an existing technology to address this unmet need?

Mucus engineering

Petursson Madsen says he "spent around two years talking to different researchers" to track down a technology that could work. This included an academic who was developing bioengineered silk. But it was when he met Dr. Thomas Crouzier, a researcher from France who is at the Royal Institute of Technology in Stockholm, that he felt he found the "perfect match between the user need and the technology to create a real breakthrough in contraception."

Shortly after that, Crouzier, the mucus expert, joins our conversation in the lobby. I want to know more about mucus. "It's a gel, it lubricates, it hydrates. You can think of your eyeballs—your eyelids are sliding on a layer of mucus." Mucus is everywhere. "You don't get sick every day, although we do breathe in millions of viruses and bacteria through our lungs, for instance." That's thanks to the defense provided by our airway mucus.

And then, there's cervical mucus, which protects the uterus from bacteria. During pregnancy, it turns itself into a "mucus plug" like the knot at the bottom of a balloon, that protects the womb and the fetus. Outside of a pregnancy, cervical mucus follows the menstrual cycle—it's thick outside of ovulation and acts as a barrier stopping sperm. At the time of ovulation, the mucus loosens up and becomes watery, allowing sperm to swim through.

Even during ovulation, the mucus is "still a very good filter," notes Petursson Madsen. Out of millions and millions of sperm cells, only a few 100,000 make it up to the fallopian tubes.

"Our approach is that we modify that barrier to bring it back to that naturally impenetrable state. We have a small biopolymer that interacts with the components of the mucus at a molecular level," Petursson Madsen says. "What we do is we modify that mucus layer."

Their contraceptive product is called Oui, and in early design ideas it looks like a translucent piece of gummy candy. It would be applied vaginally to dissolve before sex.

Oui

For their initial proof of concept, Crouzier leveraged his university funding to set up a partnership with a Swedish hospital. They created an artificial cervix, using cervical mucus from female donors and sperm cells to show that Oui blocked the sperm.

I ask if it's made of chemicals. "Everything's a chemical!" Petursson Madsen laughs. They use an ingredient called chitosan. "You can derive it from the shell of crustacean and fungi; it is used in a lot of biomedical applications." It's used to stop bleeding and to regenerate nerves. It's also used to preserve food. They have shown that the concept works in a lab setting and got a patent.

"We did our pre-seed round with RH Capital." Their

investors' specialist expertise and due diligence paved the way for them to get the BII funding and raise $1.8 million overall.

As with most areas of women's health, there has not been much research on mucus. "We had to establish our own animal model," he says. Oui is currently tested on sheep. Mice or rodents are typically used in the early stages of health research. How did they land on the sheep? "The issue with rabbits was that there is no evidence they have a cervix filled with mucus that has a filtering and barrier property," Petursson Madsen says. "But that is the case in sheep as one of few animals!"

They went through several iterations to arrive at a gel formulation that blocked all sperm cells. In the first round, 30 sheep did not get pregnant. There will be 200 sheep in the next round, before proceeding to clinical trials with human participants. Oui is regulated by European regulators. The team wants to avoid any side effects of their contraceptive, but as of yet, that is an unknown. If everything goes well, the process from idea to market could take a decade. "I didn't know that it would take so long when I started," Petursson Madsen admits with a somewhat resigned laugh. But I think it's only a matter of time.

The Adam of contraception

Liquid contraception could also work in an entirely different way. About a decade ago, when Kevin Eisenfrats was a seventeen-year-old teenager, he watched the American MTV reality television series 16 and Pregnant. "The women were talking about how the guy obviously didn't use a condom; that's why they're sixteen and pregnant," says Eisenfrats. "And it's always about *her, her, her*—and the guy gets no blame, to be honest. They're like, 'sorry'," he says, imitating them with a goofy smile and a hapless shrug.

In his application for university, Eisenfrats wrote his essay lamenting that there is no male birth control pill. By the time of our interview, he had raised $16 million to develop a nonhormonal and reversible contraceptive for men. It's called ADAM. It seems a bit ironic, given that Adam and Eve were told to be fruitful and multiply. But on another level, it's the first of its kind for men, so it makes sense.

Now, you may wish to point out that a company focused on male contraception is not "femtech"—and you're right. I'm including this company because women have borne the brunt of long-term contraception for too long. To this day, three-quarters of couples in the United States rely on women for birth control. To make contraception a more equitable affair, we need better male contraception.

Traditionally, male contraception has largely been limited to condoms and vasectomies. Is it culture that is holding us back, rather than what's technically possible? And are men ready to step up? These are some of the thoughts on my mind as I speak to Eisenfrats, the charismatic young founder and CEO of Contraline, the company that's creating ADAM, based in Charlottesville, Virginia.

"I wanted to be a doctor from a very early age," says Eisenfrats. Once his essay on the absence of the male pill got him into the University of Virginia, he joined the research lab of Professor John Herr, who spun multiple companies out of his lab, including an at-home sperm count test.

"I was an engineer who was doing reproductive health research," Eisenfrats says. The next step of his plan was to go to medical school, but some friends convinced him to enter an entrepreneurship competition. Despite never having taken a business class, he won. "I came up with an idea that basically was Contraline," he says. But, at the time of the competition, he had another target population: "I wanted to replace neutering for male cats and dogs!"

Time to pivot

Once he graduated, Eisenfrats decided to focus on the company full-time. "Because I was feeling..." His voice trails off and a smile dances around his mouth. "It was exhilarating!" He was twenty-two years old when he started Contraline with Professor Herr.

"We were doing all this market research, talking to veterinarians and dog owners—and there was a lot of pushback." It turned out they were happy with neutering. Instead, they asked Eisenfrats, "Why doesn't this exist for me?" Or "Why doesn't this exist for my husband?" A better unmet need emerged. "We abandoned pet contraception and then pivoted to working on male contraception."

The idea is to put an implant into the vas deferens—the tube that carries sperm from each testicle to the penis—to create a sperm barrier. "People have been trying to work on that since the 1970s," he says. "However, it's never been commercialized, it's never fully worked."

In the 1990s, some twelve thousand men in China were injected with polyurethane. "But polyurethane is actually toxic;

it causes cancer. They shut down that program," says Eisenfrats. In another case, researchers used a form of plastic, which was hard to reverse. "It's very technically challenging to create something that's safe, effective, and it also has to be reversible," says Eisenfrats. He realized that the problem was a material science problem. "You need the right choice of materials.

"Our biggest 'aha moment' was using what's called a hydrogel," he says. Hydrogels are frequently used in the medical device industry, as they can adapt to tissues in the body. "It's like Play-Doh or Jell-O," he says. "We spent about four years creating the product's chemistry. We've done animal studies, manufacturing studies, and we are starting clinical trials. It's been quite a journey to get here."

If the product makes it to the market, what would getting an ADAM hydrogel injected look like? The procedure is done by a urologist, and it's similar to a no-scalpel vasectomy. "It's a minimally invasive procedure," he says. "The doctor finds the vas deferens in a scrotum and applies local anesthesia. They then make a very small puncture in the skin and basically take a couple centimeters of the vas deferens out of the skin. With a vasectomy, they would cut it or cauterize it; with ours, they put a catheter inside, and we have a delivery device that injects the gel—and then they put the tube back under the skin." He estimates that it takes about fifteen minutes for both sides, and recovery time is minimal. The description gives me pause, but I'll leave it to those with a vas deferens to judge.

And how does it feel? "It doesn't affect the ejaculation, it doesn't affect sensation, because most of the vas deferens is pretty early on in the whole 'tubing system'. Most of the ejaculate comes after that toward the prostate. What we're doing is we're just blocking the sperm cells. But the guy will have no idea that there's anything different about his ejaculate because the only difference is that there are no cells to fertilize an egg—everything else is the same."

The goal is not to replace vasectomies. "Our goal is to create a reversible product that can satisfy the whole unmet need of younger men, who don't want to use condoms and they're not even thinking about a vasectomy, or they have partners who don't use their birth control anymore because of side effects," Eisenfrats says. He adds that the gel will be designed to last for years and can be removed at a doctor's office or degrade on its own after a specific amount of time.

Are men ready to step up?

One question that is typically raised about new forms of male contraception is: Would men be willing to use it? "We have done market research with thousands of men and have seen that about 52 percent of men are very or somewhat interested," says Eisenfrats.

When I look at large-scale, multinational studies that have been conducted on this question, an unexpected picture emerges. One survey of men in nine countries found that 55 percent of respondents said they were "willing" or "very willing" to take a pill, injection, or patch. Favorable responses ranged from 71 percent in Spain to 28 percent in Indonesia.

The next objection that is typically voiced is: But would heterosexual women trust their partners? A survey of 1894 women attending family planning clinics in Edinburgh, Shanghai, Hong Kong, and Cape Town found that 90 percent of women surveyed in Edinburgh and Cape Town thought that a male pill was a good idea, with 87 percent in Shanghai and 71 percent in Hong Kong. Overall, only 13 percent thought it was not a good idea, and only 2 percent said they wouldn't trust their partners to take it. Then again, answering a survey in cold daylight is not the same as making a decision in the heat of a moment.

Has Eisenfrats encountered any resistance based on cultural attitudes? "Very occasionally, I'll meet a guy that's like, 'Isn't that a woman's job?' But that rarely ever happens—one in a hundred men. Times are changing. Men want to play a role in family planning."

In 2016, it was reported that clinical trials of a male contraceptive pill were abandoned, due to the side effects men encountered—mood changes, muscle pain, and acne—in other words, the same side effects that women are expected to suffer. In the same year, a male hormonal injection was found to be effective, but this trial was also terminated early because of side effects, including acne and mood disorder. There is, however, a revealing detail in the latter study.

At the end of the trial, the men who participated were asked whether they would continue taking a contraceptive like this: a staggering 82 percent said yes. The development of a safe and effective reversible method of male contraception continues to be an unmet need. Perhaps we can be optimistic about how it might be received.

Men are getting in touch with Contraline. "They want to be part of our trials. We now have two thousand men who have signed up," says Eisenfrats as he shows me some of their videos.

"I am excited about the potential of what that can mean for our relationship and what that can mean for me," says a tall bald man from Texas, who sports a large smile. "We hope that we get to be part of the trials and even see it revolutionize the birth control industry as a whole," says another guy. "Why am I interested in male contraception?" says a young man, who is sitting on a squishy couch next to his wife. "Because I want to be a better husband!"

8

FERTILITYTECH

ALICE IN FERTILITY CLINIC WONDERLAND

My friend Alice is a high-flying professional at one of those companies that cover their employees' fertility benefits. It's straightforward, so long as you're straight. If Alice's wife were a husband who was infertile, the policy would cover them. If the husband's testicles got blown off in an accident, they'd be covered. But as it stands, there's no provision for Alice and her wife. "My wife cannot get me pregnant. So why is it that male factor infertility is covered and yet we are not?" Never one to despair, Alice convinced her company to include an add-on to its existing policy to partially cover their fertility treatment.

Then, there was the fertility clinic. "It's difficult to navigate," she says. "Unless you are clever enough, or have the time, to do loads of your own research, you can get drawn into unnecessary, expensive, and not necessarily harmless add-on treatments." Treatments were pushed onto them to test whether their fallopian tubes are blocked, a test that makes sense for women who have been struggling to conceive. But Alice and her wife are not infertile; they just don't want to have sex with men. Meanwhile, the test increases the cost and time spent. Curiouser and curiouser.

Egg sharing, where one woman provides the egg and the other woman carries the pregnancy, is another procedure pushed on lesbian couples. "It's not necessary," says Alice. "It's sold to lesbians as 'this will make sure that you're both involved,' which is silly, because you're involved by being a hands-on partner helping the pregnant one, and once you have a child, you're both involved 24/7." Yet another procedure to drive up the cost.

To those who plan to conceive with donor sperm, she recommends the documentaries *The Vikings Are Coming* and *25 Siblings & Me*. Alice got pregnant after multiple rounds of IUI. A common form of fertility treatment, IUI stands for intrauterine insemination, whereby sperm is inserted into the uterus. But if at-home insemination with a registered sperm donor was possible in the UK, it could have been a much simpler journey.

If we look at the wider fertility space, the largest companies are either new chains of fertility clinics like Kindbody or employee benefit providers like Progyny or Carrot, which do include benefits for single parents and same-sex couples. Instead of focusing on companies that are, broadly speaking, a more inclusive extension of existing fertility clinics, I talk to the founders of two smaller start-ups.

I exist for this reason. Why would anybody need something else?

"You spend so many years thinking about how intimate and beautiful it's going to be," says Maureen Brown, CEO of Mosie Baby. But the day she conceived her first child was not the way she had imagined it. "You're on the table, that traditional cold environment that women are used to in the medical office," she says.

After struggling to conceive naturally for over two years, Brown and her husband, who are based in Austin, Texas, turned to a fertility clinic. Testing confirmed that she was ovulating, and they both had no underlying fertility issues. "We ended up going through IUI," she says, referring to the fertility treatment where sperm is inserted into the uterus.

First, Brown monitored her cycle with LH strips. "We got to pay extra for ovulating on the weekend," she says with a wry laugh. Coming into the clinic, she was met by a doctor she didn't know and has never seen since. "He came in and he showed me the sample." It was labeled with her husband's name. With natural conception, cervical mucus filters down the load on its way to the uterus, whereas in this case, the sperm is "washed" at the clinic so that a small portion can be injected into the uterus.

"He injected it through a catheter. There was some cramping. He tapped my knee. We waited for 15 minutes; then I could get dressed." Throughout the procedure, her husband was not allowed in the room. "He felt really neglected," says Brown. "It was not a joyful occasion for us. It left us feeling kind of dejected."

This off-putting experience inspired their venture. The
couple spent eighteen months designing a less invasive form of
artificial insemination: a syringe with a rounded tip that can be
used at home. It comes in a kit that includes ovulation tracking
guidance. In 2015, Brown and her husband used it to conceive
their son over one weekend. "He's the first Mosie baby," she says.
In January 2016, they launched the company.

Mosie Baby

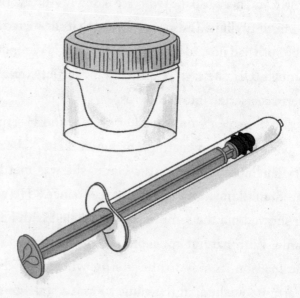

"There's more than one way to do insemination at home,"
says Brown. Sex is the obvious one, and then there is intravagi-
nal insemination (IVI), which is often used interchangeably with
the term intracervical insemination (ICI). "I think, oftentimes,
people are directed straight to IUI. They're not directed to try
IVI, even though they have no real reason to go for that invasive
procedure."

What's more, IUI can cost up to $4,000 per cycle in the United States, and up to £1,600 in the UK. It can take several rounds of IUI to have a successful pregnancy. In comparison, a Mosie Baby kit with two syringes costs $99. They are pursuing FDA 510(k) clearance as a Class II medical device.

Both IVI and IUI happen inside the body and are not to be confused with in vitro fertilization (IVF). With IVF, the sperm and egg are fertilized outside of the body in a petri dish, grown, and then transferred into the uterus in hope of creating a successful pregnancy. It's the most invasive and most expensive procedure, typically recommended once other methods haven't worked.

To fund the business, Brown and her husband mortgaged their house. It's common for some start-ups to raise funds in what's known as a "friends and family round"—but, of course, not everybody is surrounded by people who are flush with spare cash.

Finding a manufacturer was not easy. It's never easy to find a facility that can produce an initial small batch, but femtech entrepreneurs face an extra hurdle. "It was not a product that they are familiar with," says Brown.

There are simple reasons why an option like Mosie Baby should exist. It can help lesbian couples and single mothers conceive with donor sperm. It can also potentially help those who experience vaginismus and painful intercourse. "We are not claiming to treat vaginismus, but we have found that this user base has been able to comfortably use our product," she says.

"In the same regard, there are people like us who were frustrated. Your sex life starts to break down pretty quickly when you're doing timed intercourse," she says. "So much so that 40 percent of men have experienced erectile dysfunction while trying to conceive and having timed intercourse. It's just the pressure of performing."

A previous study has found that IUI has higher success rates than IVI, but more research is needed on lesbian couples, for example, who don't tend to have an infertility diagnosis.

Brown argues there is no incentive for the fertility industry to study IVI. "It's a low-cost pathway, less money for many people to make, right? They're not going to validate it."

Anecdotally, women have used everything from turkey basters to needleless syringes and menstrual cups for at-home insemination. Now, an increasing number of start-ups focus on simple devices made for specifically this purpose. In London, Béa Fertility is working on an applicator. In Amsterdam, Ferti Lily has developed a cervical cup. So far, Mosie Baby has sold over 100,000 kits.

"I'm at a conference right now where it's easily 95 percent men," says Brown. She encounters resistance from investors. "Because instinctually, we're replacing a penis in this process, right?" It's a fear of becoming futile. "I exist for this reason. Why would anybody need something else?"

"Unexplained" is not acceptable

Ravid Israel's journey to motherhood has been everything but straightforward. It took fifteen years for her to be diagnosed with severe endometriosis, when she was nearing thirty-five. "Nobody told me what impact it would have on my fertility," she says.

She decided to freeze her eggs but could only retrieve two eggs, which didn't turn out to be viable. "I learned that I would need IVF to have a child, and I fell in love with the medical system here for women's health in Israel." She decided to move from the United States to Tel Aviv. "They pay for IVF," she says. "Whether you are a single woman or a same-sex couple, you can have a child here with the help of the country. I decided to do that."

She had three cycles of IVF that didn't implant and then a miscarriage. At the time, she was active in infertility communities on Facebook and Instagram. "I saw some woman talking about a link between endometriosis and autoimmune disease," says Israel. That's how she knew to ask her doctor for an autoimmune disease test. It came back positive. But the doctor dismissed it as irrelevant to her fertility.

In her previous job at a record label, Israel created a digital dashboard that combined disparate strands of data. To figure out how she might conceive, she took a similar approach. Charting her medication in an Excel spreadsheet, she wrote down how her body responded, while reading studies on Google Scholar and PubMed on the links between endometriosis, autoimmune disease, and IVF.

Based on her research, she asked another doctor to adjust her "protocol," which is the treatment plan. "I was back to being single." Her boyfriend had left. "He couldn't stand the pressure of all the IVF." But she proceeded with her plan—and the protocol succeeded. "I got pregnant, choosing my own path," she says.

"I don't think that Ravid is necessarily representative, but I don't think that she's fundamentally dissimilar. The term 'IVF warriors'—these are not passive women. These are people who invest tremendous amounts of personal energy, time—financially and emotionally," says Josh Gottesman, the CEO she recently hired to raise investment alongside her.

The discourse about infertility tends to solely focus on women, but of course, women are just part of the equation. It is estimated that one-third of infertility cases are due to male reproductive issues, one-third are due to female issues—and the remaining third are "unexplained." Commenting on the large number of unexplained cases, Gottesman says, "That's just unacceptable."

"It was on Facebook, where I saw the post. What if I hadn't?" says Israel. One day a post is there; the next day it is gone. The insights people post about their infertility journey on Facebook are not collected or analyzed anywhere. Israel decided to create an app that could do these things. On the Embie app, users track their treatments. There is a lively discussion forum. There are explainer videos with medical experts. For each point of information, Embie cites the academic source, or whether the insight is gleaned from their own data set.

Within five months of launching, Embie was the number one tracking app focused on infertility in the Apple Store, with nearly 30,000 registered users. Their users are 33.4 years old on average, and 27 percent have been diagnosed with PCOS.

Embie is available in English. "We're hoping to add Spanish next, because Spain has some of the highest success rates of IVF," says Gottesman. There is a lot of geographical variation. "In the UK, they take autoimmune issues very seriously. In the

States, not so much, in Israel not so much—Ravid had to shop around for a doctor who would take it seriously, and adjust the protocol accordingly," says Gottesman. "We have a window into understanding what is working in all of these different countries."

While their data isn't published or peer-reviewed yet, they tell me they have so far gleaned the following insights:

"In the U.S., the frozen embryo success rate is higher than outside of the U.S., and so that might be due to technology, it might be due to the fact that there's a lot of genetic testing that's done on embryos in the U.S.," says Israel. Comparing the data of 5000 Embie users, they found that women with endometriosis have a higher chance of a successful pregnancy with a frozen embryo transfer rather than with a fresh embryo transfer.

They have also found there's little personalization in the space. "At present 80 percent of women are starting with the same exact IVF protocol, regardless of diagnosis," says Gottesman. "Eighty percent of women are not that identical!" They plan to use machine learning and AI to analyze what has worked for different groups of people on a large scale, so that one day, they can fill the gaps and explain the "unexplained."

Ice, Ice... baby?

"This is Marina. She leads a feminist organization." This is how I am introduced at the entrance of an event that aims to "normalize egg freezing," run by a start-up collaborating with a private fertility clinic. It's a misunderstanding, but for a moment

I contemplate whether that's what I should be doing, and my mind wanders.

The event is taking place at a private members' club in a bougie part of London. We are gathering on pastel-colored chairs, and the air in the room feels like cold wool. I sit and listen, alongside other women, as if I'm here to learn about my fertility, as if I am wondering whether to freeze my eggs. Because I'm here to find out how the organizers talk about egg freezing.

In the United States, some clinics throw "egg freezing parties" with champagne and canapés. They create a sense of solidarity around "taking control" of our "biological clock." There are pop-up buses that provide free fertility tests. Whenever a company hands something out for free, it's worth considering what their business model is and whether you are about to become the product. There is no champagne at the event I have come to, and despite the buoyed empowerment language that was used on the invitation, the mood is gloomy.

The women in the audience are in their twenties and thirties, almost exclusively white, clad in black leather skirts and cashmere sweaters. At the start, we're asked to fill out a survey, and the woman in front of me puts her copy beneath her chair, so the moment I look down at my feet, I can't help seeing that she earns between £70,000 to £100,000 annually. That's more than double the average income of a Londoner.

The fertility clinic presenter says, "I fully appreciate that thinking about fertility is something that feels overwhelming and something that many of us push to the side until we need it." She says that while women are good at eating well and exercising, we neglect our fertility. "Those aren't easy conversations to have," she continues. With urgency in her voice, she says the conversation we are about to have is still easier than conversations she has with clients who have struggled to conceive for years and have run out of options. She congratulates the audience for taking the first step to understanding their fertility by attending this event.

And herein lies the first problem. The women in the audience know nothing about fertility. I don't blame them: it's not part of our education, and it's not a topic that health providers routinely address. That, however, means anything the presenters say is likely to be accepted as a fact. Women who have come to learn about their fertility for the very first time are in a vulnerable position.

Is this the full picture?

I have done a lot of research before coming to this fertility event. This is how I know when I hear messages that evening that do not show the full picture. One woman in her thirties, who sits in the audience, asks how many eggs she would need to freeze to have a child later on. "I'm promise I'm not trying to be coy—it's really hard to answer questions about the success rate," says the presenter. She says that some of their clients only choose to have one egg retrieval cycle—that might yield a few eggs—and that is fine.

At that point, I'd like to hand the inquirer an evidence-based chart on the number of eggs she needs to freeze depending on her age. Just a few eggs are a bad idea. But I realize that if I produce a research paper out of my tote bag, in the eyes of the audience, the presenters run a clinic and I'm just an unknown woman with a bright orange umbrella.

Each curve shows the percentage likelihood by age of having at least one live birth based on the number of mature eggs (oocytes) retrieved and frozen.

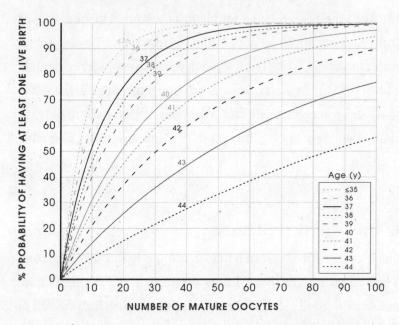

Goldman et al., 2017.

This chart illustrates the typical number of eggs one needs to retrieve to have a certain probability of a live birth. For women below the age of thirty-five, freezing 20 eggs provides a 90 percent chance of a live birth. At the age of thirty-eight, one would need 40 eggs for a 90 percent chance. A larger number of eggs typically means multiple rounds of egg retrieval. A lot of what the presenters say is factual, but the danger is in the detail. They imply that having a low ovarian reserve—which is assessed through the fertility tests they sell: the anti-Müllerian hormone (AMH) test and antral follicle count—means you should freeze your eggs to avoid disappointment further down the line. It's a fear-based claim without any nuance.

Even if you have a low AMH level relative to your age group, that doesn't mean you're less likely to conceive naturally. Because one egg typically gets released naturally by one of your ovaries each month regardless of AMH levels. The AMH test is not a measure of egg quality; it's a measure of egg quantity.

The AMH level matters if you plan to have children at an advanced age, as a low AMH can indicate a slightly earlier onset of menopause. Research has shown that if your AMH level is at an average level, the onset of your menopause is likely to occur at about fifty-two. If your AMH level is low compared to that of the general population, for example, if it's in the bottom 5 percent, your menopause age is forty-nine, on average. If your AMH level is high, let's say you're in the top 5 percent, then the median age is fifty-five. Overall, that doesn't seem like a massive difference, and most women probably don't expect to have children at a very advanced age.

It's worth knowing that the AMH test was developed in the context of reproductive technology to find out how many eggs can be retrieved in a cycle to be used for IVF or egg freezing. It wasn't originally intended as a routine test, and it doesn't reliably predict fertility.

An ovary contains follicles, which are tiny, fluid-filled sacs. Each follicle contains an immature egg. In the first half of the menstrual cycle, hormones (including AMH) trigger a few of these follicles to grow, but only one follicle goes all the way to maturity, while the rest of the cohort gets expelled through what's called "apoptosis." It's typically only the dominant follicle that releases an egg at ovulation, and the egg goes on to travel down the fallopian tube, ready to fuse with sperm.

Through medication, it's possible to stimulate the ovaries to produce multiple eggs to then retrieve them for IVF or egg freezing. Looking at AMH levels can help us estimate how many follicles could be stimulated to grow mature eggs for that purpose.

AMH looks at the quantity, but we have no way to assess egg quality. For conception, egg quality is crucial. And age is an important factor for egg quality. But clinics couldn't possibly charge for consultations where all they do is point out your age.

Tests are useful in that they can help to diagnose conditions like PCOS or an underactive thyroid, which can affect fertility. They can identify issues with ovulation and hormonal imbalances. PCOS, for example, can present with symptoms ranging from irregular periods to excessive hair growth, difficulty getting pregnant, and weight gain, and it's estimated that 75 percent of patients with PCOS are unidentified in clinical practice. A combination of tests can help with a PCOS diagnosis.

In each case, the interpretation of the test matters. If a test is used to sell something else, it's worth questioning what that next product is or does. Beware if anything you are sold triggers strong emotions of fear—you're running out of eggs!—scarcity, and pressure. Clinics can present you with an accurate test result, but that's not the same as an accurate interpretation of the result.

The age thirty-five is often seen as a fertility cliff for women. Female fertility peaks between our late teens and late twenties and it does statistically decline more after thirty-five, but it declines in a slope—it does not fall off a cliff—and there are many individual variations.

The thought behind egg freezing is to preserve eggs that are statistically likely to be of a higher quality at a younger age for a pregnancy at a later stage. When frozen eggs are thawed, their survival rates vary by clinic. The presenters emphasize that 95 percent of eggs they have frozen at their clinic survive the thawing process. But that figure is just one of many factors that need to be considered. Taken in isolation, the figure makes it sound like the egg is guaranteed to be fine. According to the American Society for Reproductive Medicine, the chance for a single egg resulting in a birth is between 2 percent and 12 percent. The egg has to survive freezing, storage, and thawing; it has to be genetically viable; it has to fertilize; and the pregnancy has to work out—there are many steps on the way.

The presenters never use the word "IVF" or "ICSI" (intracytoplasmic sperm injection, which is a similar fertility treatment), even though a fertility treatment is the logical conclusion of freezing and thawing your eggs. They therefore omit that such a treatment carries an additional price tag and that resulting pregnancies tend to be higher risk.

On top of that, success rates vary. Out of 2.5 million IVF cycles performed around the world per year, about 500,000 result in a birth. That means 80 percent of IVF cycles don't succeed.

They also don't mention potential side effects of the medication that's used to stimulate the ovaries for egg retrieval, such as headaches, fatigue, cramping, and nausea, and they don't mention rare but potentially serious complications such as ovarian hyperstimulation syndrome. At one point, they say they don't want to get "too technical." But if I were planning to freeze my eggs, I would like to know the evidence, risks, and cost up front.

Egg freezing is an expensive procedure, although prices vary by geography. One cycle of egg freezing can cost $10,000 in the United States and £7,500 in the UK. The cost can be as low as €2,750 in Spain, not dissimilar from a full set of Invisalign braces. It's not surprising Spain has already become an egg-freezing tourism hub.

There are multiple components that make up the cost of the procedure. There's the consultation, medication, blood tests and screening, as well as the actual egg retrieval and freezing cycle or, more likely, several cycles. The second part is the egg storage fee, which is typically annual, and the third part is the transfer of the eggs to attempt a pregnancy once they're thawed. It's often the case that fertility clinics don't reveal all the costs involved up front.

Modern reproductive technologies like IVF and egg freezing are worth celebrating, as they help millions of people start a family in a way that was impossible in previous decades. They can be a lifeline. The reason I focus on the nuances and risks here is that the space urgently needs more regulation and transparency: we deserve the full picture.

No longer experimental

Egg freezing—or its technical name, "oocyte cryopreservation"—was developed in the 1980s, to be used for medical reasons. The idea behind "medical egg freezing" is to preserve the eggs of someone who is about to have a fertility-threatening procedure. It can be a protective measure against chemotherapy, which diminishes fertility, as well as medical conditions including autoimmune disorders and severe endometriosis. It is also used by trans men who would like to preserve their fertility.

With the development of "vitrification"—a more reliable freezing technique—egg freezing was commercialized for nonmedical reasons. In 2012, both the American Society of Reproductive Medicine (ASRM) and the European Society of Human Reproduction and Embryology decided to lift the "experimental" label of the egg freezing procedure.

Since then, "social egg freezing" has been on the rise. It is offered to healthy, younger women, who wish to postpone motherhood. Kim Kardashian froze her eggs. Jennifer Aniston has said she regrets not freezing her eggs. On TikTok, influencers upload videos of their daily injections and reels about their trips abroad to have their eggs frozen.

Every woman is different when it comes to how age affects her fertility. Some women do not suffer infertility in their early forties. Egg freezing typically works best for those in their twenties and thirties and is not usually recommended for women over 38 years, according to ASRM. And yet, research shows that the average age of egg freezing in the UK and United States is 38. The main motivation is to "buy time" to find a partner, according to research done at Yale University.

The procedure involves daily injections for about eight to fourteen days to stimulate a group of eggs to mature and develop. During this time, ultrasounds and blood tests determine whether the medication is working. Retrieving the eggs is usually done under general anesthetic or sedation. Once the eggs are inspected by an embryologist and deemed usable, they can be frozen.

It's possible to freeze our eggs and therefore preserve their quality. What about carrying a pregnancy at a more advanced age? "It's definitely harder to carry in your thirties than in your twenties, and harder to carry in your forties than in your thirties," says Dr. Timothy Hickman, the president of the Society for Assisted Reproductive Technology (SART).

Pregnancy puts pressure on our organs, including our lungs, heart, and kidneys. Our blood volume increases by half, the center of gravity changes, and ligaments become loose. But, he adds, "in general, it's very feasible to carry. We've had women who are menopausal, that use donor eggs, for example, carry into their late forties, early fifties." In those cases, pregnancies are supported by medication.

But Dr. Hickman also has some words of caution. "I often hear the phrase 'this is insurance,'" he says. But that's misleading. "Life insurance is a policy: if you need it, it pays off; this may not pay off."

For those who are trying to conceive naturally, the general guidelines are "If you are having regular cycles, and you don't know of a reason why you shouldn't get pregnant for you or your partner, and you're under thirty-five, then try naturally for about a year. If you're between thirty-five and thirty-eight to forty, you try for six months naturally. If you're forty, you have an evaluation and think about doing treatments."

Egg freezing is a clinical procedure. Whether venture-backed start-ups, which have launched new fertility clinics, further women's health or not depends on whether they show the full picture. Or whether they maximize their profits by aiming fear-based claims at people who would do anything to have children.

What would be truly revolutionary is to find ways to bring down the prices of fertility treatments substantially and make them transparent and accessible to all, ideally covered by health-care, as is already the case in some countries.

The future of egg freezing

For now, our data on egg freezing is limited, while the uptake continues to increase. Most studies showing successful pregnancies with frozen eggs focus on women freezing their eggs in their twenties and early thirties, but that does not necessarily reflect the current demographic. Research has often focused on donor eggs. We do not have large-scale data on women freezing and using their own eggs, because most eggs frozen recently have not been thawed yet.

In a few decades' time, egg freezing might look radically different. The procedure might become so safe, accessible, and effective that women in their twenties confidently freeze a small number of eggs to preserve their quality just in case.

Clinics vary in how good they are at fertilization. The air quality inside the laboratory matters. It has been shown that shining a red light on sperm cells improves their performance— they seem to like the spotlight—and that a petri dish covered in a thin layer of diamond could help human cells live. All of this could improve the process.

Egg freezing could also fall out of favor for cultural reasons, if governments introduced better childcare policies and addressed wealth inequalities and if workplaces acknowledged the importance of families, so that people no longer delayed having children and being a single parent would become easier. It's very sad that this scenario seems less likely than the technology-focused ones.

Alternatively, the procedure may no longer exist, because it's been replaced by another technological advance. In 2023, researchers at Osaka University in Japan led by Professor Katsuhiko Hayashi managed to turn the stem cells of male mice into egg cells. These egg cells were implanted in female mice who gave birth to seven babies. Perhaps, this could eventually translate into human research. Or perhaps, scientists find a way to shield our egg quality from declining with age.

9

FAMILY TECH

WHERE'S YOUR VILLAGE NOW?

"Our nation has the highest maternal mortality rate of any high-income country," said Lauren Underwood, representative to the U.S. Congress at the Black Maternal Health Conference organized by the Motherlab and Tufts University Medical School in 2022. "And the majority of these deaths are preventable. The pregnancy-related mortality rate for African Americans is three or four times higher than the rate for white Americans." But this is not just a reminder of tragic, unacceptable statistics. It's a call to action.

To address the maternal health crisis in America, Representative Underwood introduced a package of policies, the Black Maternal Health Momnibus Act of 2021. "The new bills include investments to grow and diversify the perinatal workforce, address social determinants of health, improve data collection, provide funding to community-based organizations, and support moms with mental health conditions and substance use disorders," she said.

Out of all pregnancy-related deaths in the United States, 52 percent occur after delivery, according to a study by the Commonwealth Fund. The most frequent underlying causes include mental health conditions, hemorrhage, cardiac and coronary conditions, infection, and cardiomyopathy, according to the CDC—and 80 percent of such deaths are preventable.

Part of the solution is increasing knowledge about the warning signs around complications—and empowering women to communicate with their providers while also ensuring that providers take them seriously. I have found three professors who are paving the way. They call themselves the "Synergistic Sisters in Science."

Based in Atlanta, Georgia, they are Professor Rasheeta Chandler of the Nell Hodgson School of Nursing at Emory University, Professor Natalie Hernandez of the Morehouse School of Medicine, and Professor Andrea G. Parker of the School of Interactive Computing at Georgia Institute of Technology. I speak to the first two.

"Dr. Hernandez and I have known each other for some time," says Chandler. They met as PhD researchers. While Chandler has a grounded authority, Hernandez has high energy. "We have a lot of common goals as far as making sure women of color, and in particular, Black women have equitable health outcome," Chandler continues.

"We use technology within our disciplines to really leverage information, use it as a tool for social justice, and to figure out the pressing issues that are contributing to inequities among women of color," says Hernandez.

Each synergistic sister of science brings a unique skill set to the table: Chandler is a trained family nurse practitioner, and she previously created Savvy HER, an app to increase the uptake of HIV prevention behavior among Black women. Hernandez is a social behavioral scientist, trained in public health, and Parker applies human-centered design to technology. "We connect as mothers," says Chandler. "We all have two children, a boy and a girl around the same age."

Georgia is a dangerous place for pregnant women—especially pregnant Black women. More than half of the counties in Georgia lack any type of ob-gyn provider, as hospitals with a labor and delivery unit have closed down. As a result, women have to travel long distances to give birth, so that two-thirds of rural births happen outside of the mother's home county. Black women living in rural areas have double the maternal mortality rate of rural white women.

Hernandez, who is on the Maternal Mortality Review Committee in Georgia, says, "We still have about 20 percent of women in this state who don't have access to health insurance coverage." The communities they are hoping to help are often rural and low-income. In rural areas, there is a shortage of clinicians, nurses, and hospitals. This makes it difficult to address cases of preeclampsia, which is high blood pressure in pregnancy, more common among U.S.-born Black women. Added to that, says Hernandez, people in the region are affected by "social determinants of health and the deep divisions in the South of racism."

Differences in health insurance coverage and access to healthcare are crucial, but the disparities in maternal health affecting Black women in the United States persist across socioeconomic status. We also need more research on ethnic differences in how pregnancy, labor, and the postpartum phase progress.

The porch

For the development of their PM3 app, the professors assembled a community advisory board—called "the porch"—consisting of women who represent each of the local communities they are working with, as well as healthcare providers of color from those communities. "Especially in communities of color, the porch is a sacred space," says Chandler. It's a place where family and friends meet, especially after a day's work, on weekends and on holidays, to gather and exchange stories, to decompress, to be heard and to be supported.

The app PM3 stands for "Prevent Maternal Mortality Mobile," and it combines self-management, resources, and peer support. It's part of a research study, and it allows women to monitor health indicators including blood pressure, weight, physical activity, and mental health. It also comes with a FitBit. It could revolutionize the postpartum period for high-risk populations.

"We see PM3 as a personalized behavioral health tool, where we give women access to resources, so that they can learn how to self-manage their own conditions," says Hernandez. "What we're hoping is that they can use that data to have informed conversations with their provider to say 'Look, this is what has been happening.'"

For their formative research, they conducted focus groups. "What contributes to maternal mortality for Black women in the state of Georgia is cardiomyopathy, a cardiovascular condition," says Hernandez. "What came out of our focus groups was more about maternal mental health, but we know that mental health has an effect on cardiovascular health." Therefore, supporting mental health is conducive to good heart health.

What came up in their focus groups was "the strong Black woman narrative," says Hernandez. "A lot of the partners didn't see their place in how to support the mother of their child." Simultaneously, the women didn't know how to ask for help.

Initially, they planned to focus their app solely on the mothers, but their formative work showed that they need to include information on the child as well to keep mothers engaged. "It is a dyad," says Hernandez. "That's how they're going to really engage within the mobile application." The app's timeline for the mother's health evolves in conjunction with the baby's development. There are also positive affirmations to build self-esteem and peer-support groups.

The app explains policy changes around Medicaid in an accessible way. It provides resources about healthcare facilities and food banks based on location. "They are not just general resources; they're specific for Black women," says Hernandez. "So, if they are more prone to preeclampsia, they'll get more information about preeclampsia. If they indicated that they have significant mental health challenges, they'll get more information about mental health." The app adjusts to each woman and where she is in the postpartum period.

One of the key behavioral changes the Synergistic Sisters in Science are addressing is this: most maternal deaths occur in the postpartum period, but fewer than 50 percent of women in rural Georgia attend the recommended postpartum appointment. By providing evidence-based information and engaging tools through their app, the professors hope to close that gap. Ultimately, they aim to eliminate preventable postpartum emergency department visits and hospital readmissions among rural Black women. What could be more important than for the Synergistic Sisters' vision to become a reality?

Remote monitoring

There is another company that is hoping to address the limited access to maternity care in rural areas of the United States. "You have this increasing rate of moms that need more care, and a decreasing number of medical providers that can support them," says Eric Dy, the CEO of San Francisco–based Bloomlife. In the United States, 36 percent of counties are considered "maternity care deserts," without hospitals or birth centers offering obstetric care.

"The system is breaking," he says. "If you look at the high rates of maternal mortality and morbidity, clearly we're going in the wrong direction." One promise of wearable technology is that it can move routine procedures from the clinic to the home. One such procedure is the fetal non-stress test. It's done to check a baby's health in pregnancy, or during delivery, and it's called "non-stress" because it doesn't cause the baby any stress.

In a clinical setting, it's done with a cardiotocogram, whereby two elastic belts with sensors are placed across the belly: one sensor tracks the baby's heart rate, and the other tracks contractions. The test takes about half an hour to complete. It measures whether there are any contractions and analyzes the baby's heart rate and movements. The goal is to detect, for example, whether the baby's heart beats faster when they move, to see whether the baby is getting enough oxygen.

Not all pregnant women need a non-stress test. It's typically recommended for high-risk pregnancies, which can include preexisting chronic diseases, hypertension, pregestational and gestational diabetes, or prior preterm birth as well as multiple pregnancies.

The goal, says Dy, is "to prevent long-term neurological impairment to the baby due to not getting enough oxygen. Or if it's really severe, the baby might die." The non-stress test helps to mitigate these risks. "Women are having babies later in life, there are increased rates of IVF, and with IVF you're likely going to have a high-risk pregnancy," says Dy.

"You're uncomfortable getting around, and you essentially have to get to the doctor's office twice a week and get monitored for about 30 or 40 minutes. And that's not counting travel time and the waiting room. It's super inconvenient." With about $16 million raised from VCs, angel investors, and a foundation, Bloomlife is building a wearable device to perform the non-stress test remotely. The device is

Bloomlife

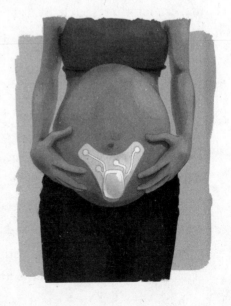

in clinical trials as a Class II medical device, and it would allow doctors to monitor their patients from afar.

The FDA has decided that the monitoring needs to be done by doctors rather than the patients themselves. As I talk to Dy at a conference, he shouts across the room to another entrepreneur. They both lament this attitude toward women's capacity to handle information about their own bodies. "It's a very paternalistic view," he says.

"I think there's oftentimes this belief that patients are helpless people," says Dy. "That's just not the case. If you actually empower people with tools and information to better care for themselves, it gives them greater confidence." He cites the practice of Group Prenatal Care, where women attend prenatal appointments and educational sessions together. This practice has shown to decrease preterm birth among low-income and African American women.

In the long run, Dy hopes to collect longitudinal data sets that can inform research. By using machine learning and AI, this data could one day be analyzed to help predict adverse events such as a preterm birth.

A smart shield

The birth of a baby brings a new set of questions in its wake. Whether to breastfeed or not is one such question, and there is a company that could offer unprecedented insights. Before becoming the CEO of Coroflo, Dublin-based Rosanne Longmore was a financial adviser, working with high-net-worth individuals. "There was a lot of inherited wealth; there were people who won the lotto," she says. "But the people I loved talking to were people who've built a business."

At the time, her cousin James Travers and his wife, Dr. Helen Barry, had their first baby. "He was tiny but not premature," says Longmore. Because the baby only weighed four and a half pounds full term, a public health nurse came to their house with a pair of scales and weighed the baby after he was fed. The intention was to measure whether the baby was getting enough breast milk. Barry, who is a doctor, was taken aback by this method. "She knew this was a nonsense; it wasn't accurate," says Longmore. Weighing a moving baby with scales that are not motion-compensated is not an accurate method.

Travers, an electronic engineer, felt there must be a better method, so the couple spent two years developing just that. "Jamie developed the technology and filed the patent," says Longmore. "Helen, in the meantime, was looking at the commercial side," she says. "Initially, our focus groups were just coffee mornings, and women with new babies would come along." Longmore asked them to include her in the company if it went ahead. "I thought I'd go in as a head of sales, and then they said, 'No, no, you're the CEO!'"

The World Health Organization recommends that women exclusively breastfeed for six months. Breast milk is a great source of nutrition for babies. It contains antibodies that protect babies from infection. It adapts to the time of the day and has an increased water content in times of hot weather. Breastfeeding also triggers the release of the hormone oxytocin, which helps the mother's uterus contract and return to its original size.

In Europe, 13 percent of mothers reach the six-month target;

in the United States, it's 19 percent; and in China, it's 26 percent. Some stop because they need to go back to work, while others stop because they find it physically uncomfortable. According to Coroflo's analysis, 60 percent of mothers who stopped breast-feeding did so because they didn't know if their baby was getting enough milk.

Longmore shows me the "Coro" prototype. It looks like a standard silicone nipple shield, but it has a sensor. Nipple shields are typically used for skin protection. Throughout history, they have been made from animal skins, plant leaves, pewter, and glass. Nowadays, they're made of soft, ultrathin silicone. "We have patented a micro flow sensor that sits in here," she says, pointing to one side of the shield.

"The mother wears this like any other normal shield, and as she's feeding her baby, the data comes up in real time on the app, on how much milk her baby is getting." What's more, the app allows you to swap between left and right breast. As Longmore says, "That came out of one of our original focus groups."

Coro

They raised €2.1 million from the European Commission to create the product and test it comprehensively. The research opportunities are endless. "We have huge inbound contact from hospitals and universities around the world," she says. "One of the first things they look to establish is, what is a normal milk supply? Nobody knows. Every government in the world has a different guideline."

Other research questions could be: What are the external factors that impact breast milk supply? Does the mother's BMI impact her supply? If a mother is on diabetes medication, does that impact her supply? If it's the mother's fourth child, how's that different from her first child for breastfeeding? Having answers to these questions can potentially inform breastfeeding guidelines in the future.

Fed is best

Breastfeeding is a highly emotive subject. "Women who want to and can't, or don't, feel like they failed," says Longmore. The phrase "giving up" is used to talk about breastfeeding. Longmore prefers to say "if a woman stops." Giving up implies failure, carrying shame in its wings.

For decades, "breast is best" has been touted by health organizations and campaigners to promote breastfeeding. As ever with female bodies, it's time to rethink the mantra.

I get the sense that sometimes, the benefits of breastfeeding are overstated, while the negative impact of the pressure put on new mothers to breastfeed has been ignored.

Breastfeeding has some short-term benefits for the baby, such as a slightly decreased risk of diarrhea. But there is a lack of randomized controlled trials to confirm any long-term benefits for the child. Some existing research on the long-term benefits for children being breastfed has been clouded by the high socio-economic status of those who tend to breastfeed in the West. One long-term benefit of breastfeeding that does have a strong evidence base is for the mother: it's linked to a decreased risk of breast cancer. In developing countries, breastfeeding has increased benefits, because unlike formula, breast milk doesn't have the risk of being mixed with contaminated water. For an in-depth analysis on the scientific evidence base around breast-feeding, turn to Emily Oster's book *Cribsheet*.

It's worth noting that breastfeeding can be a complicated and even painful experience. Innovative start-ups like Barcelona-based LactApp provide evidence-based support on their app covering everything from breastfeeding positions and latching to nipple shields, breast milk storage, and also formula milk.

Breastfeeding can be a wonderful bonding experience, but it's not for everybody, and certainly not at all costs. Breast milk is not liquid gold, and formula is not the devil's elixir.

Or as Oster writes, "If it doesn't work out, it's not a tragedy for your baby or for you. It is almost certainly worse if you spend a year sitting around feeling bad about not nursing."

Longmore says, "Sometimes women hear about our product, or they see me coming, and they might think, 'Oh, no.'" They suspect she's a breastfeeding proselytizer who's about to preach "breast is best." But Longmore supports the shift to "Fed is best," a slogan that has been gaining popularity among activist groups in the United States.

"Fed is best" is a more feminist approach. It acknowledges that not everyone can or wants to breastfeed. "Anecdotally, doctors believe about 15 to 20 percent of mothers do have a low supply issue, and those mothers need formula," says Longmore. "Formula is life-saving and life-giving—and mothers shouldn't be polarized for not breastfeeding their baby."

It takes a village

Given that large family structures are less common these days, especially in big cities, there's a strong need to create new communities, whether those are friendship groups, professional networks, or parental support groups. In the world of femtech, the next entrepreneur has been leading the way.

"I was the first of my friends to have a baby," says Michelle Kennedy, based in London. At two o'clock on a typical Wednesday afternoon, she would be at home with her newborn baby. Her partner is at work. "All of my girlfriends are at work; there is no one to hang out with." The baby is tiny. "He's just lying there in my arms, probably crying, and I probably haven't even managed to get dressed.

"That is very, very isolating. And you start to think about and question your identity," she says. "You are thrown into this seismic life change, which is new motherhood. You're responsible for another little person."

Big cosmopolitan cities like London and New York attract people from other cities and countries who may not have extended family nearby. "We don't necessarily live where we grew up, right? We don't live around the corner from our mom or sister." Traditional support networks—it takes a village to raise a child—have changed fundamentally. As Kennedy says, "Well, where's your village now?

"What does that look like, and in a new, imagined world, where I've just moved halfway across the country, for a new job, and now I don't know anyone, I've got a tiny baby?" I think about all the ready-made communities we have—at school, at university, at work.

"That's how we operate as people; we look for commonality," she says. "And yet, when it comes to this core element of our life, there's nothing to support us and help us emotionally connect with other people." There's no ready-made community for mothers. All the while, we know that loneliness is damaging to our health; in fact, some say it's as damaging as smoking 15 cigarettes a day. For new mothers, isolation can feed into and exacerbate postpartum depression.

That is why Kennedy decided to create new communities with her app Peanut. It's Tinder for new mothers. Since launching in 2017, they have put over three million mothers in touch with each other. They have a team of 35 and raised $23 million in funding.

On the app, women create a profile to describe themselves. "Women want to have an initial sense of, I understand why Peanut is suggesting that you and I be friends," says Kennedy. The app matches them on elements of commonality. Simply being mothers is not necessarily enough for a friendship.

There are times when parents who are out and about with their baby are able to strike up a conversation with one another—"How old is yours?"—but as Kennedy puts it, "It's not like I can walk up to someone on the street and say, 'Hi, fertility challenges?'" Or in menopause, "Oh, hi. Don't suppose you're having night sweats, are you?" To address this issue, Peanut launched versions focused on fertility, and menopause.

"I think as soon as your identity is challenged, that's when loneliness creeps in," says Kennedy. "You feel like you must be the only person, because you feel like it's taboo to talk about it, which makes the isolation even worse." That's not only true for new motherhood but other life stages as well.

The concept behind Peanut seems like a no-brainer. I ask: Are there any other solutions for unmet needs that are hiding in plain sight? Within a heartbeat she says, "It's childcare. But I don't know what the answer is. Women are contributing toward the economy in a way that we never have before.

"But we don't have an infrastructure in place that supports our return to work in order to support our contribution. You have a situation where we lose critical women from the workforce." In countries where childcare is as expensive as in the UK, women are likely to drop out of their jobs to look after their children. "Childcare is fundamentally broken. Anyone who is taking that challenge on and trying to address it is a hero in my eyes."

Childcare policies vary widely by country—from free childcare to extortionate prices. It fundamentally comes down to policy. But, as ever, technology can play a role. As Kennedy says, "In the same way that Uber transformed how we think about transport, is there an answer to transforming how we think about childcare? I don't know. But I feel strongly that there must be something."

Mother-in-law learns best

In each local context, innovators have to figure out what the specific challenges are. In the case of Govandi in northeast Mumbai, it's the extended family that needs to be considered on topics of female health. "If you look at a typical family construct, there's a middle-aged couple with children who are in school and they're most likely responsible for one parent or more who's also part of their immediate family," says Aditi Hazra-Ganju, cofounder of Mumbai-based Saathealth. A suburb of informal settlements located next to a rubbish dump, Govandi is home to about 600,000 of the city's poorest residents.

"Most decisions are made by the whole family together, including, if a woman is about to deliver a child, which clinic is she going to? Who's the doctor? It's not just her and the husband but very often the extended family. So, the husband's elder brother, his wife, or mother-in-law, everyone will have a say."

For health content to be effective, it needs to consider the social construct of the whole family. For this reason, some public health programs specifically target the mother-in-law. The idea is to convey "Here's what you could do to take care of your pregnant daughter-in-law." It's an effective strategy, and I notice that the mother-in-law is not thought of as someone who arrives at the house on a broomstick.

Hazra-Ganju, a soft-spoken biochemist, her hair cut in an immaculate bob, cofounded Saathealth—*saath* means "together" in Hindi—with Aakash Ganju, a physician, in 2018. "We're a husband-and-wife couple with two kids," she says. After careers in the pharma industry, the duo turned to entrepreneurship. Saathealth partners with healthcare providers and foundations to create apps where underserved communities can access healthcare information and services.

So far, their apps have reached thirty million people across India. For their maternal and child health app, Saathealth put together a multidisciplinary team of healthcare professionals, behavioral scientists, designers, and user researchers who spent time with members of the Govandi community to understand their needs.

The typical middle-aged couple tends to have "concerns

around children's health, around their own health with respect to blood pressure, hypertension, and diabetes." Added to that, they have concerns about infectious diseases, seasonal mosquito-borne diseases, and the health of their parents. Depending on how a person interacts with the app, the health content is person-alized to them through algorithms.

The apps created by Saathealth are wide-ranging, including everything from videos about periods and ways to make your own reusable menstrual products to information for female healthcare workers known as ASHA to apps that provide infor-mation on the nutritional value of foods together with vouchers and apps that connect people to local healthcare providers. Their apps are mainly in Hindi, and some content has been produced in Gujarati, Marathi, and Kannada. Each app is created on the basis of extensive user research and testing.

"The other part, which is the cultural relevance, is much more touchy-feely, where we go interact with users and under-stand what it is that they want and then respond to that," says Hazra-Ganju. Many members of the Govandi community are migrant workers. "They could be domestic help; they could be owners of small businesses, a shop, or a local grocery store; or working in a factory or delivery jobs; they could be people who have school-level education."

As the Saath team was testing the app, they noticed a surge of engagement late at night. "In a lot of families, the husband's phone is used for work, and the wife's phone becomes common property between the wife and the in-laws and the children," she says. "We realized that's when the woman has finished all her jobs and put the rest of the family to bed, and then she has time on her phone to do what she wants to do." They used that insight to time their uploads and notifications.

King Khan, the role model

Equality always starts in the home. That's why it's critical for femtech to include fathers, partners, and other male role models as part of the audience for its apps and devices. To change the system, we have to address everyone.

Women around the world spend double the amount of time than men on caregiving and doing housework, according to a study in *The Lancet Public Health*. India has one of the world's lowest rates of labor force participation among women and a high rate of gender inequality. I want to know more about the role of fathers.

"We had content which was directed toward fathers saying here are ways in which you can help raise a child," says Hazra-Ganju with a bright smile. "And how important it is for you to be an involved father, because you will build a bond with your child," she says. "Why should it only be the mother who's enjoying the benefits of parenthood? It should be you and the mother together!"

Play is central for a child's healthy development. Saathealth created an animated series to show fathers how to play games with their children that involve counting beads and stacking boxes. To make the characters relatable, an animator spent time with the community to find out how they picture typical men. "How would they dress? Would they have a mustache or not? What would they carry? A bag? When he did the design, it was based on one of Shah Rukh Khan's characters from one of his movies from about a decade back."

Nicknamed King Khan, he is India's Brad Pitt. In her book *Desperately Seeking Shah Rukh*, the economist Shrayana Bhattacharya maps the economic and personal trajectories of six women from diverse backgrounds in India who are united by their search for the ideal man, expressed in Khan.

"We feel quite strongly that Bollywood has a profound effect on the Indian populace," says Hazra-Ganju. So, they chose instrumental versions of Bollywood songs for the background music of their videos. "Much like cricket, football, or the royal family in the UK, it's something I could discuss with someone who comes to maybe deliver food for me. I saw the same movie as he did, and we both liked it."

The games-for-fathers content was well received. "When we visited the communities, they would tell us, 'Now that you've told me that these are games I can play with my son, I play them and I enjoy the time I spend'," she says. "It's not that they don't want to; they just don't have the tools for it. So, we gave them some games that fathers could play with the children, things that are good for cognitive development at the same time they build a bond between the father and child."

This content was created for the Govandi community, but the lesson is universal. If heterosexual couples shared parental leave and childcare responsibilities equally, the world of work and business would become a radically different place.

Saathealth involves the whole family. Peanut alleviates loneliness. The Synergistic Sisters of Science improve access by providing tools. Bloomlife and Coroflo allow us to track the womb and breast milk. Each innovation shows us that health issues are intertwined with their social context, their local place and culture.

The "family tech" in this chapter is a subcategory of femtech in that it considers female health or well-being as well as considering the child's health or well-being. There is, separately, also a category of "child tech" products that primarily address the needs of babies and children: the Tueo Health device, for example, helps parents monitor asthma symptoms in sleeping children. Novonate is a device that stabilizes umbilical cord catheters in newborn babies.

But, of course, the baby doesn't seek out its own technology. As the pediatrician and psychoanalyst Donald Winnicot said, "There is no such thing as a baby; there is a baby and someone."

10

MENOPAUSETECH

WHEN AGEISM MEETS SEXISM

"Did you know that female humans and killer whales are the only two creatures on planet Earth to go through menopause?" asks the stand-up comedian Karen Mills in one of her routines. "And I'm guessing they weren't 'killer' whales until after they went through it!"

There are women who experience no menopause symptoms, though for up to 80 percent of women, the most common symptoms include hot flashes, night sweats and vaginal dryness, aches in muscles and joints, fatigue, mood swings, low mood, and anxiety.

As Mills puts it, "There cannot be very menopausal women in hell, because they wouldn't put up with it. They'd band together, overthrow the devil, and get the air turned on. You don't know a fiery pit until you've had a hot flash."

"Menopause" comes from the Greek *month*, rooted in the word "moon," combined with "pause." It occurs naturally when our estrogen levels drop as our ovaries stop producing eggs. It officially sets in when a woman hasn't had a period for twelve consecutive months. It is no ovary action. The phase that sets in before menopause is called "perimenopause" and lasts between four to ten years.

The role of estrogen

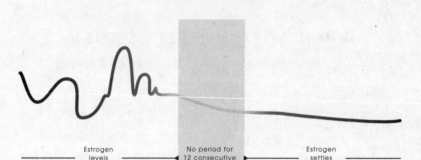

Estrogen levels fluctuate	No period for 12 consecutive months	Estrogen settles down
PERIMENOPAUSE	**MENOPAUSE**	**POST MENOPAUSE**

In the Western world, the average age for menopause is fifty-one; globally it's between forty-five and fifty-five years. About 1 percent of women experience early menopause before the age of forty. Medical treatments and surgeries, including radiation therapy or hysterectomy with removal of the ovaries, lead to the onset of menopause.

In the femtech space, menopause is still an underserved area compared to periods and fertility. There are more than twice as many period-focused companies than menopause ones, according to data from FemHealth Insights. It seems that menopause is where ageism and sexism meet. And yet, this could be the biggest market of all. Around 1.2 billion women will experience menopause worldwide by 2030, and the innovation in this market could address the needs of multiple generations to come.

In the 1990s, the go-to treatment for menopause was hormone replacement therapy (HRT), now often referred to as menopause hormone therapy (MHT). In 2002, the Women's Health Initiative (WHI) released a large-scale study that later turned out to have flaws. It said that postmenopausal women who took combination hormone therapy (estrogen and progestin) had an increased risk of breast cancer and heart disease. HRT prescriptions plummeted by 70 percent.

More recently, the benefits and risks of HRT have been reconsidered as research continues to emerge. "The benefits of HRT usually outweigh the risks for most women," according to the British National Health Service. But it depends on individual circumstances—some women can't take it for health reasons, and it depends on how long it's taken for. Some research has found that women commencing HRT within ten years of the onset of menopause, or under the age of sixty, had a lower risk of cardiovascular disease. The treatment continues to carry risks, just like the contraceptive pill does, but these results have led to a renewed increase in uptake.

In the femtech space, the telehealth company Evernow has raised $28.5 million in funding with support from celebrity investors including Cameron Diaz and Abby Wambach to create a platform where women can access treatments and talk to menopause specialists. In the UK, the TV presenter Davina McCall and the GP and menopause specialist Dr. Louise Newson have brought renewed attention to the treatment.

While new ventures blaze a trail, the medical establishment

is unprepared. In the UK, a survey found 41 percent of medical universities have no mandatory menopause education. In the United States, it is estimated that only one in five ob-gyns are trained in menopause. All the while one in ten women quit their jobs because of menopause symptoms. We can no longer ignore one of the largest underserved groups of all: menopausal women.

Our physical well-being is never separate from our environment, culture, and the people around us. I found some fascinating surveys on how that can play out. One survey of 453 married women in India found that those who ranked their husbands' attitude as indifferent toward menopause had more severe menopause symptoms than those who said their husbands were supportive.

One study conducted in China surveyed menopausal women from the patriarchal Han ethnic majority, and another group of women from the Mosuo, a tribe that passes property and surnames down the female line. Mosuo women reported "milder melancholia" in menopause and "less psychological suffering." In other words, menopause is better under matriarchy.

We never thought we were radical

Vaginal dryness can be a consequence of menopause and is yet another worthy subject that is addressed by femtech entrepreneurs. As women approach and go through menopause, estrogen levels fall, causing the vaginal tissue to thin. This can lead to dryness and irritation as well as pain with sex and daily activities like wearing jeans or walking. Thinner vaginal skin is also more prone to infections like UTIs.

So far, the main solutions have been HRT and lubricants. I am particularly interested in novel, nonhormonal solutions. We have already encountered Madorra, which is working on an external medical device that uses ultrasound to create heat within the vaginal tissue, which, in turn, creates more blood flow and lubrication. If Madorra makes it through clinical trials, it will be possible to say how effective it is and whether it has any side effects.

We also encountered Joylux, which created a consumer tech device that uses vibration, light, and heat. In contrast to the regulatory tests medical devices have to pass, it's not possible to evaluate how well a consumer tech device works in the same way, as the regulatory hurdle is lower. Reviews or the opinions of friends might help.

Another new product to address vaginal dryness is a gel stick developed by Tel Aviv–based Aquafit Intimate, who are a team of four women led by Rebecca Sternberg. After going through radiotherapy for cervical cancer, Sternberg suffered from vaginal adhesions. The go-to treatment was a dilator, but she found it impossible to use.

So, she galvanized a team to create something new that could help her. She brought on Varda Messer, a designer with experience in manufacturing and sales. They had previously completed a triathlon together—Sternberg did the running and Messer the cycling. Then, they convinced Vered Italiano, an applied chemist and industry leader in advanced materials, to come on board, and, finally, they were joined by Dr. Amy Kesselman, an ob-gyn.

The lemon-colored stick they have come up with looks deceptively simple, but it is based on patented technology. It has a way of slowly releasing the gel while it's used as a vaginal trainer.

During perimenopause, a drop in estrogen can cause the lining of the vagina to become thinner and less elastic. "Your elasticity and your pH are influenced by the presence or absence of estrogen, and estrogen changes as we go along," says Sternberg. The gel stick does not include any estrogen; instead, its ingredients address the pH imbalance created by the loss of estrogen. It's regulated as a cosmetic, not a medical device.

The team received $650k in government innovation grants as well as raising funding from The Case for Her. To date, they have developed two gel sticks that can help with a range of issues, including vaginal dryness and vaginismus. The sticks are biodegradable, and they need to be kept in the fridge.

So far, they have about 700 customers and have spoken to most of them on the phone. Messer has become the company's chief educator, who takes phone calls and explains vaginal anatomy to women. When the team first got together to set up the company, they didn't anticipate the amount of stigma in the space. "We never thought we were radical," says Sternberg. But what else could this gel stick be, if not radical?

Time to cool down

Our next consumer tech device did not begin with menopausal women at all; it began with one sweltering summer day in Boston. A small group of engineering students were freezing in their air-conditioned laboratory at MIT. Even though it was hot outside, they had to wear down jackets indoors to keep warm. The lab was mostly empty, while the air conditioner was on full blast—what a waste of energy. It led the students to wonder: what if we could heat or cool people in a more local way?

Delving into research on "thermal comfort"—the sensation of holding a warm mug of tea on a winter day, for example— they created a wristband that could replicate this effect. After winning a material science hackathon with their thermoelectric wristband, MIT put out a press release and the story was picked up by *Wired* and the Weather Channel. Emails arrived asking if the wristband was for sale. Women who experienced hot flashes were interested.

After raising over $600,000 on Kickstarter to develop and manufacture the device, the team decided to hire an experienced CEO. "They ended up hiring me," says Elizabeth Gazda with a warm smile, "which is really a story in itself—because I would challenge you to find another technology company founded by three men that hired a female CEO. It just doesn't happen." Gazda is a serial entrepreneur and has been the CEO of Embr Labs since 2018.

Hot flashes are the most common reported symptom of menopause. In Europe, 69 percent of women report having them; it's 68 percent in the United States and 61 percent in Japan. There are geographic differences and ethnicity-based differences. African American women tend to report high rates of hot flashes and night sweats, followed by white women, while Asian women tend to report lower rates.

"What most people don't know is that when a woman is in menopause, the hot flashes are caused by an overactivation of the sympathetic nervous system." says Gazda. "You have your sympathetic and parasympathetic response in your body, which is your 'fight or flight' response, and your 'rest and digest' response."

Our skin has thermal receptors, and "if you stimulate those receptors, you hit networks and regions of the brain responsible for temperature perception, but also balancing the autonomic nervous system," says Gazda. "The wrist is an area with a high density of both warm and cold thermal receptors. Maybe your grandmother told you—when you're too hot—to run your wrist under water," she says.

The wristband, called Embr Wave, has a thermoelectric tile that changes temperature through an electric current. The bracelet doesn't change the wearer's core body temperature, instead, it changes the perception of temperature slightly, to help the wearer feel refreshed or toasty.

It delivers the heat in waves. Otherwise, our bodies tend to acclimatize to temperature. When we jump into a swimming pool, for example, the water that at first seems icy cold gets more comfortable within minutes.

In a small study of 39 perimenopausal or postmenopausal women, about half felt they had more control over the degree of sleep disruption caused by night-time hot flashes while using the device.

Gazda estimates that 75 percent of their customers use it for cooling and 25 percent for heating. She notes there's a link between temperature and a person's inner state. Studies have shown that people who are socially isolated are more likely to feel cold. Our language captures this link between temperature and emotion: "He gave me the cold shoulder." "Did you see her icy stare?" "She flashed a warm smile."

Growth stage

Gazda says most femtech funds go up to Seed and Series A. "We're now in our growth stage. We've outgrown many of the femtech investors. So, we are talking to traditional growth investors, and unfortunately, it's primarily populated by men. If they don't really understand the problem, it's hard for them to identify with it."

This led her to develop a strategy. "When I'm talking to men, I describe to them what a hot flush feels like, in a way that they can relate," says Gazda. "I want you to imagine the last time you were in your car, and you had a near-miss accident." Or when you think you're going to fall but you catch yourself. That sensation of tingling, perspiration on your forehead, the hair on the back of your neck standing up. That's the fight-or-flight response. "That's what a menopausal hot flash feels like," she says. "Now imagine having ten to twenty a day, and at night, interrupting your sleep."

"Another way we got the attention of all the male investors is we ran a clinical study and proved the device's ability to mitigate hot flashes in men undergoing prostate cancer treatment," she says. "We thought, 'Well, maybe if we're talking about men and their prostate, they'll pay attention.'" It paid off. So far, the company has raised $21 million.

How has her leadership style evolved over time? "What starts to happen as you get older, you just start to become more confident about what you believe in," she says. "We not only have almost gender parity in the company; we have people on the gender spectrum, we have 13 native languages spoken, we also have four generations working together."

Living and working in the Netherlands for a decade had a

lasting impact on her leadership style. "There's no reason you can't have a very successful company and still have work-life balance and pursue your own interests outside." At the end of our conversation, she says "Stay cool." I do try.

From NASA to menopause

Menopause can also affect our bones. Women have a lower bone mass on average, and following menopause, women can lose 3 percent of bone per year for about a decade. Osteoporosis, which literally means "porous bones," and its earlier stage version, osteopenia, make bones brittle and more susceptible to fracture.

Bone health might seem a gender-neutral issue, but according to the Bone Health and Osteoporosis Foundation, 80 percent of the ten million Americans who have osteoporosis are women. And tragically, a study has shown that women who experience a hip fracture because of osteoporosis are five times more likely to die within the first year. Around the world, Japan has a high rate of osteoporosis, and so do Korea and China.

Not unlike menopausal women, astronauts in space can lose an average of 1 percent to 2 percent of their bone mass for every month they spend in a microgravity environment. Over the last three decades, NASA-sponsored scientists have addressed this issue. A team led by Professor Clinton Rubin and Professor Meilin "Ete" Chan of SUNY Stony Brook found that depending on the magnitude and frequency, standing on large vibration plates can improve bone strength.

Though vibration plates are not used by American astronauts in space, the research findings—that vibration can improve bone strength—could serve the needs of postmenopausal women on Earth. San Francisco–based Bone Health Technologies is applying the research to develop a new wearable device, the Osteoboost.

It looks like a thick black belt worn across the lower back and it sends gentle vibrations across the hips and spine. In their clinical trial, participants wore it for 30 minutes a day in an upright position, five days a week, while doing chores at home or walking their dog.

Osteoboost

"Vibration is essentially simulating exercise," says Laura Yecies, CEO of Bone Health Technologies. "It challenges the bones, it puts stress on them, just like it puts stress on the muscles. That stress slows down bone cell destruction and speeds up bone cell creation." We typically think of our bones as "these hard, dead things, because we think of skeletons." But our bones are in a constant state of renewal. Bone density peaks in our early thirties.

"Mineral density is measured in grams per centimeter squared," she says. "Just like lead has higher density than limestone, right? Your bones have different density levels." Bone density is analyzed with a DEXA scan, a type of X-ray. There is also an online risk calculator called FRAX, developed by the University of Sheffield, to calculate a person's risk factors. Just like mammograms and cholesterol testing, earlier screening of bone density for those at risk can lead to better care.

Bone Health Technologies has raised close to $10 million, about half of which is grant money from the NIH. At times, Yecies encountered investors who were not keen. "They didn't have the embarrassment and awkwardness of using the word 'vagina' like it was in your article, but they just were very dismissive," she says. It's time for good vibrations.

Women started finding me

Some issues are so taboo most women don't know about them at all. When Sherrie Palm, who lives in Milwaukee, Wisconsin, was diagnosed with pelvic organ prolapse at the age of fifty-four, she had never heard of it before. "I jumped into the Google rabbit hole and discovered how common it is." According to some studies, 50 percent of women experience it globally. "I was like, 'How is this possible? We're not being told about this!' I was smoking ticked off!"

The most common cause of pelvic organ prolapse (POP) is childbirth, and the second most common one is menopause. Older women are most likely to be affected. POP happens when the muscles and tissue supporting the pelvic organs become weak or loose. This can lead to one or more of the pelvic organs dropping or pressing into or out of the vagina: the bladder, rectum, uterus, small intestine, or the vaginal wall may drop after a hysterectomy. "Women typically have two to three types at the same time," she says.

Palm notes that in most hysterectomies, which are done by a gynecologist, the "vaginal vault at the top is still not being secured, despite the fact we know it can cause vaginal wall prolapse. It's not being addressed; it's not taught in the curriculum." As a patient turned advocate, Palm has become a leading expert with four books on POP since having her own surgery almost three decades ago.

After her first book came out, she says, "Slowly women started finding me." Many phone conversations followed. "The big picture for supporting women kind of just evolved organically." She set up a nonprofit, the Association for Pelvic Organ Prolapse Support (APOPS). She leads a Facebook group, which has over 23,000 members from 177 countries and six volunteer admins.

Palm posts on APOPS social media every workday. "By and large, it's women helping women. I'm just helping to steer the ship," she says. The women in her Facebook community can be grouped into decades. She says there are young women in their twenties who are terrified that their sex life is over. They are often gymnasts and double-jointed, or they have Ehlers-Danlos syndrome, a tissue integrity condition. Then there are women in their thirties and forties who had babies. Women going through menopause in their fifties.

Those over sixty-five can be split into two groups. "The women who say, 'Okay, well now I'm officially done with sex,' whatever, they're still active other ways. But then, there are those that are like, 'Oh, no, I'm not giving it up. I'll be screwin' in my coffin!' I've met some incredible women in their seventies that are very, very sexually active—their energy!—they're just amazing to talk with."

POP is treated either through surgery or a pessary, which is a removable device that is inserted into the vagina. Pessaries come in different shapes. "It's pretty normal for it to take two to three fittings to get the right size," says Palm. "You can't see inside. Another problem is that there's very little effective pessary training for practitioners." She adds, "Pessaries do fail for about 30 to 40 percent of women." But there is innovation on the horizon. Palm is keeping an eye on medical device companies working to develop 3D-printed pessaries that can be created based on vaginal imagery.

Kegel exercises can be preventative. "Say a woman is twenty-three years old and leaks pee when she coughs or sneezes; she should be using a Kegel trainer or at least doing Kegels," says Palm. "If a woman has had a baby, and it feels loose down there—she should be doing Kegel exercises." The same goes for marathon runners. Because every time your foot hits the pavement hard, gravity creates downward pressure.

But doing Kegel exercises the wrong way can lead to overly tight muscles. A pelvic floor physiotherapist can show patients exactly which exercises to perform—they can be Kegel exercises but also lunges and squats.. Unfortunately, not all women have access to a pelvic floor specialist. Is it possible to learn Kegels on YouTube? "Don't look at just one video. Do your homework. Watch several videos, read information on several websites to get that balanced picture," says Palm. "Dr. Kegel is rolling over in his grave, because the medical system dropped the ball."

Palm argues women should routinely be examined for POP. "Women complain of incontinence and chronic constipation to their doctors all the time, but the docs don't know these symptoms are classic POP indicators," she says. "The shortfall in screening, curriculum, and best practice is absurd. I share this info often, but the medical community by and large ignores it."

Nevertheless, Palm is optimistic. "I've watched how women in our space have morphed over time." They used to barely interact with each other online. "But now"—she roars like a tiger—"in our space, oh boy, it's like the mob is forming!"

Menopause has entered the public discourse in unparalleled ways. But not all taboos are equal. There are areas of femtech that will take a long time to destigmatize. I seek out more of those who are pioneers on the final frontier of taboos.

11

FINAL FRONTIER

THE HARDEST TABOOS TO BREAK

What is a taboo? It is something that is usually hidden. It must not be spoken about. The word was introduced into the English language by the British explorer Captain James Cook in the late eighteenth century. It's based on the word *tapu* from the Polynesian language of the island Tonga, where it means "forbidden" though it also means "sacred." It seems like the last meaning was lost in translation on its way into the English language, but there's great power in seeing the holy in the profane.

Taboos have surrounded female bodies throughout the ages. If an activity is taboo, it usually still goes on in a clandestine way. If a topic is seen as taboo, people are less likely to seek help or speak out. In women's health, it's good to draw a line between what is rightfully private and what is a detrimental taboo.

The echo of "no vaginas on Monday morning" reverberates through most of women's health, from menstruation to menopause. But where is it most persistent?

When Gloria Kolb, CEO of Elidah, presents her product to

investors, it's not just embarrassment she encounters, it's disbelief—so much so that recounting a pitch competition, she says,
"I still remember the judges saying, 'Oh, if this is such a great
concept, someone would have invented it already.'"

On another occasion, she pitched a group of angel investors
and once she left the room, the first comment from one investor
to another was "If this is such a big problem, we would have heard
about it. And we haven't heard about it even from our wives."

But as Kolb, who has easy gravitas, points out, "Just because
women are quiet doesn't mean that it's not significant. It really is
significant."

"I have a lot in common with our customers," says Kolb. "I
had a nine-and-a-half-pound baby girl, which is really big, and
then thirteen pounds of twins, and I was leaking. Like a lot of
women, you leak and then you wear pads, and you think you're
in control." Then, she ran a 5k race, constantly worrying that
the pad was too full. "I felt like it was just going to fall out of my
shorts and be so embarrassing." She ran past the finish line and
straight to the bathroom. "It was horrible," she says. "I was like
OK, this is an issue. I really need to start looking for a solution."

It is estimated that about one in four women in the UK and
United States experience urinary incontinence. It's when urine
leaks as soon as pressure is put on the bladder by coughing,
sneezing, exercising, lifting heavy objects, or laughing. It can
occur at any age but is more common in women over the age of
fifty.

Kolb attended physical therapy to strengthen her pelvic
floor muscles. This includes hands-on exercises. "There was a
thin curtain separating me and some big guy, right next to me,

getting his knee worked on." Only 30 percent of women who are prescribed pelvic floor physical therapy complete their sessions. That's because it's too invasive, argues Kolb.

Physical therapy can teach you how to do Kegel exercises correctly. But after that, devices are often used, such as Kegel trainers that provide biofeedback, or electrical stimulation (e-stim) devices that stimulate the muscles. For Kolb, the e-stim was not a good option. "It does work," she says, but "it's very strong and I felt violated." In addition, it "requires you to lock yourself in your bedroom and be flat on your back. I had toddlers running around, and you just don't have that much private time."

Kolb is an engineer, one of the most male-dominated professions, with women making up only 13 percent of engineers in the United States and 16.5 percent in the UK. "I think it was God's plan for me to have all the incontinence and be an MIT engineer, so that I could pair the two together and create a solution that can help these women," she says. "It's more than just 'this is a great market opportunity.'"

The medical device Kolb created with her husband is called the Elitone. It's a thin, rechargeable gel pad, and it's worn like a period pad. "We've tried so many different substrates and materials and gels, and different lengths," she says. "I believe that it is the only one on the market that is wearable underneath your clothes." They went through several rounds of clinical studies to get FDA

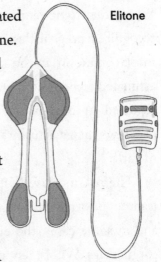

Elitone

clearance and a CE mark, including a randomized controlled trial with a sham device and an ultrasound study to visualize the effect. It's sold over the counter and can be also covered by Medicare through a prescription.

Their customers tend to be between forty and sixty years old. On average, the participants who joined Elidah's clinical research had incontinence for eleven years. "I really advocate that women start to take care of their bodies sooner," says Kolb.

"We've raised $1.8 million in grants," she says, "that got us through everything to commercialization." They raised a further $600,000 from angel investors. The grants have come from the National Science Foundation, and they also raised money from the Department of Defense to create the equivalent device for men. "I joke that had we come up with the male device first, we probably would have had no problem fundraising."

Getting support through loss

Yet another topic remains in the shadows. Out of all clinically recognized pregnancies, some 10 percent end in miscarriage, most commonly in the first trimester. The overall number is estimated to be even higher, as most early pregnancies are not reported. "A lot of people think that it is a problem that affects very few, when it actually affects many," says Lina Chan, the CEO of Parla.

The risk increases with age. For some, pregnancy loss can lead to posttraumatic stress, severe anxiety, and depression, and in some cases, the emotional toll can impact subsequent pregnancies. Within femtech, Chan's company is very much in the minority by focusing on pregnancy loss. "It's a really under-served area that's ripe for disruption."

As we begin our conversation, I wonder about the termi-nology we use. "Miscarriage" sounds like "mishap" or "mistake," and it's not a great connotation. "Miscarriage is, by definition, losing a baby before 12 weeks. Stillbirth is after 24 weeks," says Chan. Between 12 and 24 weeks it's described as "late miscar-riage" in the UK. In the US, the terminology changes at 20 weeks. "Pregnancy loss" is a broader term. Chan says, "There is this misconception that if you didn't carry the baby for that long that's not really a pregnancy loss." She advocates for a broader sense of empathy. "Women who have to go through an abortion, that's a pregnancy loss. Women who have to terminate for medical reasons, that's a pregnancy loss." Whether it's due to a failed IVF cycle or an ectopic pregnancy, grief should not be disparaged.

London-based Chan was born to Chinese immigrant parents and raised in Brazil She spent most of her career as an inves-tor before turning to entrepreneurship. "I didn't start thinking about having children until after I was thirty-five." Sadly, her first pregnancy ended in stillbirth. "I had to labor and deliver that baby," she says. "It took me a while to just realize how that experi-ence really affected me emotionally." A miscarriage followed.

"I'd go to a doctor, and he'd help answer some questions, and I'd still feel horrible. So, then I'd have to go and work with somebody on my mental health. And then I wanted to feel strong again, so I went to find a nutritionist. I was paying insane amounts of money, dealing with ten different people," she says. "Through that I realized just how fragmented the whole woman's health experience is." Chan went on to have three children in her late thirties and early forties.

After joining the accelerator Zinc Venture Capital, she raised a pre-seed round of £250,000 and cofounded Parla. The idea was to develop a digital platform to support women through their fertility journey.

In an unusual move for a start-up, Chan won a grant from the Wellcome Trust, which funds research in the academic world, to partner with researchers at University College London and conduct a study on whether providing evidence-based information on Parla can improve health literacy.

Previous studies have shown that taking folic acid supplements in the months leading up to conception and in the first trimester reduces the risk of neural tube defects for the baby and yet, only 31 percent of women take folic acid before pregnancy. Smoking in pregnancy increases risks of miscarriage and premature births. Poor preconception mental health is associated with increased odds of pregnancy complications. Unlike age, these risk factors can be mitigated. Tracking 400 Parla users over 90 days, they found that self-reported knowledge about fertility health increased by 16 percent, while levels of stress decreased by 27 percent.

Cohort-based learning

During the Covid pandemic, healthcare systems around the world were at a breaking point. "Women going through a miscarriage had to be at the hospital by themselves at a time of extreme vulnerability," says Chan.

With a second grant from the Wellcome Trust, they surveyed 600 women on Parla who experienced pregnancy loss, 500 who did not, as well as an additional 300 women who are not on Parla. What they found is a searing indictment to the strength of this taboo. About 85 percent of women didn't know pregnancy loss could occur until it happened to them.

Approximately 75 percent of women said they felt they did not receive appropriate care. Some 55 percent reported that they received no care whatsoever after the loss; most were just sent home with a pamphlet to read, and 65 percent of women wanted better access to a grief midwife or counselor. Many reported that the healthcare professionals who looked after them didn't know how to support them after loss, and some of the most traumatizing experiences were caused by a lack of empathy.

It's common to announce a pregnancy only after the first trimester, when the odds of miscarriage are lower. "You go from not announcing your pregnancy to trying to explain to people that you've had a pregnancy loss, and you're feeling horrible," says Chan.

"Pregnancy loss is something that you experience very physically. It's so easy to condition yourself to think that you must have done something wrong, right? Did you go for a run? Or did you not eat properly?" The pernicious self-critic can be extremely loud for women.

"If you go to the doctor, they don't believe your pain. Or you're going through pregnancy loss, and it's so taboo, it's extremely isolating," she says. That's why they've designed an approach that's built on peer support with six-week-long programs. They have sponsored spaces for those who can't afford the program. Each cohort has 15 participants and is led by a medical professional, a therapist, and a wellness coach.

Only four years after Parla was founded, it was acquired by the UK retailer Holland & Barrett. The amount they were acquired for is not public. Can Chan retire? "I wouldn't want to retire!" Can she go on a trip around the world? She laughs. Now I think I'm warmer.

Citizen Endo

"I've had endometriosis my whole life pretty much from the age of thirteen," says Noémie Elhadad, who is a professor and chair of the Department of Biomedical Informatics at Columbia University. Growing up in a family of doctors in France, she says, "I was very lucky to be diagnosed early within a year." On average, it takes endometriosis patients eight years to get a diagnosis.

"From a clinical standpoint, there were many mysteries." After each period, Elhadad noticed that her shoulder pain would flare up. "My doctors were like, 'You cannot have endometriosis in your shoulder, end of story, you're imagining this.'"

It turned out Elhadad was right. "Now it's recognized that when you have endometriosis on your diaphragm, the pain can be projected onto your shoulder." She says, "It was extremely validating to know that I was right the whole time." The location of the lesions and the pain don't always correlate.

With endometriosis, endometrium-like tissue is found outside of the uterus. "It can make organs adhere to each other; it can touch on nerves, which is painful. Sometimes it's not a lesion as much as it is a cyst," says Elhadad. The lesions can cause excruciating pain, especially at the time of menstruation.

It's estimated that 10 percent of women worldwide have endometriosis. It's a similar figure to the number of women who have diabetes, but diabetes research receives significantly more funding. In 2020, the U.S. government announced $26 million of funding for endometriosis research. In the same year, the NIH spent $1.1 billion on diabetes research. Even if we allocate half of that funding to female diabetes patients, that still means funding for diabetes research is 22 *times higher* than for endometriosis research. Besides, the $26 million promised to the NIH has yet to materialize.

Ultrasound can be used to help with an endometriosis diagnosis, and the definitive way to diagnose it is through a laparoscopic surgery. Some doctors recommend the contraceptive pill as a way to reduce levels of estrogen, which can relieve symptoms. The current standard of care is to remove lesions through excision surgery, but they have a high recurrence rate. Endometriosis has been detected in female fetuses, indicating that the cells for the lesions are even present before birth.

Surgery hugely improved Elhadad's quality of life. The surgeon encouraged her to use her expertise in machine learning for endometriosis research. "It was really, really difficult emotionally, because I didn't want to think about it," she says. But if scientists, who are patients, don't do this research, then who will?

Once she got a tenured position, Elhadad set up Citizen Endo as a research project at Columbia University, bootstrapping the development of the app Phendo, launched in 2017.

Since then, over 17,000 endometriosis patients use the app to track their symptoms.

What motivated her was the gap she saw between how she experienced endometriosis and what doctors told her about it. "There's a lot of talk in terms of infertility, and I was very lucky to have a child, for example." She realized there needs to be more quality data to enable innovation.

The ultimate goal is to use this data to define the disease. So far, the Phendo team has grouped users into severity-based phenotypes. "What our analysis emphasizes is that the disease is systemic. When it's severe in one part of your body, it's severe in other parts of your body as well—all parts react in concert to the disease."

Their analysis suggests the hypothesis that endometriosis could be an "inflammation-based condition as opposed to a surgical condition." If the hypothesis proves to be true, she says, "then we can start looking for gene expressions that are related to inflammation; we can start looking at whether it has a link to the gut microbiome," she says. "My hope is that there's medication that can be repurposed for endometriosis."

To self-manage their pain, Phendo users turn to heat packs, acupuncture, and changes in nutrition. Some turn to alcohol. "Patients with endometriosis are more likely to have allergies, food sensitivities, and autoimmune conditions," she says. "There's evidence that nutrition has an impact on inflammation."

Physical activity can help to relieve the pain—but, and this is a crucial caveat—it helps those who habitually exercise three times a week or more. For those who don't typically work out, exercise can increase the pain. It's a case of correlation rather than causation. Those who work out might do so because they know it helps them feel better—and vice versa.

Phendo users would like to be able to predict a flare up. "They say, even two days in advance would be amazing, because I can tell my partner the next two days will be bad, or I can cancel an event," says Elhadad. The Phendo team now analyzes whether changes in a user's voice can predict a flare up. "A lot of my research is based on my own experience," she says. Elhadad's mother, who is in France, can tell whether her daughter is unwell by how she sounds on the phone. Elsewhere, studies have already shown that changes in voice can indicate postpartum depression.

The rising awareness around endometriosis harbors risks too. "I think as there's more recognition of the disease, there's also more potential for exploitation," says Elhadad. "The big worry is, are women going to be exploited in one way or another? We see how much distress and need for help there is. It's a very vulnerable population, and technology can easily exploit people."

A cause for optimism is that the femtech movement is happening at a time when the medical establishment is more willing to hear patients. "It wasn't the case when I started doing research in 2007," she says. "I've had grants rescinded for me when I said I was going to ask patients how they experience a disease. I hate to talk in such general terms, but the belief in the medical establishment was patients don't know what they're talking about, they have an agenda, they can't be trusted—and I think that has changed tremendously."

Developing a noninvasive diagnostic test

Cécile Réal first heard about endometriosis from a friend who told her she suffered terrible pain during her period. "There is nothing wrong—it's probably in your head," doctors told her, until one doctor paid attention and diagnosed her with endometriosis. As a biomedical engineer based in Paris, Réal had launched her first company at the age of twenty-five and sold it eight years later. She felt thirty-three was too young to retire.

Réal wanted to use the experience she gained as an innovator and went on to establish herself as a serial entrepreneur in the medical technology space "I've cofounded at least five or six med tech companies, and I'm also involved on boards of the same number," she says, radiating a sense of restless energy.

When she realized how underserved endometriosis was, she knew she had to do something about it. In 2011, she launched her company, Endodiag, to create a noninvasive blood test to detect endometriosis. She raised about €10 million, half of which is grant money from the European Commission, French government grants, and private foundations.

"We're still learning a lot while we're progressing," says Réal. They have decided to enroll an additional 1,000 patients to their clinical trial. "I think everybody underestimated the number of patients we needed for validation," she says. What makes the development of a test challenging is the complexity of endometriosis.

"The disease is extremely heterogeneous," says Réal. "Even more so than we were all thinking ten or fifteen years ago." Over the last few years, several start-ups have launched—including DotLab and Hera Biotech in the United States, Proteomics in Australia, and Sision Medical in Ireland—to develop a noninvasive endometriosis test. Some are working on a blood test, while others analyze saliva or endometrial tissue.

"At the beginning, the holy grail was to have one test for everybody," says Réal. It's likely that different tests might detect different types of endometrioses.

Out of all the med tech companies Réal has worked on, she says, "I think this one is particularly challenging." As with other areas of female health, there is still—as you will by now know—a lack of research.

"Usually, this research is done at an academic level and then transferred to private organizations," she says. But in femtech, entrepreneurs shoulder the work that should have already been done by academics. "There's much more work to do."

Réal has set up a seed fund called Medevice for med tech companies and they have just made their first femtech investment: Emagina, an app-connected medical device focused on the perineum pre-birth. Once again, she notes, "A very limited number of studies has been done, which is surprising." The lack of research never fails to be surprising. But there has been a marked change in the levels of awareness about endometriosis.

"When we started the company in 2011 and I said I work on endometriosis, people asked, 'Endo-what?'" But a few days ago, she attended a conference that could barely accommodate a thousand attendees in the room.

Once there is an easy diagnostic test, patients will no longer have to be diagnosed through surgery. "Without the need of doing surgery to detect it, clinical trials become much faster, much easier, and much cheaper." This, in turn, will accelerate the development of new treatments.

A moving target

In reality there is no final frontier in women's health, because there will always be a new frontier of taboos. The femtech industry flashes a light on these issues like a lightning storm. As we move forward, the horizon keeps extending and there will always be a need for innovation.

It's time to end the normalization of female pain during medical procedures. Several companies are working on a gentler, more accurate form of breast screening to replace mammograms, which compress the breast tissue in a painful or uncomfortable way. San Francisco–based iSono Health is working on a portable, breast screening wearable device that looks a bit like Xena the warrior princess's breastplate. Meanwhile, Delphinus Medical Technologies in Michigan is developing a breast screening device that looks like a bed for patients to lie down on.

The Swiss start-up Aspivix is working on the Carevix, a gentler alternative to the tenaculum, which is a pair of scissors with sharp-pointed hooks that's used for IUD insertion, for example, and can pierce cervical tissue (it was first developed to remove bullets on a battlefield). The new device uses suction technology instead to gently stabilize the cervix.

In the diagnostic space, Boston-based AOA Dx is working on an early-stage, noninvasive diagnostic test for ovarian cancer. Barcelona-based MiMark is working on a less invasive test for endometrial cancer.

Tampons are cast in a new role going beyond periods. London-based Daye and Oakland-based NextGen Jane are leading the way in turning tampons into diagnostic tools for everything from vaginal microbiome screening to STIs. At-home testing is increasingly possible. London-based Juno Bio offers an at-home vaginal microbiome test.

Conditions that have long been overlooked are beginning to receive more attention, and existing treatments are improved. Cambridge-based medical device company Ablatus Therapeutics is developing an enhanced form of tissue ablation to treat fibroids while protecting the surrounding tissue. London-based Femspace is creating an evidence-based platform for pelvic pain issues such as vulvodynia. Modi'in-based Ocon Healthcare, which has created a ball-shaped copper IUD, is reinventing the ball so that it can also deliver medication straight to the uterus to treat abnormal uterine bleeding.

New start-ups are emerging to provide sexual health solutions for the LGBTQ+ community. London-based Lvndr Health aims to facilitate remote clinical care, and it's collaborating with Sexual Health London to research and improve medical adherence for users of PrEP, a medication taken to help prevent HIV. Boston-based Folx Health provides remote access to clinicians and hormonal treatments for people who are transitioning.

We are only beginning to see the potential of personalized medicine and of predictive and generative AI on women's health. For AI to be trained on data sets that are truly inclusive, we need to first close existing gender data gaps in health research. In the fertility space, Haifa-based Embryonics is using AI to improve an IVF cycle's success rate by an average of 15 percent. Given that many femtech companies collect unprecedented data sets, it's likely that AI will become an integral part of many ventures.

Since her early days of fundraising when Farah Kabir, the cofounder of Hanx, was asked to demonstrate how to put on a condom, she has gone on to raise £1.8 million. Her company has produced over a million biodegradable condoms.

With all forms of innovation, it's time to stop putting the planet last. That's why an increasing number of companies in the femtech space create products that are biodegradable. There are flushable period pads, created by Fluus and Planera. There is a pregnancy test made of 99 percent paper created by Hoopsy. Such products are sustainable by design. One day, all products should be.

PART III

OUT INTO THE WORLD

12

COMMUNITY

SOCIAL REVOLUTIONS ARE FUN

"Come closer—I want to hear you," says Gloria Steinem, fixing me with her attentive eyes. I lean toward the world's most iconic feminist. We are sitting on a gray couch at Soho House in New York, where she's about to give a talk with Ann Olivarius, a renowned attorney, in honor of the fiftieth anniversary of Title IX, an American federal law that banned sex-based discrimination in government-funded educational programs.

Is it her magnetism or my chutzpah? I don't know, but I could feel my feet marching across the room, and now I have struck up a conversation. I hear myself saying that Pamela Anderson is fabulous as Roxie Hart in the musical *Chicago* on Broadway. Gloria smiles. She's one of those rare people who listen intently. In photos of her at second-wave feminist protests, I have often noticed that her fingers are very long. I'm looking at them up close, graced by the fringed sleeves of her jet-black suede jacket. She is eighty-eight years old.

I tell her about this book. I mention *Our Bodies, Ourselves,* the feminist book written over fifty years ago, before ABBA even sang "Waterloo" at Eurovision. The book strikes me as uncannily relevant to what I'm writing. The Boston Women's Collective argued that women don't determine medical priorities, that we are alienated from our own bodies. Am I right in seeing all these echoes today? "Of course!" says Gloria. "It's because we still have the same bodies."

There is nothing new I can tell her, nothing she hasn't heard before, and yet, I continue. What can be done for society to overcome the stigma around female bodies? "Keep talking about it," says Gloria with calm urgency. "The more you talk about it, the more we overcome stigma."

At the age of twenty-two, Steinem had an illegal abortion in London and would later dedicate her memoir to the doctor who performed it. "You must promise me two things," the doctor told her at the time. "First, you will not tell anyone my name. Second, you will do what you want to do with your life." This life-changing moment sparked her feminism and led her to campaign for women's rights.

Steinem gained national attention as a journalist in 1963, when she went undercover for her investigative story "I Was a Playboy Bunny," exposing the underpaid and sexist world of bunny-waitresses at Hugh Hefner's clubs. In 1969, she wrote "After Black Power, Women's Liberation" and spoke out at an event advocating for the legalization of abortion in New York State, where she shared the story of her own illegal abortion.

"If you're ever feeling discouraged, I think all you need to do is look at the '70s," says Steinem as she takes her seat on stage. Fifty years ago, there was no word for "sexual harassment." Women could easily be fired for being pregnant. Unequal pay was the way of the world. "Everything we think of now as a matter of simple justice was then called life," she says.

It was much less common to think that men could raise children or that women could represent the world politically. "Take your ruler and measure from the '70s to now—and this is at least the same distance we're going to do from now forward," says Steinem.

"Equality is never dull," says Olivarius. "It's a powerful motivator." Her achievements are testament to that. The two women met in the early days of the second-wave feminist movement. Since then, Olivarius coined the term "date rape" and represented scores of women who experienced sexual harassment and assault, in lawsuits against major banks, hedge funds, law firms, and universities.

"What I would like to say to you, which is really the case for me—and it's rarely said—is that making social revolutions is fun," says Steinem. "It is interesting. It is way more fun than conforming." A woman at the back of the room shouts "Woo!" and Steinem continues, "It will bring you friends and colleagues with whom you share values, and a kind of chosen family that will be with you for years to come and throughout life.

"We are communal animals. We are not meant to be alone. The purpose of entire social justice movements, of girlfriends having lunch, is to give each other that support," says Steinem.

They talk about our need for each other. "Our need not only to speak up but to find a person or two who's had a similar experience—somebody in our family, somebody in our office, in our factory, and stand up together—that's what movements are for. Not to be alone, not to feel that you're the only victim, and to be able to tell the truth." Steinem looks around the room, electrifying. "Shared hopes and dreams and a determination to take no shit—this is what a movement is!"

Feminism and femtech

It was the smart bra that first drew me to women's health tech. But it was the community I discovered in its wake that made me stay. Once I wrote about the smart bra, I was invited to chair a panel on data security at the first ever Femtech Summit organized by Women of Wearables in 2020. I stayed to listen to all the other panels. I was curious. I had expected to learn more about technology, but I was amazed to discover I was learning more about another subject: my own body.

In the 1960s and 1970s, small groups of women would meet up in each other's living rooms, make tea, sit together, and share their experiences on a chosen topic—work, sex, relationships. Oftentimes, they would realize, for the first time, that the experience they had long thought of as solely their own was actually one many women shared. The personal, they realized, is political. Such "consciousness-raising circles" were the backbone of second-wave feminism.

Listening to large groups of female entrepreneurs, researchers, and investors share their experiences, I felt a strong sense of recognition. Each one articulated invisible expectations, norms, and obstacles. They were voicing shared hopes and dreams. I realized that what I am witnessing is a sisterhood in action, a social revolution—and yes, it is fun.

In a world where women are still raised to judge each other as competition, where some older women pull the drawbridge up behind them so that younger women "suffer as much" as they had to, where some women continue to uphold the patriarchy as much as some men do—it's not enough to talk about "the sisterhood" in the abstract.

The femtech industry is a powerful case study of how women can thrive when we are supportive of each other in business and in life. Over the years, I have observed direct competitors who are friends. I have seen information and advice shared freely. I have seen women celebrate each other's successes, time and again. It only makes sense that women, who work on improving other women's lives, are supportive of women who run businesses too.

Critics might argue that femtech has no place in feminism because it's an ecosystem of businesses. This view assumes that social movements are over here—the people waving placards at a protest—separate from the innovators, medical professionals, and everybody else who goes to work. But what do businesses consist of, if not people?

In my experience, entrepreneurs are motivated by something bigger than just personal gain. The stamina required to weather the highs and lows of entrepreneurship is best maintained by a combination of intrinsic and extrinsic motivation.

Compared to the fatigued housewives Betty Friedan interviewed for her groundbreaking book *The Feminine Mystique*, their daughters and granddaughters are significantly more likely to be doctors and to run businesses today. In the United States, women control a third of total household financial assets, more than $10 trillion, and a wealth transfer is predicted to triple this figure by 2030. Women are poised to make larger financial decisions as consumers and as investors of their own wealth, putting money into the things we want.

Critics might say that "things" have no part in feminism, while femtech is about products and services. As a matter of fact, the contraceptive pill was at the forefront of feminist debates from its inception—for its advocates, it was the precondition to liberation, but for its critics, it was proof that men controlled the medical establishment, burdening us with contraceptive responsibility, a debate that continues to this day.

Vibrators were presented by sex educators like Betty Dodson at feminist conferences in 1970s. Abortion pills allow grassroots feminist movements to provide safe access to abortion where there is none. "Things" are inextricable from society. Commerce and culture have always been intertwined.

At the same time, we have to recognize that everything that's going on in the femtech space, from the emerging research on women's health to the products and their thriving client base, firmly stands on the shoulders of the hard-won radical activism for women's rights, reproductive or otherwise. I call this feminism. Some founders skirt around the word, calling themselves "equalists," or they say, "It's just about women's health." But that doesn't tell the full story.

Generalized terms like "equalist" and "believer in human rights" have their place. But in the health, technology, and business space, not focusing on women ignores historic and existing power dynamics and gender gaps. When we talk about "gender equality," who do we really mean? Women and gender minorities. Half of the population has been oppressed for centuries, so it's only fair for us to acknowledge that feminism is what brings equality to women.

Of course, women's reproductive rights are a matter of legislation. Of course, we need to make sure that businesses don't exploit us—they always need regulation and oversight. So do politicians, nonprofits, and academic institutions. What I am arguing is that we cannot afford to ignore technology as a feminist issue. If we do, then it will continue to fail serving us. Innovation is born, as women research, build, launch, and lead businesses—and this sea change is contagious and irresistible.

Women of Wearables

The largest and most active femtech community is Women of Wearables, with over 20,000 members. "We have very diverse members: innovators, start-up founders and serial entrepreneurs, but also people who are researchers, academics, designers, technologists. We have a lot of investors; we have people with portfolio careers, who are doing multiple things at the same time—like me," says Marija Butkovic, the founder and CEO of Women of Wearables (WOW).

"Almost half of our members are from the U.S. at this point, and the rest is spread across the UK, Europe, Middle East, even Asia. We have members in Latin America, we have some members in Africa," she says. It shows that innovation is borderless. It also maps itself onto the geographical spread of femtech companies.

"People need the same things when it comes to the community and support wherever they are," says Butkovic. "Amazing innovators can come from any part of the world—not just big tech hubs like London, San Francisco, New York, and so on.

"I was a corporate lawyer for eight years before I got into tech," says Butkovic, who is charismatic and talks a thousand words a minute. In 2014, her husband got a job in London, where they moved from Croatia. "I decided to completely reinvent myself." Drawn to the world of wearable technology, she coinvented a smart umbrella called Kisha that could be traced on an app if it was mistakenly left behind on public transport.

"I realized that there are not many women in the wearable tech space," she says. "Not to mention that back then, London was so much—and still is—about fintech, traditional banking, all these old industries." To meet other women in wearable tech, Butkovic set up a small Meetup Group.

In 2016, she hosted the first event focused on femtech with speakers from Elvie, MysteryVibe, and a hypnobirthing expert. "It was amazing. Although there were people who asked me, 'Oh, is this a FinTech meetup?'—we had, like, 100-plus women showing up."

It was then she felt that "femtech could be one of those industries that can really make a difference, not only for female founders, because two-thirds of founders in femtech are female, but as a category. Until that point, it never occurred to me how underserved and underresearched women's health is.

"And then I got pregnant with my son, and I gave birth to him in August 2018, and since the moment I got pregnant, I became intoxicated with femtech, because, no one teaches you about your body. You go through so many changes mentally and physically throughout pregnancy. I saw so many gaps where healthcare could be improved for women, especially women going through pregnancy."

The birth was complicated by an emergency C-section. "Postpartum care was super traumatic for me. I ended up having three rounds of mastitis," she says. It's a breast tissue inflammation that can involve an infection, common when breastfeeding. "And I ended up having an abscess, which is a lump." Four GPs failed to diagnose it. Butkovic diagnosed it herself and insisted on treatment.

"From that moment, I realized, I need to start paying better attention to my health, because if I don't advocate for myself, doctors might brush me off again," she says. "I think support and community is tremendously important, whether you're a start-up founder, or a regular woman."

While the smart umbrella didn't take off, the community is soaring. WOW has become her full-time job, and in 2019, she hired her best friend, Anja Streicher, as the chief marketing officer at WOW. How did they meet? They were part of a Facebook group for Croatian people in London, where Butkovic asked for apartment recommendations and Streicher promptly suggested her own block. "You don't even know her—she might be a psycho—and you offered her to come live in our building?" was how Streicher's husband reacted at the time. "Everything ended up well," Butkovic laughs.

"Her husband actually works with my husband now. She works with me. We have children of similar age," says Butkovic. As they don't have other family members in the UK, they have become an extended modern family, relying on each other. "We are super, super close."

The goal of WOW is to showcase the latest tech innovation, emphasize the importance of investing in women, and highlight female role models. "This world is a man's world; although we think it's not, it still is, unfortunately. But things are slowly changing.

"We decided that we want to be a community for women and allies in healthcare technology," she says. "Women deserve to get the same amount of funding as men. We deserve to get the same quality of healthcare as men. We deserve to be seen and be heard," she says.

"I never thought that this could become a proper, full-time job and a business," she says. For the first three years, she ran the community alongside her freelance work as a marketing and social media professional. She organized free events, wrote a blog, created databases. In 2020, she launched a paid option that has about 1000 members, and events are sponsored.

"Success doesn't mean that it has to be super quick, and you have to raise a ton of money and that you have to grow tremendously. That's only one version of success, and as a founder, what I can say is that each of us has the power to define what success means for you. I think that's one of the biggest lessons I've learned in this industry: define what success means for you, and then find a way to achieve that. You don't have to follow someone else's; you can create your own.

"You have to start doing something because you really want to make a difference and you want to see a change, not because you want to make money. Because money will come inevitably. But you have to start doing something because you really want it, and that will shine through everything you do—and people will recognize that."

Femtech communities have formed across the world. The best place to find them is LinkedIn. They can be professional networks like the Femtech Community Japan, FemTech Israel, Women of SexTech in New York, and FemTech Association Asia.

Or they can be incubators or accelerators, which are organizations that serve as springboards for early-stage start-ups, including the FemTech Lab in London and Tech4Eva in Zurich. Each accelerator differs in what it provides and what it takes in return. Some make an investment in return for some equity, while others mainly provide a mentoring program and network.

I have observed a great sense of camaraderie in those spaces. As Halle Tecco puts it, "We can and should create a start-up ecosystem that is more supportive of one another." It's not a zero sum game.

Femtech in the country of romance

I wonder how the femtech community fares in a country we think of as sensual, where pleasure is accepted and communicated as a central human need. A country that gave us Andréa Martel, the charming and ruthless movie star agent from *Call My Agent*— not just the object of desire but the one who desires, the one who calls the shots. A place that created the French kiss, *le libertinage, l'éclair au chocolat*, and a national strategy to combat endometriosis.

"France is still an old country with very patriarchal organizations," says Brest-based Christel Bony, who's at the helm of SexTech For Good. "Talking about pleasure for men is OK, Viagra is fine," adds Delphine Moulu, founder of the nonprofit

Femtech France in Paris, "but women's pleasure is still a big taboo." *Plus ça change*, I think.

The two women met at the Paris-based incubator Station F, where Moulu set up the femtech program. "Pleasure for elderly or disabled people is also very taboo," she says. That's why SexTech For Good is leading a research program on sexuality at old-age homes. It has been met with reticence from healthcare professionals. "For them sexual pleasure is not part of health," Christel says. "But we know that when you allow people to have a sexual life with intimacy, they eat better, they require less medication— it's great and it's natural."

Even though they praise some aspects of the national strategy against endometriosis, it is not enough. Bony says, "We would love to have a national strategy on women's health overall." Moulu continues, "There may now be too many French endometriosis start-ups. What about PCOS? We know that more women, in France at least, are touched by this than endometriosis." What's more, menopause and postpartum depression remain very underserved.

Given that France has a strong healthcare system that covers fertility treatments and pelvic floor therapy, I wonder which business model French femtech companies tend to adopt— whether they sell directly to people or to the healthcare system. "Most of the French femtech start-ups haven't found their business model yet," says Moulu. Investors are less keen to fund direct-to-consumer companies. The majority of French femtech start-ups hope to get reimbursed by the healthcare system one day, but that requires them to conduct further studies, which in turn, requires more funding.

Bony argues that France needs more public voices on women's health, citing the United States, where Meghan Markle wrote about her miscarriage, and Angelina Jolie spoke about her mastectomy. Bony says there needs to be greater willingness to talk about failure and promptly sets an example by talking about the start-up she launched, Little Bird, a sex toy that would vibrate as erotic stories are read on an app. It won a Consumer Electronics Show award in 2016 but no longer exists.

Moulu launched Femtech France because she felt "the ecosystem was too fragmented with start-ups on one hand, healthcare professionals and investors on the other." The goal is to accelerate innovation in women's health in France. "Women are leaving their very comfy finance job to launch their own fertility start-ups because they had fertility problems," she says. "There is momentum. We see more and more companies."

The number of European femtech companies has been increasing. At the same time, one East Asian country that has been making waves in the world of femtech is Japan. My next stop is the world's biggest expo of femtech products, which takes place in Tokyo.

13

BIG IN JAPAN

THE WORLD'S LARGEST FEMTECH EXPO

Tokyo is misty when I arrive, the business district, Roppongi, dotted with amber streetlights in the drizzling October rain. People carry see-through umbrellas that are lit up like milky domes while pink, blue, and yellow bottles of sweet teas stand illuminated in vending machines. The cash point plays music and has buttons that feel like velvet. At a convenience store, I buy almonds stuck to crackers with cheese.

I make my way to Roppongi Hills. A giant spider by Louise Bourgeois stands at the entrance, dwarfed by the group of skyscrapers that house beautifully designed shops, restaurants, and bars. I think of Andy Warhol, who said, "Someday, all department stores will become museums, and all museums will become department stores."

Walking through the bladed door, I take an elevator up to the "Femtech Fes," the world's largest femtech expo, organized by Fermata, the Japanese femtech hub and marketplace. At the entrance, visitors choose between a pink or a blue sticker to signal whether they would like to be photographed while they ponder the objects on display. Not everyone wants to be seen looking at femtech and sextech devices.

The devices are neatly arranged on long tables that run like branches of a tree across two large halls. Each device has a square place mat, with descriptions in Japanese and English. A small flag on each place mat indicates the country the device is from, accompanied by the founder smiling from a circular photo.

Wearable breast pumps sit inside the bras of mannequins. The rings of Ohnut are displayed on a banana. Menstrual disks roll around the table, and cycle tracking watches are accompanied by signs saying "Touch Me!" I'm told for Japanese customers, it's important to touch, see, and feel products. Fermata staff members answer questions. The idea is to show Japanese audiences the innovation that exists abroad and get their feedback on what they would like to have in Japan. Over the next two days, I wander the rooms and corridors of the Femtech Fes touching products alongside the crowd of visitors.

I notice there is a significant proportion of men. "I'm here because of her," one guy tells me pointing at his friend. "We want to have a baby soon, so we're here to learn how to take care of her body," says another one, who is here with his wife.

Most products on display were created in the United States and Europe. Some Japanese companies create their own products in existing categories like period underwear. And then, there are creative local variations. I spot a display of what looks like oversize mochi desserts. I touch them and they feel like mochi too. They are external sex toys developed by a female-led team called Iroha based at a larger company. They also developed a small gel-based flower toy that dissolves when it's used.

Iroha

On another table, there is a peppermint-colored vibrating ball called Nopole—a sex toy created by fifty people from the LGBTQ community led by Juntaro Morita. Elsewhere, there's a small sex toy that's half vibrator and half razor. It seems to me like a dangerous combination. Then, somebody explains that it's meant to be a sex toy in disguise.

Throughout the day, there are panel sessions with local and international speakers. Anna Lee from Lioness talks about orgasm data. Her product is already sold at Fermata, together with other products including mucus tracker kegg, the Ohnut ring buffer, Dame products, the Elvie pelvic floor trainer, and the Kegelbell vaginal weights. Eric Dy from Bloomlife talks about preterm labor. Brittany Barreto of FemHealth Insights covers trends in the femtech industry. Ivonne Altamirano of Inne, the saliva-based hormone tracker, and Hana Janebdar of at-home vaginal microbiome test Juno Bio are here to explore the Japanese market.

Others yet are here with an early prototype. Hungary-based Anna Zsofia Kormos of Alpha Femtech presents a bodysuit that provides period pain relief through heated patches and microvibrations. Israel-based Hilla Shaviv has brought a prototype of the Tulipon, a device that can contain period blood without absorbing it. It looks like a tampon but works like a moon cup. At her presentation, Shaviv pours her cup of coffee into the device—to spontaneous applause from the audience.

In sessions held in Japanese, I notice that the word "orgasm" is used in English; so are "sexual wellness," "innovation," and "taboo." I ask Lia Camargo from the Fermata team about this. Isn't there a Japanese word for "orgasm"? She says the Japanese term *kairaku* sounds archaic and it means "pleasure"; it is therefore not always precise enough.

In Japan, a confluence of trends has aligned. The country's aging population and strict immigration laws mean the workforce has been shrinking rapidly. In an attempt to reinvigorate the economy, the government has been incentivizing women to join the workforce and take on managerial positions. It only makes sense that politicians have taken note of a tech sector that supports female health.

There is a parliamentary working group focused on femtech, called the "Femtech Giren." The group works on legislation to enable Western femtech companies to enter the Japanese market. Since 2021, "femtech" has been part of the annual federal budget, channeling investment into the sector. It's fair to say that femtech is big in Japan.

Found in translation

The woman who leads femtech in Japan is Dr. Amina Sugimoto. She launched the femtech hub Fermata in 2019, headquartered in Tokyo with a branch in Singapore. Growing up in Tanzania with a Japanese mother and a Malaysian father, she remembers observing that malaria products didn't always reach local people who needed them, when clinics sold them to tourists at a premium instead. Sugimoto went on to do a PhD on public health and health economics in London.

After that, "I was working in policy for a while, and I got really bored," she laughs. At the time, she met Taizo Son, the CEO of Mistletoe, a start-up ecosystem, and brother of Masayoshi Son, Softbank's CEO. At Mistletoe, Sugimoto realized that innovative companies who want to enter the Japanese market face multiple barriers. "Not only just culture and language, but then there's the regulation, and the legal side," she says.

Fermata is an online marketplace and a one-stop shop for femtech companies. If a company wants to enter the Japanese market, as a gateway to Asia, Fermata handles the licenses for software, hardware, medical devices up to Class II, cosmetics, and "quasi drugs," a pharmaceutical legal category that exists in Japan and Korea.

"We do the packaging, localization, language changes, marketing," she says with the energy of a woman who can do anything. "We also have a brick-and-mortar store in Tokyo and Osaka." They have a warehouse and they're involved in political lobbying. Fermata also consults big Japanese corporations like Sony and Panasonic. So far, they have brought over twenty femtech products from the West to Japan. Period underwear has been the biggest hit.

"People ask me: Why are we so behind compared to the West? Or why is sexual wellness or sex such a taboo in Japan? But as someone who grew up outside of Japan for most of my life and came back here, to me, this country is super open when it comes to sexuality," says Sugimoto. "We use the same word 'taboo,' but people see it differently."

I think of Japanese woodblock prints that have a long history of representing vagina ghosts. Every spring, street festivals at Japanese shrines celebrate the power of fertility and the harvest with graphic sculptures of penises. These are centuries-old folk rites. "People just carry around a penis," says Sugimoto of those festival parades, making a gesture like she's lugging a log over her shoulder. "How's that not taboo?

"When we opened the brick-and-mortar store, we had a lot of media attention, because it was the first femtech store," she continues. A reporter came along from the six o'clock nationwide evening news. She picked up a dildo and asked viewers, "What do you think this is?" And Sugimoto was thinking, "BBC? CNN? Nah, I don't think that would happen there!"

There is no doubt that taboos are culturally dependent. Genitals have a rich visual language here, but their actions are still grappling for words. Terms like "sexual wellness" are in English. Sugimoto observes that the concept of Zen, of wellness, of meditation, originated there. "But people have somehow forgotten that in the last fifty years, so now we're reimporting back the concept."

In women's health, Sugimoto noticed "people themselves are not even realizing what they need." The English term "femtech" resonates with Japanese consumers. "People see it as a movement, as the right to know their own body."

In the room

This is the first time that international guests are invited to attend the Femtech Fes and I'm shown to a conference room where they have gathered. As I lean against a low table carrying cans of water, I look around. I recognize many of the entrepreneurs. I have already interviewed some of them; others I recognize from LinkedIn. Now, they laugh and talk in three dimensions, seated around tables. Some are upright, and some are slouching. Here we all are.

At the opening night in a bar called The Moon, the woman who made all of this happen, Amina Sugimoto, gives a speech. The Femtech Fes began with only 20 companies. The following year, 150 companies participated. This year, there are 200 companies from all over the world and 3,000 visitors. I could have touched the anticipation in the room, it was so palpable. Behind Sugimoto and her eminent guests of senior politicians and entrepreneurs, a slideshow captures the expo. There are moon cups, illustrations of vaginal anatomy, and sex toys. I can't picture a British politician standing comfortably in front of these images.

The bar is abuzz with entrepreneurs and investors. I talk to Kumi Takahashi, a charismatic entrepreneur whose company Bé-A created period shorts that can measure the amount of blood they absorb. "Ninety percent of Japanese women use pads," she tells me. Tampons are not big in Japan. But the strongest growing new category is period underwear. The shorts Takahashi created can contain up to 150 milliliters of period blood. "How much is that?" I ask. She points to the top of her champagne flute.

We turn to talk to Takuma Miyaji, a member of the House of Representatives. "I am a Liberal Democrat, a man, and the district I represent is Kagoshima—all of this marks me out as conservative," he says, and yet, he is known as Mr. Femtech, and he set up the parliamentary group. "It has been a big challenge. I was told to just focus on infrastructure or farming policy." But Miyaji is adamant to keep talking about women's health. He says, "If femtech is known in *my* district, we can change all of Japan!"

I walk around, twirling the ice in my drink, until I recognize some other people. "We are eight to ten years behind Europe and the U.S.," one expert says about the Japanese femtech landscape. "Businesses are run by men in their sixties and seventies who don't even know their wives stopped having their period," she adds.

Then I talk to Francesca Geary, who runs the Singapore branch of Fermata. When she first got involved in the field, her work was met with little understanding. "This is my friend who sells sex toys" is how her friends used to introduce her. With growing recognition around female health needs and what femtech can do, they now say, "This is Fran—she's changing the world!"

The final dinner for international guests turns into a karaoke night. As the evening progresses, people talk about orgasms with the intensity that comes after the third cocktail. We move on to a dance bar. Brittany Barreto orders a round of multicolored shots, and the barman sounds a large bell. We are joined by a group of Japanese women on the dance floor. One of them comes up to me and shouts, "You're so sexy!" and jolts me out of my dance routine. I stumble across the sticky floor and survey the bar. Could this be the reason we don't treat each other as competitors? On some level, we see each other as potential partners. Perhaps I'm having a Freudian revelation.

A voice for women

In the morning, I interview Hiromi Marissa Ozaki—known as Sputniko!—who is a Japanese pop star. "I'm half British, half Japanese," she tells me as we sit down at a small round table inside the conference hall. Growing up as a teenager in Japan, she had bad period pain and PMS. When she decided to see a doctor about it, he told her to just "deal with it."

She went on to study mathematics and computer science at Imperial College in London, where it struck her that "we have neural networks, bioinformatics, all this amazing tech. But why am I still bleeding every month? Why am I still in pain every month? Something so primitive is still happening to me. Tech and science have solved so many problems in the world, but they haven't solved *my* problem and many other women's problems."

When she was a student in London, the NHS gave her the Pill—it was free and it helped with her cramps. "Why didn't I know about the Pill and how it could help my pain? And I found out that Japan only approved the Pill in 1999, which is 40 years after the U.S. and Europe."

For her master's degree at the Royal College of Art, she created a music video called "The Menstruation Machine." In the video, she plays Takashi, a young man who builds a wearable metal device, shaped like a chastity belt, to experience what it's like to have a period. The device stimulates pain and dispenses blood. Takashi wears it on a night out, striding around a shopping mall, suddenly doubling over in pain.

The music video went viral on YouTube. "A curator saw my work and invited me to show it at the MoMA," she says. It launched her onto the firmament of the art world. "I was in a lot of women's magazines and television, talking about menstruation," she says. *Vogue Japan* made her Woman of the Year.

In Japan, the Pill took 40 years to get regulatory approval. "Many male politicians in Japan said the Pill could make women too sexually outward. But on the other hand, when Viagra came out, Japan approved it in just six months," she says. "And to me it felt like it could make men too sexually outward!" Our laughter echoes through the exhibition hall that hasn't filled with people yet.

As we talk, she combines the charisma of a pop star with the critical mind of a professor, which is also a role she has held at the MIT Media Lab and the Tokyo University of Arts. "There are only about 20 percent female doctors, and it's because of deliberate exam rigging," she says. In 2018, it was revealed that Tokyo Medical University had been rigging entrance exams to discriminate against female candidates.

We talk about abortion in Japan. "You can get an abortion," she says, "But many hospitals require the woman to get permission from her boyfriend or husband." Even though Japan's health ministry has released guidelines that women who've experienced domestic violence do not need spousal consent to get an abortion, clinics don't necessarily implement that. "The default is you need the man's permission, which is ridiculous," says Sputniko!

When she moved back to Tokyo after living in the UK and United States, many of her friends had launched start-ups. She wondered: Could she "go beyond museums and try to create a service or product that changes women's lives and changes society in a positive way?"

Raising $1.5 million from angel investors, she launched her femtech start-up Cradle. It's an educational platform and employee benefits provider with clients like Shiseido and Honda to provide their employees with information on women's health and access to clinics.

I tell her that in Europe and the United States, there is a sense that women have been overmedicalized in some ways, as research on the side effects of hormonal contraception continues to emerge. "In Japan, only 3 percent of women take the contraceptive pill," she says, and only 1.7 percent of menopausal women have hormone replacement therapy. We note that the dynamics are reversed.

I mention the natural birth movement in the West, which pushes back against the medicalization of birth. She mentions that 94 percent of births in Japan are natural, while only 6 percent of women get an epidural. "And this is without a movement!" She says, "It's because traditional families think that if you remove the pain, you're not going to love your daughter."

"Everything looks like it's so futuristic and high tech," she says, waving her hand at the skyscrapers that stretch out of the window. "I think because of the language barrier, a lot of Japanese women don't even know that they're in a strange situation.

"I hope people try to understand these choices," she says. "And I think Femtech Fes is all about that." We look around the hall as new visitors trickle in. "A lot of them appear to be very polite," she says, holding my gaze. "But I can feel a hidden anger among the women."

14

THE INSIDIOUS SIDE

MONETIZING INSECURITIES

"Hygienic," "clean," and perfect for "those on the go" is how two start-up founders describe their product. They are standing in front of a jury of investors on the German version of *Shark Tank*, called The Den of Lions.

The founders are two thirty-two-year-old guys, and they have been working on this idea for four years. One of them has ginger stubble, and the other one has a hairstyle and way of speaking that can both be described as slick. "We really understand what women want," he says. "And we want to make the lives of women easier." Their invention: "Pinky" gloves—a single-use pair of pink plastic gloves for women to remove and dispose of our tampons.

The panel of "lions," or angel investors, consists of three men and two women, who decide whether they'd like to invest €30,000 for 20 percent of equity in the company. "Something is bothering me," says a lion in an indigo suit. "I'm missing a woman on your team. Is there a woman who has equity in your company?"

"No, just the two of us," says the slick one. "But I am married!"

Nodding his head at his cofounder, he adds, "And so is he…by now." The lions smirk.

A glamorous lioness pipes up, asking: How are these gloves different from little tampon disposal bags? How are they better than existing single-use latex gloves? She listens patiently, heaps praise on them, but decides not to invest. "It's not my subject area."

The other female investor, also full of praise, bows out. "It's simply not my kind of thing."

Indigo Suit is not convinced either. "You need a woman, or someone who can help you with this subject—that's just not me. For this reason, I'm out."

The other two men, however, offer to invest. "That nobody has ever thought of this!" an investor in an extremely shiny suit exclaims in disbelief while fingering one of the pink gloves. "I am totally into this, because you are cool guys." He goes on to reiterate three times that the founders are cool guys, then offers to invest.

"Our goal is to be in every lady's handbag. To get this product onto the market," say the founders as they walk out of the pitch. Except it wasn't to be. The market told them what it thought of Pinky gloves in what became a social media storm.

Not only is the product not an "invention," but a basic set of rubber gloves—it's capitalizing on period shame. In a flood of #pinkygate memes, women "invented" latex gloves for men to remove condoms and "despaired" because they needed to take their tampon out but only had white latex gloves at home. Ultimately, Pinky gloves was taken off the market, and the founders and investor apologized. I accept their apology.

No matter how far we think that we have come in destigmatizing menstruation, since the Roman scholar and admiral Pliny the Elder argued that period blood is what "causes the fruit of trees to fall off," "dims the bright surface of mirrors," and "kills bees"—a tall order!—the tale of Pinky gloves shows how stigma persists.

The gloves help us recognize a category of products that "Monetize Shame"—their strategy is: Shame them, then sell them. It's not the first and not the last time for a company to do this—there is, in fact, a long history.

The empress's new clothes

"I'm not going to lie—we did groan when we saw your order," a librarian tells me at the counter of the National Archives in London's Kew. The documents I ordered are "hard to maneuver, and awkward." I'm here to inspect copyrighted designs for inventions registered in the 1800s. The books are burgundy red with yellow lattice, containing thousands of Victorian designs and they are so big they have to be wheeled out on a silver trolley.

Some of the pages are parchment-paper thin and crumbling. To touch those pages, I was expecting to wear gloves, perhaps even Pinky gloves, but I'm told that would make my fingers less sensitive.

Gingerly turning the pages of design drawings from 1881, I find a bowler hat with built-in ventilation. I find an "advertising lamp" designed by a Victorian Don Draper to position ads in the frames of streetlights. I find a combined knife-and-fork. I find it astonishing that many Victorian inventions forever changed the way we live—the telephone, railroad, electric telegraph, and light bulb—but that most inventions never see the light of day.

Two Victorian designs stand out to me. There's the "anti-cholera belt," a wide strip of flannel wrapped around the abdomen, worn by men and women. The link between poor sanitation and contagious disease was not well understood, and the anti-cholera belt fit the medical knowledge of its era—it was believed that a chilled abdomen was prone to diseases. Medical doctors endorsed the belts. Newspapers recommended them. Today, we know that cholera is a bacterial disease and that all a flannel belt can do is provide a false sense of protection.

What the belt shows is that we have always been limited by the current medical knowledge of our day. Future scientists might look back at us and say we didn't know the most basic things about the menstrual cycle. That it's no wonder women are routinely misdiagnosed given how little we knew. That we used crude and inadequate methods of contraception, so it's hardly surprising half our pregnancies were unplanned.

The second design that stands out is a corset from 1881. It's drawn in a beautiful aquamarine, and it has two protruding "air bags." According to the inventor, F. Parsons, they are "made of a form to represent as nearly as possible when distended the shape of the human breasts." Uh-oh. It's a corset with inflatable boobs. A short tube tangles

Inflatable Boob Corset

at the boob. Just like the lifejacket that's under your seat on a plane, the mouthpiece can be used to top up the air.

Today, we know that the average corset's tight lacing exerted a force of 21 pounds on the body, causing constipation and deformation by compressing organs. Like other corsets, the air boob corset was therefore actively harmful. It's an illustration of toxic beauty standards. What the air boob corset sells is "beauty is pain"—a sales pitch that has an incarnation in every generation.

Today, start-ups that fall into the "beauty is pain" category have begun to exploit the femtech label. A company called "Mia femtech" says it "brings harmony to your body by shaping your breasts." What it actually sells is plastic surgery. It does not mention the plethora of side effects and illnesses associated with breast implants. This is *not* femtech.

As the femtech category continues to expand, we will inevitably see more insidious companies abusing the term and the narratives around female health and empowerment.

Danger! Danger!

"Ancient feminine wisdom" and a "time-honored tradition" are how the next company describes its at-home vaginal steaming kit on a Kickstarter fundraising page. The founder "had a transformative vaginal steaming experience after attending a local women's circle in Brooklyn."

Vagina steaming gained widespread attention when it was advertised on Gwyneth Paltrow's Goop in 2015, which claimed the practice "cleanses your uterus." As we know, that's not possible, because the uterus is protected by the cervix.

Besides, vaginas are self-cleaning. It's well documented that vaginal steaming and vaginal douching are dangerous practices. They have been linked with adverse pregnancy outcomes, including ectopic pregnancy, reduced fertility, and preterm birth. They can increase the risk of cervical cancer, pelvic inflammatory disease, inflammation of the uterine lining, and sexually transmitted infections, including HIV.

These practices alter the vaginal microbiome and predispose women to develop bacterial vaginosis (BV). The vaginal microbiome influences our health, and steaming can disrupt the vaginal microbiome and pH balance. Anything that steams, douches, sprays, wipes, or cleanses your vagina is not just unnecessary but actively harmful.

On another occasion, Goop advertised vaginal jade eggs that "increase vaginal muscle tone, hormonal balance, and feminine energy in general." For this false claim and another one about a blend of essential oils they claimed can fight depression, Goop has paid $145,000 to settle a false advertising lawsuit in California.

Jade eggs were a "strictly guarded secret of Chinese royalty," stated an article on Goop at the time. In a study of over 5,000 Chinese jade objects across art and archaeology collections, Jen Gunter found no evidence to support the claim that vaginal jade eggs were ever used in sexual health practices or for pelvic muscle exercises in ancient Chinese culture. Instead of being an ancient Chinese practice, they are a modern marketing myth.

In my research, I was amazed to find that two other objects were probably never used in the way we think of them, even though they are often mentioned in discussions of female bodies. First, the chastity belt. While the artifact itself exists, historians doubt that chastity belts were ever used to enforce medieval fidelity. It's likely they were merely curiosities to be displayed in cabinets like large seashells. Just like virginity has little grounding in anatomy, chastity belts had no practical use. But that doesn't make the symbolism of the chastity belt—or the demand for female virginity—any less insidious.

It is also now considered a myth that it was a common practice for Victorian doctors to use vibrators to treat their patients' hysteria by stimulating them to orgasm. This claim can be traced back to Rachel Maines's influential 1999 book *The Technology of Orgasm*. In 2018, two academics at the Georgia Institute of Technology found there is scant evidence to support this claim.

Medical device failure

The majority of medical devices are life-saving and life-improving, but there have been several medical devices focused on women that have failed with catastrophic consequences.

Medical devices came under regulatory control by the FDA in 1976—before that, only drugs were regulated. The decision to regulate medical devices was made in the wake of the scandal surrounding the Dalkon Shield, an IUD that was sold in the 1970s. It was made of plastic and was the shape of a small flat crab. Over 200,000 women said it caused them serious health issues, including miscarriage and loss of fertility.

The Dalkon Shield had a design flaw: its string was made of filaments harboring bacteria that could enter the uterus. It led to severe infections and a number of fatalities. The manufacturer knew about this flaw but refused to make changes, as that would increase their costs. After a range of lawsuits against the manufacturer, the product was withdrawn from the market.

Essure was a type of permanent birth control launched in 2002. The devices consisted of metal coils inserted into the fallopian tubes through the vagina and uterus. The coils were intended to cause a local inflammation that was supposed to close off the tubes, as an alternative to tubal ligation. The device caused serious health issues, leading 39,000 women to file lawsuits. The clinical data the company had provided for FDA approval was not long-term enough to capture its damaging effects.

In 2018, Bayer removed Essure from the market, shortly after it was covered in *The Bleeding Edge* documentary. The "Essure Problems" Facebook group, founded by Angie Firmalino, has over 43,000 members and in 2020, Bayer agreed to pay $1.6 billion to settle nearly 39,000 Essure injury claims.

Mesh is a flexible plastic scaffold that has long been used for hernia repair. In the late 1990s, vaginal mesh was introduced to treat pelvic organ prolapse, which led to horrific complications. Vaginal mesh "can fragment, twist, degrade, or shrink to slice into nerves, tissue, and organs," according to the Sling the Mesh campaign. In some countries it has been removed from the market; in others it still exists as a surgical option.

In some cases, as with vaginal mesh, medical devices weren't tested rigorously enough. The FDA's 510(k) process allows medical device manufacturers to demonstrate a product's safety and effectiveness based on it being "substantially equivalent" to an existing product, as was the case for vaginal mesh, rather than conducting new clinical studies. This means companies only need to convince the regulator their product is similar enough to previous ones, even if those previous products have been pulled from the market or are decades old.

I've asked the FDA how they plan to address these issues to avoid further tragedies.

"The FDA believes firmly in the merits of the 510(k) process," an FDA official told me, though they had rolled out changes to modernize this process in 2018. "Those changes continue to be intended to help keep pace with the increasing complexity of rapidly evolving technology."

Potions and lotions

I'm calling the next category of products potions and lotions. Many supplements are evidence-backed and recommended— like taking Vitamin D supplements in British winter months— but others are not.

"While the FDA has the responsibility to approve the use of any conventional pharmaceutical and to monitor how it is manufactured, the FDA has no such responsibility with regard to supplements," according to Harvard Health. "That means unscrupulous companies can sell any products they like, and the supplements won't be pulled from the shelves until and unless the FDA proves they're unsafe."

Dubious supplements are targeted at postmenopausal women. "Compounded bio-identical hormones and testosterone pellets are hawked on the internet very aggressively in the U.S. with all kinds of promises that do not require data to back up the claims made," says Nanette Santoro, MD, Professor and E. Stewart Taylor Chair of Obstetrics & Gynecology at the University of Colorado. "There is really no end. The market is large."

The companies that sell them list vague benefits like "balance." They claim that their nonregulated "bio-identical hormones"—typically made from plants—used for "pellet hormonal therapy" are "safer" and have "fewer side effects" than FDA-regulated hormonal therapy. But a 2021 study has found that women on "pellet hormonal therapy" are more likely to experience side effects, abnormal uterine bleeding, and hysterectomies, compared to those on FDA-regulated hormone therapy.

If you look at the websites of snake oil products, it's noticeable that they like to describe themselves as "naturally sourced" and "all-natural"—even though everything is a chemical. Besides, natural doesn't necessarily mean good: a flu is natural too.

Potions and lotions like to claim they are "anti-aging," "antioxidant-rich," and "clinically proven"—but it's always worth doing more research on what that means. Their packaging is slick, and their claims are seductive.

The FDA and FTC issued warnings to five companies for selling supplements that claim to cure, treat, mitigate, or prevent infertility. The names of their supplements are ConceiveEasy, NaturaCure, FertilHerb, EU Natural Conception, and Conflam Forte. These supplements claimed "to boost your chance of pregnancy or improve your IVF success rate." They claimed to prevent miscarriage by making sure "your body is ready for conception and pregnancy at the cellular level."

Joining the group of potions and lotions are most libido-enhancing supplements. Sexual desire is complex—emotionally and psychologically. Most pills that claim to improve your sex life are not supported by scientific evidence. Just like aphrodisiacs, these products could work nonetheless, thanks to the power of sensual suggestion—the placebo effect is powerful and it can be beneficial. But sugar pills that make big claims become dangerous if they keep people from seeking actual help for serious medical conditions.

What's the business model?

The business model tells us a lot about the nature of a company. In the egg freezing space, a few clinics offer the option to freeze your eggs for free, if you give half of those eggs to the clinic. This is usually framed in altruistic terms as a "donation" to those who can't conceive, rather than saying: if you can't afford to freeze your eggs, you can do it here by paying with half your potential offspring.

This model, which is sometimes called "egg sharing," raises more ethical questions than I can cover here, but to name a few: What happens if the donor changes her mind at any point? In an investigation for *Undark Magazine*, Alison Motluk reported several cases of would-be donors in the United States who pulled out before an egg donation and were consequently threatened with bills and legal action by fertility clinics. In the case of "donated eggs", the clinic could also hold half of the donor's frozen eggs hostage.

So, what is the small print? How transparent—and how risky—is the process for the donor and for the recipient?

Besides, there is no limit on how much clinics can charge egg recipients for the procedure. Should there be? How much profit should be made on something that is advertised as a "donation"? Is egg sharing preferable to egg selling? Do the financial circumstances and motivations of donors matter? For now, the model raises more questions than answers.

The bigger question is: Should eggs and sperm be sold at all? In the UK, for instance, egg donors can only be paid £750 per donation cycle. And sperm donors get up to £35 per clinic visit.

Then there are apps whose business model seems to be to sell your data. According to a report in the *Washington Post*, the pregnancy and fertility app company Ovia Health has shared private information on employees with their employers who offer the app as an employee benefit.

It's always worth asking: What does the product actually do? And perhaps, the answer is: nothing or nothing good. How does this company make money? Is it possible that you are the product they are selling? What are the risks? What is the current evidence? What emotions do they trigger with what they sell?

Misinformation is used to hawk products and services online. There are, for instance, websites and social media posts on "natural ways to reverse PCOS," which isn't possible. The way misinformation spreads is by grabbing our attention with outlandish claims.

Anti-abortion organizations that masquerade as "pregnancy crisis centers" around the world are spreading lies. They falsely claim that abortion increases the risk of mental illness, that hospitals wouldn't treat any arising complications, and "that abortion can 'turn' a woman's partner gay," according to an investigation by openDemocracy. It's bizarre.

Femtech or scamtech?

A gap has opened between the demands of patients and the mores of the medical establishment. The question is: Who steps into the gap? Good actors and bad actors. In either case, it's interesting that the market knows to take women's needs seriously—"Oh, you have abdominal pain? Here's a pill!"— rather than dismissing them, even if the goal of some companies is ultimately to exploit.

Being a bad actor is cheap; you don't need much of an R&D budget. There's no need to employ expensive medical professionals. No need to pay for studies to get on the regulatory pathway. Just repackage some existing gel or pill and slap on some unfounded marketing claims.

It's hard to estimate how big the overall scamtech market is. But, as an example, global vaginal plastic surgery, often described as "vaginal rejuvenation," is estimated to be a $5 billion market. Some of that surgery is necessary, but a lot of it isn't. The global "intimate wash" market could reach $6 billion by 2029. None of that wash is necessary.

We need to keep drawing the line between "scamtech" and "femtech" so that we can get the innovation we deserve. To detect scamtech ask: Does this product monetize shame? Does it imply your body is dirty? Does it sell "beauty is pain"? Does it provide a false sense of safety? Is it actively harmful in some way? Is it under-regulated for what it is? Does it hide what kind of data it collects? Does it make outrageous claims that are not based on any evidence? Does it fall into the category of potions and lotions? Does it trigger fear or anxiety? If the answer to any of these questions is yes, then it's probably scamtech.

The femtech community is good at filtering out bad actors. But I have seen cases where the term "femtech" was used to include "intimate washes" and vaginal douches. By not excluding such companies entirely from their conferences, events, and reports, the femtech industry risks discrediting itself.

To separate the femtech from the scamtech, we need regulators but also experts who can rank and analyze what's on the market. I go on a search to find them.

15

VIGILANTES

EVERYBODY DESERVES TO BE SAFE

When Brad "RenderMan" Haines travels to a conference, he always brings along his silver suitcase. At airport security, the baggage handlers detect a big wad of cords and a bunch of electronics on the X-ray. The suitcase is taken aside and unzipped. What the silicone hell is this? RenderMan looks around to make sure there are no children nearby. After all, this is a public area.

Underneath the suitcase lid, the haul is covered with a towel that reads "No Panic," a reference to *The Hitchhiker's Guide to the Galaxy* by Douglas Adams. Lifting the towel reveals that the suitcase is full of dildos. Though the baggage staff have seen it all, this sight never fails to surprise them."They always skip a beat," says RenderMan. "They rarely see them in bulk. And particularly so well organized!"

Each dildo has its own laser-cut crevice, so that they don't rattle around turning themselves on. What happens next depends on who's appraising the suitcase. Some ask RenderMan where he's going. "Oh, Las Vegas," he says. "I can hear the guy's thoughts: 'Dude knows how to party.'" Once, a group of female baggage screeners looked inside the suitcase and proceeded to nod at each other. "The thing that amuses me is, he actually gets less shocked reactions when traveling with bulk sex toys than me when I travel with one," says Nicole Schwartz, who goes by "CircuitSwan." She continues, "I get people who look at it, look at me, look at it, look at me, and turn beet red, and I'm like, 'It is a vibrator. Lots of people have them.'"

As we speak online, RenderMan is sitting in his basement, drenched in dark-blue light—like all the hackers in stock images. You see, RenderMan is a hacker: a sex toy hacker. He is wearing a black T-shirt with what looks like the print of an EKG on it. Behind him, the walls are stacked high with cables and antenna. In the far corner, there is a banner for Def Con, the annual hacker convention held in Las Vegas.

When I comment on his office, RenderMan smiles thoughtfully and waves his hand, saying as he does so, "That's just a stage!" It serves to impress clients who see the basement and think "He must be the real deal!" I admit that's also why I sit in front of stacks of books for our conversation.

Schwartz joins our call from a business trip. She's sitting in front of both an illuminated keyboard *and* a bookshelf. It appears she is double-qualified. When I point out that they both wear hoodies, although hackers would usually cover their face, they both immediately pull their hoods down over their heads, laughing, "Is this better?" RenderMan and CircuitSwan are a married couple who live in suburban Alberta, Canada. In the world of hackers, they are known as the sextech power couple.

The internet of dongs

In the romantic comedy *The Ugly Truth*, the protagonist, played by Katherine Heigl, wears vibrating underwear to a business dinner. When the remote control accidentally rolls out of her bag, a young boy picks up the remote and starts playing with it, sending Heigl into a shivering orgasm. "The crowd of my talk is laughing at this," says RenderMan. But then he points out, "She was not anticipating it being activated at that time, so there's the potential for physical harm. The kid did not have her permission, or consent; therefore, in many jurisdictions, that would be considered sexual assault." The audience recoils—what seemed hilarious has quickly turned serious.

With the rise of the "Internet of Things," everyday devices— fridges, doorbells—have been plugged into digital networks. Sex toys have joined the fold in a phenomenon dubbed "teledildonics" so that they can be controlled remotely. CircuitSwan says they are used by people in long-distance relationships or those whose partners are deployed.

As RenderMan followed the rise of the IoT, he noticed analysts were monitoring the vulnerabilities of internet-controlled thermostats, baby monitors, and fridges—but nobody was looking at sex toys. "I have no shame or dignity, and so I didn't mind being associated with this." He asked an adult store called the Traveling Tickle Trunk if he could have their old display devices to analyze their security.

If vendors fail to secure their sex toys, the contents of bedside drawers could be weaponized for remote takeover, data breaches, and even revenge porn. "If you're a woman, your husband's away, and you get a message saying, 'Hey, let's play'. You put the device on, have a good time. Husband comes back a few days later and you say 'Oh, thank you, that was such a fun time.' 'What are you talking about?' 'When you sent that message that we should use the vibrator.' 'That wasn't me!' That sense of violation. It wasn't a physical assault, but in a way, it's on par with it," says RenderMan.

CircuitSwan notes vendors of physical hardware have "tacked on this added new technology, to upsell a more premium product, without actually fully understanding they have now entered the world of software," she says. In 2016, We-Vibe was sued for collecting more customer data than they declared. "Companies want diagnostic data, so they can find out what the popular features of a product are," she says. Presumably, most people don't care if a company knows how many times a day they're at their fridge, unless they're cheating on a diet, but a sex toy is a different matter.

To take his project further, RenderMan spontaneously sent Pornhub a drunken email asking for funding to purchase more devices. To his surprise, they gave him a budget. Then, Pornhub sent him a twelve-pound twerking silicone rubber butt. "It had motors and actuators that actually twerked," he says. "To see this thing sitting on the table was ridiculous!

"I became the face of sextech security, making my mother proud," he says. "And your mother-in-law as well!" says CircuitSwan, who joined the project a few years ago. To date, they have analyzed over thirty devices. By day, RenderMan works as a cybersecurity expert for a large company, and CircuitSwan is a project manager at a software company. In their spare time, they run The Internet of Dongs.

Dissecting toys and looking under the hood of their apps and websites, RenderMan has managed to access full user databases with a single command, including email addresses, phone numbers, home addresses, and GPS coordinates of where users were, and he also managed to download their profile photos. "An unfortunate decision," says RenderMan, as the download turned out to be "two and a half gigs of dick pics."

Holding your junk for ransom

Once RenderMan detects a vulnerability, he alerts the vendor. A phone call is usually better than a message. "I can talk them down from the roof because their first reaction is to panic and call their lawyers." Ransomware is common in the space. Established tech companies like Microsoft have a robust way for security-related reports to be delivered, but sex toy vendors often don't. "It's very simple stuff," he says. Companies should provide an email where security issues can be reported. "You don't have to put it on your front page but in a FAQ."

RenderMan and CircuitSwan are so-called "white hat hackers," whose intention is to protect customers rather than demand ransom. The term was inspired by early Western films, where heroes wear white hats to help audiences follow fast-paced fight scenes. "I'm doing this altruistically, trying to make the world a better place," says RenderMan.

In one case, RenderMan had concerns about a "chastity cage" device produced by China-based company Qiui. But the company ignored several warnings. Shortly after, there were cries of help from users who were locked into the "chastity cage" by hackers. "It's literally like holding your junk for ransom," says

RenderMan. Such devices need to have a physical override mechanism.

As more devices are paired with apps, the amount of data collected is only going to increase. As RenderMan says, "I'm still waiting to hear about the first divorce case where they use evidence that the app on the husband's phone was paired to the account of his secretary."

A data breach can reveal users' sexual orientation. In 2021, an American Catholic blog outed a group of priests for using Grindr. The consequences can be lethal in countries where gay sex is criminalized. A study of court files found that police forces in Egypt, Tunisia, and Lebanon confiscate phones to look for apps like Grindr, messages, and photos to persecute LGBTQ+ people. In some cases, sex toys have been used as evidence.

"I've started looking at cam model sites," says CircuitSwan. From her kitchen table, she signs up to these sites, and uploads videos of herself making cups of tea, shouting downstairs to RenderMan—still in the basement—"Go find my latest video, and then get the Wireshark of it!" This analyzes the sites' traffic to see whether it leaks IP data.

CircuitSwan teaches webcam models to avoid any photo backgrounds that can identify their location. She advises them, "Imagine you're in a spy film and you have to create a persona," which includes an email account with fake data for sex toys.

"I've learned a great deal from her," RenderMan says about CircuitSwan. "It's nice to be able to bounce ideas off somebody and not have to be, you know, sheepish about it." To educate the hacker community at Def Con, they hosted a butt plug hacking contest. CircuitSwan wore one, and contestants were asked to hack into it. "Oh my God, I'm so sorry," the winner told CircuitSwan, "I'm, like, I signed up for this. I consented," she says. Or as RenderMan puts it, she "was willing to literally put her ass on the line."

Safety standards for sex toys have been created, but so far, they focus on materials and electronics, neglecting cybersecurity. As RenderMan says, "Everybody deserves safety and security, be it your baby monitor, your thermostat, or your sex toy."

"I run a nonprofit, the Diana Initiative, where we're trying to get more women and underrepresented people into information security," says CircuitSwan. "When you have people coming in from the different perspectives, you can get better coverage of all your risk surface area."

When the sextech couple is at work, their two little tuxedo cats nest on top of the silver suitcase in the corner. The Internet of Dongs embodies civil society, the idea that members of a community rise up like vigilantes to protect their own.

When I talk about vigilantes, I mean experts who test, rank, and evaluate—yes, and hack—products to protect the interests of those who use them. It's an absence of regulation and transparency that motivates their work. To my mind, they are an integral part of the ecosystem.

Just like there is a lack of research into women's health, there's a lack of research comparing femtech products, beyond the studies provided by companies to regulators, or the internal studies competitors conduct on each other. For now, I continue to look for those rare individuals who have emerged as vigilantes out of their own accord.

Does your table have a heartbeat?

A few years ago, Professor Katherine T. Chen had just given a talk, when a gynecologist, who was in the audience, approached her. She said, "My patient came to me with an app that says it can measure the fetal heart rate. I put the phone on the examining table, and it was reading the table as having a heartbeat of 150. That's when I knew something was wrong."

Chen, who is the Vice Chair of Education at the ob-gyn department at the Icahn School of Medicine at Mount Sinai, decided to take a closer look. Her team downloaded 22 of these apps from the Apple iTunes store. "One of my residents was pregnant, so she put the phone on her abdomen while we used a real tool," says Chen. What they found was astonishing. "They were all inaccurate," she says. "Zero of these apps that advertise they would detect fetal heart rates could do that. It was pretty much fraud."

When I first uncovered the work of Chen and her associates, it felt miraculous, like finding an affordable apartment in central London. Because on the whole it has been frustrating for me to discover how little comparative research there is on femtech in the academic world. What's more, the research that exists is often run by the company itself rather than independent researchers.

Every now and then, there's a paper on femtech, written by an academic from a humanities department, who assumes that all businesses are evil and exploitative by nature, and that the only solution is, therefore, to abandon our period products and embrace free bleeding. Good luck with that.

One of the changes I'd like to see is practical, large-scale, comparative, independent analysis of women's health products across categories as the industry continues to emerge. This will, as always, require funding. Perhaps the Bill & Melinda Gates Foundation could fund it.

That's why Chen's work stands out. In a second study, her team has found that only 28 percent of pregnancy-tracking apps cite medical literature. In a third study, they looked at pregnancy wheel apps, which are used by doctors to figure out their patient's due date in pregnancy. They found that over 50 percent were inaccurate.

In another study, they ranked menstrual cycle tracking apps by accuracy, with Germany-based Clue coming out on top, followed by U.S.-based Glow, and India-based Maya. They have ranked apps for patients with pelvic floor disorders, identifying the top-ranking apps as the UK-based NHS app Squeezy, U.S.-based LeakFreeMe, and Sweden-based Stop UTI. I want to know why it is so hard to find studies like hers, even though they are desperately needed.

App overload

Apps have a huge potential to make a positive contribution to healthcare. Doctors are time-strapped, and apps can increase compliance with treatment recommendations, even among older individuals, as educational components are increasingly personalized. How can we know if an app is accurate?

"It's really, really challenging," says Chen. When she first began her research over a decade ago, it was possible to have an overview of the existing health apps, but the field has mushroomed exponentially. "I am very concerned about app overload." When researching apps, Chen and her team tend to focus on the top results on Google, as that's how patients might find them. But with its slow peer-review and journal submission process, academia cannot keep up with the pace of tech companies.

Academics also shy away from this research to avoid legal issues. "I know that even the journals get a little nervous," she says. Some journals didn't want her to identify the apps by name in the main text but provide numbers instead with a separate key in the appendix.

In a typically academic manner, Chen proceeds to critique her own methodology. There is no agreed scoring system for apps. When evaluating period apps, she thought it was fun to create a scoring system based on each letter of the word "Applications." The "L" stands for literature, for example, and each app that includes medical literature got a point. They also analyzed whether an app predicted the next menstrual cycle based on averages of past cycles instead of a default—and as we know, mythical—28-day cycle.

But in other parts of the scoring system, apps got points if they were free, if they didn't require an internet connection, and if they didn't show any ads—that doesn't tell us whether one app is better than another. "One of the things we've been advocating is that you discuss your app with your doctor," she says.

Unlike drugs, which go through rigorous regulatory processes, apps are not necessarily regulated. "The FDA doesn't really regulate all the apps; they only regulate the ones where the software can be used as a medical device," she says.

"It's just very challenging. There's no oversight. There are not enough people like myself," she says. This I already knew. But then she goes on to say, "I do this for fun, but I have another job, which is running education programs for our department." I realize the app analysis is her side hustle. She says, "It has really helped with my career." Even though analyzing apps takes a lot of time, it has led to publications and speaking engagements. In the academic world, she says, there is "no grant money for this."

The ideal scenario would be for national organizations focused on gynecology and fertility to have dedicated teams to evaluate apps in their field. "You don't want patients to find apps that are harmful," says Chen. Once again, I feel I'm reporting on the absence of something that should exist. For now, what is clear is that if your app claims to track a heart rate—try it on a table first.

How to choose a cup

"Put A Cup In It" (PACII) is a site and community focused on menstrual cups, founded by Cincinnati-based Amanda Hearn. What is a menstrual cup? "I usually say it's a tampon alternative, except it's not going to absorb any blood—it collects it, you empty it, wash and reuse," she says.

Whenever Hearn asks her audience why they have switched to menstrual cups, the number one reason is the environment. It is estimated that 2 billion pads and tampons are flushed down British toilets every year. They pollute our oceans, and they have become one of the most common items found on European beaches.

"Growing up, I didn't want to talk about periods at all. I went straight to using tampons, because that was the most 'out of sight, out of mind' method," she says. In her twenties, Hearn began to explore eco-products, after her middle child was born prematurely. "I learned about how tampons leave micro-abrasions," she says. Once she started using a menstrual cup, she noticed a difference within a cycle or two. "I was surprised by how my vaginal environment changed." For years, she had vaginal dryness, but now she no longer used lubricant for sex.

As she learned more about menstrual cups, she decided to share what she learned online. Today, her chart surveys over 100 menstrual cups, listing their capacity and size, and firmness. It has between 200,000 and 500,000 views per month. She uses affiliate marketing codes and advertising to monetize the site.

There's a menstrual cup quiz for people to identify the best fit. "There are so many individual differences," says Hearn. The quiz asks about your age; the number of children you've birthed, if any; fitness level; and the position of your cervix. It then provides a handy video on how to find and measure your cervix.

How do the shapes of cups differ? "There are cups that are more bullet-shaped," she says, while others are bell-shaped, or ball shaped. Others yet are slanted or "ergonomic." Hearn estimates there are four or five main cup shapes. Cups sit in the vaginal canal. Meanwhile, menstrual discs are shaped like flat bowls, and they sit higher up in the top part of the vaginal canal, the fornix, right below the cervix.

In the United States, menstrual cups are considered a Class II medical device, and therefore, they must be registered with the FDA. They should be made of medical-grade silicone. As with tampons, they carry a very small risk of toxic shock syndrome, a very rare infection, if left inside for too long.

PACII has a large community on Facebook. "If you have any questions about your particular period, how your cup fits, or particular problems, you're guaranteed that somebody in that group has it," says Hearn, whether it's vaginismus or ways to use a cup with two uteruses. "It's always amazing to me," she says.

Chem fatale

When we buy period products, we hardly know what's in them. Pads and tampons are used to being grabbed so furtively at the shop, hardly anyone pauses in the aisle to read what we're putting in our bodies—though it may be worth lingering over the ingredients list for a moment. Since 2021, period products sold in New York State have to disclose their ingredients on the label.

Only few researchers dissect the ingredients of period products and make their research into various brands available online. It took some effort to find Alexandra Scranton, Director of Science and Research at the nonprofit Women's Voices for the Earth, who analyzes period product ingredients as intently as if she had come upon the Rosetta Stone.

What do we need to consider when choosing period products? "Try to avoid products that have extra bells and whistles," says Scranton. Fragrance is one to avoid, for example. "There are a lot of chemicals that can be in fragrances that are harmful," including not only allergens but also reproductive toxins. A shorter list of ingredients can reduce such risks.

Generally, pads and tampons that are 100 percent cotton are considered a good option. But Scranton points out that there are some "deceiving ones where it'll say 100 percent 'cotton core.'"

This sounds like 100 percent cotton, but it only refers to the inside of the tampon, which could then still be covered in plastic.

When you're looking at menstrual cups, she recommends avoiding cups that are dyed (better to go for a clear one), cups that have a fragrance, as well as cups with raised lettering on the silicone. Bacteria could potentially get stuck in the crevices of the letters. "You don't want growth of bacteria on your menstrual cup because that can potentially lead to toxic shock," she says.

She recommends avoiding any "antibacterial layers." She says, "You're putting this antibacterial layer adjacent to an area of your body where the bacteria is really, really important." Nanosilver, for example, kills lactobacilli, which make up a healthy vaginal microbiome. "Silver is like glitter—it gets everywhere, and it's impossible to clean up," she says. Look out for nanosilver in period underwear and athletic clothing, including products marketed as having "ion technology" or as being "antibacterial." Besides, there is no evidence to show such ingredients "fight odor" or whatever else it is they claim to do.

Another concern are "forever chemicals," technically known as perfluoroalkyl and polyfluoroalkyl substances (PFAS). These are human-made chemicals that don't break down easily and can have adverse health effects.

The company Thinx has settled a class-action lawsuit over the discovery of PFAS in its period underwear. Even in a laboratory, it's not always easy to detect PFAS, because there are over 5,000 kinds of them. But all PFAS contain fluorine, notes Scranton. Therefore high levels of fluorine indicate the presence of PFAS, which have also been found in pads and tampons in reports by Mamavation.

It is possible to completely reimagine what period products are made of. The Berlin-based start-up Vyld, for instance, is making tampons out of seaweed. Could this be the answer? Scranton says it depends on the production process. The creation process of rayon, which is the pulp tampons are typically made of, is a chemically intensive process. So, with all new materials, it would depend on what chemicals are released in the production process.

Though the New York state law is a step in the right direction, Scranton notes that it does not have great enforcement mechanisms. In addition, some companies write "adhesives" or "fragrance" on their label, rather than revealing what the chemical components of those are. California introduced a similar but weaker law, which allows companies to not disclose certain ingredients if they're trade secrets.

The first step is to have more disclosure and transparency on the ingredients. For an in-depth analysis of what different ingredients mean, head to the Women's Voices for the Earth website. The next step should be for certain ingredients to be banned entirely.

Depending on the chemical, vaginal skin can be tens of times more absorbent than the skin on your hand. Some companies use self-reported surveys to evaluate new period products they create, others hire gynecologists to take an actual look at the vulvar skin. But there is currently no standard for how an ingredient that comes in contact with vulvar or vaginal skin is tested. Does it change the pH? Does it affect the tissue? Does it impact the vaginal microbiome? All of these are questions we should be getting answers to.

In the absence of widespread transparency, Scranton recommends trying multiple period products to see if you react differently. "There are so many people who are just used to being miserable for a couple days a month, like, 'Oh, yeah, every month, I get a rash.'

"Picking period products is really personal," she says. "Everybody's flow is different. Everybody's comfort level is different. We encourage people to pay attention to how the products feel and to try different products."

If your products don't disclose their ingredients, she recommends messaging the company with questions. "The more they hear from their customers saying, 'I'm actually concerned about this,' the more they start looking into it."

Getting the lowdown

While I'm writing this book, my friend Valentina tells me she is experiencing strange symptoms: inner tremors, numb hands, insomnia. Three GPs have run some tests, but they don't know the answer. She recently came off the Pill but was told the Pill leaves the body after twenty-four hours, so her symptoms are unrelated. She says, "But if I was coming off any other drug, I'd have withdrawal symptoms, wouldn't I?"

I mention Sarah E. Hill's book *How the Pill Changes Everything*, the National Library of Medicine online, and a London-based start-up focused on contraception called the Lowdown, which offers consultations with GPs trained in sexual and reproductive health. After a consultation, Valentina says, "I was finally listened to!" She has joined the Facebook group

"Support for Going Off Hormonal Birth Control" to continue her exploration. As an early customer of the Lowdown, she is invited to their community event—and brings me along. It takes place in a basement filled with balloons, bagels, and red-tinged cocktails called "moon cups."

There is a presentation led by two female GPs, who joined the start-up as freelancers to provide the kind of care they can't provide within the healthcare system. Their slides include an overview of coils: their sizes, brands, and prices. They say the IUD insertion process should be accompanied by a tray of pain medication options. They say patients can ask to put in the speculum themselves. It's possible to ask for extra lubricant. They talk about trauma-aware care. They compare contraceptive pills. Their depth of knowledge is superb.

This session should be mandatory for medical professionals, I think, as I survey the room. But the young crowd is not wearing white coats.. Instead, I recognize several Instagram influencers. For anybody wondering how technology has impacted sexual health knowledge, this audience may be the answer. It feels like a paradigm shift.

On the way out of the building, the CEO of the Lowdown, Alice Pelton, who has never met me before, gives me a massive hug. I wonder if she can sense I'm about to ask for an interview. But then, I realize, she hugs everybody.

Contraception is a minefield

Pelton's story begins with the Pill. "It took me a couple of years to realize that it was causing quite bad side effects. It changed my personality and made me feel very emotional, very out of control," she says. "Over the next ten years, I went through a journey like most women do, choosing and swapping and trying to find the right thing for me.

"I tried pretty much every contraceptive method going, and then I just had this idea in 2017 to create a review platform for contraception." She googled it, and it didn't exist. So she decided she was going to build it. "I'd worked in product management and tech for a couple of years. I knew a bit about building websites," she says in a self-deprecating manner. In a previous role, she worked on a fantasy football gaming app used by millions of people. "I put all this effort into trying to help a man choose a fantasy football team. Surely I can help a woman choose contraception. Maybe that would be a bit more impactful."

There are thousands of reviews on the Lowdown. People are more likely to review something they've had a negative experience with. But there are positive reviews on their site too. "The sad reality is that a lot of these products just aren't great. The best thing about our platform is that we are honest about that, and a lot of places and healthcare professionals aren't.

"The reviews are what gets thousands of women coming to us every day," says Pelton. The second most popular feature is their Contraception Recommender tool. It's used by 5 percent of visitors. It was built with medical guidance in mind; if someone has a BMI over 35, for example, the quiz does not recommend the combined pill.

Over the last years, the public discourse has become more critical of the contraceptive pill. But is this shift backed up by numbers? The Contraception Recommender has been used by over 20,000 people. Is there a noticeable move away from the Pill among them?

When asked "Are you open to using hormonal contraceptives?" 78 percent of respondents said yes. Are you good at remembering to do something every day? Of the respondents, 72 percent said yes. Then, 62 percent said they don't want something fitted inside their womb. Similarly, 66 percent don't want an implant inserted under the skin on the inside of their arm, and 68 percent don't want a regular injection.

"You can see therefore, why naturally, more people do end up starting the Pill," says Pelton. "There is an aversion to coil fittings, implants, injections—they have more of an ick factor for lots of people." The Lowdown has partnered with a pharmacy to provide delivery of the widest range of contraceptives in the UK. That side of the business generates the most revenue.

I say contraceptive choice seems to be an art as much as a science. Pelton agrees: "There's no point in recommending a woman the implant if she hates the thought of it in her arm." So much about contraception is down to preference: where you are in your life, your sex life, how you want your vagina to feel. "And that's why I think a community that solves that through shared experience is the best solution for that problem."

Even femtech innovators who have designed a great solution to a problem, need to find ways to make an impression. I decide to visit an experienced entrepreneur and advertising executive who has mentored scores of female entrepreneurs.

16

IMPRESSIONS

HOW TO ATTRACT AND REPEL

It's a sunny spring day and the daffodils are blooming as I walk through Bryant Park in New York City, the hem of my favorite dress billowing around my legs. In a few moments, I'm going to see Manhattan from above. The porter takes one look at me and says, "Are you here for Cindy Gallop?" I take the elevator up. Cindy Gallop opens the door and smiles. She offers me tea, coffee, or water and exits, stage right, into a kitchen nook. I feel she's giving me a moment to take it all in.

The Sky Apartment, which has its own hashtag on Instagram, sits on top of Manhattan. I'm looking everywhere all at once. It's open plan with a golden dinner table and a red antique Chinese opium bed. There's a painting of the pope cradling a gerbil. "This is better than the Saatchi Gallery," I hear myself exclaiming. There are tall altar candles called "Saint Cindy" bearing her face. A sculpture of boobs adorns the wall not far from the head of a hog baring its teeth. I feel energized just standing there.

I settle down on the couch. On the large coffee table in front of me rests an antique stone dildo. I'm delighted to recognize a familiar face next to it: the large golden alligator wearing a bedazzled choker necklace. It's in Gallop's Facebook cover photo, where she's lying down topless, with only the alligator covering her nipples; both are beaming. "We call it the Guccigator," she calls from the kitchen. I wonder if it's her spirit animal.

At my sides, two couch pillows tell a story: "Once upon a time there was a girl that said 'Fuck this shit' and did things her own way and she lived happily ever after. The end." Gallop joins me on the adjacent couch. She is wearing a "Make Love Not Porn" T-shirt. Everything is on brand. And that is exactly what I've come to talk to her about.

Gallop is known for being outspoken on business and life. "I adore being single, cannot wait to die alone, and I date younger men casually," she told Stuff, a news site in New Zealand. Born in England to a Malaysian Chinese mother and an English father, Gallop made her name as an advertising agency executive in New York before becoming a sextech entrepreneur, public speaker, and advisor to scores of entrepreneurs.

Her advice to every person, not just every founder, is to identify what you stand for: "Take a long hard look into yourself. Identify what you believe in, what you value, what you stand for. The same thing applies to your venture, your start-up, and then project that out into the world and you will attract the people who want it and repel the ones who don't."

On social media, her tagline reads "I like to blow shit up. I'm the Michael Bay of business." Gallop explains, "It's not as a bit of

creativity, a bit of whimsy, a bit of fun. I do that entirely deliberately." The goal is to attract the right audience and repel those
who are "a waste of time, effort, and money."

Gallop is known for her characteristically subversive advice
on how to succeed in business. In an article for *Harvard Business
Review*, she turned the most common advice given to women
on its head. Instead of telling women to be more assertive and
apologize less, men should say sorry a whole lot more. "The
problem isn't women's lack of confidence but men's oversupply
of it," she wrote. Instead of asking for advice, she encourages
women to listen to our gut.

I tell her that over the years of my reporting, several female
start-up founders told me they have been advised to lower their
voices and wear black. "Fuck that shit!" says Gallop, indignation
burning bright. "They don't know what the fuck they're talking
about. Drop that advisor like a hot potato!"

I mention Elizabeth Holmes, the founder of biotech start-up
Theranos, who famously spoke in a baritone voice and dressed
like Steve Jobs. Her company claimed it could detect dozens of
diseases based on a test using just a few drops of blood and it
became a unicorn. But the tech turned out to be flawed and the
founder was convicted of fraud.

It is unfortunate but not surprising that her story is often
mentioned in relation to female entrepreneurship. "One
swallow does not a summer make," says Gallop. "Every single
shitty white bro founder does not prove that all white bro
founders are shit."

xkcd.com.

I notice a stuffed mongoose fighting a cobra on the coffee table. "Don't fit yourself into the world. When you have a world-changing start-up, you've got to change the world to fit you, not the other way around," she continues.

The idea for her own venture arose out of Gallop's experience of dating younger men. She could tell that many of them had learned about sex through porn, imitating moves nobody actually takes pleasure in—a.k.a. the jackhammer syndrome. Her company Make Love Not Porn (MLNP) is a user-generated and -curated platform for videos she calls "social sex." The aim is to show consensual and communicative sex, to encourage honest conversations, and to replace porn as the default educator. "Our social sex videos role-model good sexual values and good sexual behavior," says Gallop. "We make all of that aspirational, versus what you see in porn and popular culture. Who wouldn't want to live in that world?"

She says the biggest obstacle to raising funding for MLNP is the social dynamic best described as "fear of what other people will think," which operates around sex unlike any other area.

Gallop has raised $2 million, but it has been a struggle. "Never waste your time banging your head against closed doors. It took me some time to realize this, but my investors are absolutely out there," she says. "Your willingness to fund MLNP is entirely a function of your personal sexual journey," she says. "And I have no way to research and target for that, not least because sex is the one area where you cannot tell from the outside what anybody thinks on the inside.

"The people who look like they would totally get it don't. The people who look like total prudes do," she says. I take a sip of my coffee and notice that I'm drinking it from a Little Miss Naughty mug.

Gallop decided to define and popularize the term "sextech" in 2014 with an article in *hotTopics*. "I did all of that purely to legitimize my own sector to create a climate of receptivity amongst investors. So, you could argue that when Ida Tin came along several years later, she did the same thing with 'femtech.'"

In both cases, it paid off. "Your investors are out there. But the people who get it—whether it's menstruation, menopause, fertility, health—you don't find them by going over which VCs say they're investing in health, because then they go 'Uhhh, vaginas.'" Instead, Gallop lets them find her. For the past several years, her fundraising strategy has been to be vocal online. "I blow my own trumpet across every single social channel," she says. "Because I have to rely on making synaptic connections happen that will draw those people to me."

My eyes fall on the stuffed raccoon across the coffee table from me, lounging on a chair with its legs akimbo, head lolled back, as if it had one too many martinis. Then Gallop says, "I'm going to take a picture of you and promote you on social media. Please do give me a smile. There we go. Terrific."

Censorship

While I'm writing this book, I ask women to show me with their hands how big they think their uterus is. Everybody cups their hands into the size of a mango. It's more accurate to spread your thumb and index finger and point to the tiny triangular space in between. What's more, the uterus doesn't stand up straight; it typically leans forward.

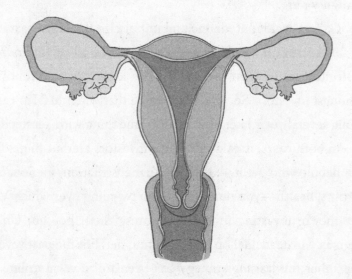

We don't have the mental pictures. We shy away from words. Censorship doesn't only happen online: what we can see and what we can say, who can be heard, and who remains voiceless reveals the underlying values of our societies.

On the New York subway, posters of drooping potted cacti advertise Viagra, but femtech ads are routinely taken down.

At my local Boots in London, a large banner proudly declares "Viagra—NEW two tablet pack only £10.99." Several aisles farther down, women furtively hover around period products, which are, at least, no longer advertised with blue liquid and named "feminine hygiene."

Femtech entrepreneurs tell me their ads are censored on social media. "We had one that was banned recently about sex education because it was deemed political," says Lyndsey Harper, the CEO of Rosy. "You can't talk about a body part that 50 percent of the world's population has, because people think it's dirty or taboo," says Colette Courtion, the CEO of Joylux. Instead of saying "vagina" on Facebook, her company says, "This is for your V." And here I was thinking V is for "vendetta."

While female sexual health is banned on Facebook, erectile dysfunction ads proudly bounce through the algorithm. Several interviewees have told me they suspect that erectile dysfunction ads pass as "family planning," which is ironic, because that's not exactly the group of people who's about to have kids.

There was a watershed moment for sextech companies in 2019, when the sex toy company Lora DiCarlo won a robotics innovation award for its micro-robotic massager, the Osé, at the Consumer Electronics Show (CES) in Las Vegas. Shortly after that, its award was revoked together with the invitation to exhibit at the show. The committee decided her creation was "immoral, obscene, indecent." Never mind that virtual reality porn for men was on show.

In an open letter, Lora Haddock DiCarlo, the company's founder and CEO, noted, "There is an obvious double standard when it comes to sexuality and sexual health." She wrote,

"This double standard makes it clear that women's sexuality is not worthy of innovation." A media outcry followed and CES reinstated her award. It amplified the conversation. "You see a lot of male-owned and male-designed products for people with vaginas," she told me. "That's something we're trying to change." The scandal brought attention to the brand, and Cara Delevingne joined as a co-owner.

From Gustave Courbet's painting of a vulva in *L'Origine du monde* to today's tech devices, female anatomy continues to shock. Vaginas are not the only censored body part. In some places, breastfeeding in public is still frowned upon. "Lactivists" across the world have been staging protests to change that. The #FreetheNipple movement points out that female nipples continue to be banned on social media. Female bodies continue to be censored.

That's why femtech companies turn to juicy grapefruits and euphemisms. It's possible that the root of this stigma can be found in terror management theory. Female bodies remind us of both birth and death, and we'd rather not think about the latter.

Ad not approved

One woman has decided to challenge the issue of ad bans head-on. When Jackie Rotman moved to Silicon Valley to do an MBA, she thought she might raise an investment fund. "I was super passionate about female sexuality and ways of improving people's relationships to their sexuality and sexual well-being." She knew that funding was an issue in the space, but she soon came to learn there was another major hurdle: entrepreneurs couldn't advertise their products on Facebook.

"I thought the venture capital model wouldn't be as successful in an industry that couldn't use the most important channels for growth, and so instead of starting a fund to get more capital to businesses—that couldn't spend it on advertising for growth—I thought it would be more catalytic and impactful to actually solve the advertising barrier."

This led her to set up the nonprofit Center for Intimacy Justice (CIJ), which has received funding from The Case for Her, among others. In their first report, CIJ surveyed 60 companies in the sexual health and well-being space about their ads, from those offering menopause consultations to posts about sexual consent education and pelvic floor health.

The report found that 100 percent of these companies had their ads rejected on Facebook. What's more, about half of them had their accounts suspended at some point. In most cases, their ads were banned because Facebook classified them as "adult content."

The report was picked up by the *New York Times*, and shortly after that, Meta, which owns Facebook and Instagram, clarified its advertising policy. It now states that "advertisers can run ads that promote sexual health, wellness and reproductive products and services." But according to Rotman, who has followed up with the companies, most haven't seen any changes. Their ads are still rejected.

The CIJ is now focused on getting Meta to change the enforcement of those policies. They're also doing investigations on censorship on TikTok, Google, and Amazon. As Rotman says, "We want women and people of all genders and all sexual orientations to experience freedom and well-being and joy when it comes to sexuality."

What can and cannot be advertised is indicative of what is and isn't a taboo, and as we have seen, female bodies continue to be at the epicenter of what is considered taboo. I decide to talk to a veteran in the space, who has advised hundreds of femtech companies, on what changes she has seen and how femtech and sextech companies can succeed.

A hidden hurdle

Twenty years ago, when Rachel Braun Scherl returned to work after having her first baby, the maternity room could be described as follows: "You're in the janitorial closet, you turned over a bucket, you sat on it, and you pumped in the dark." Since then, Braun Scherl, who is a self-described vagipreneur, has become a pioneering speaker and the cofounder of Spark Solutions for Growth, a strategic and marketing consultancy. Commenting on the change she has seen over the last two decades, she says, "We have come an extraordinary way."

It took time for companies to realize the positive impact maternity benefits had on their employees. "They've seen a real difference in productivity, lack of turnover, and reduction of fees for recruitment companies—and we're now having the same conversation about menopausal women." They are more likely to hold positions of seniority. "It's a particularly fertile time for their careers; they have a lot of institutional or category knowledge."

Celebrities have amplified the conversation around women's health, including Serena Williams, the tennis star, who has spoken about her harrowing experience of being ignored by medical professionals after giving birth to her daughter Olympia at a hospital. After the birth, Williams began to cough and feel excruciating pain. She raised concerns about her heightened risk for blood clots. It was her repeated insistence on getting a test that saved her life.

"Here's a person who has access to every single resource," says Braun Scherl. "She has a strong personality, she has a supportive husband, she has all the money in the world, she's at an A-plus facility, and still—she was ignored almost to the point of her own death." Not only has Williams spoken about her personal experience, she is also an angel investor, and she launched the VC fund Serena Ventures, which invests in several femtech companies.

While first-person perspectives help us launch femtech ventures, Braun Scherl argues that this need for personal understanding is also a hidden hurdle. If she was pitching a software to detect hackers for military organizations around the world, the guy in the room is not the customer, says Braun Scherl, "yet he still can get his head around the fact that there are people who would buy it."

Whereas when you pitch a women's health company, talking about problems with sexual arousal, you hear, "Well, my wife doesn't have that.'" "What I want to say is, 'sir, 43 percent of women have sexual difficulties. It's likely that if your wife experienced that, she's not communicating it with you.'"

As well as demonstrating the business case in figures, femtech founders have to leap over the personal hurdle. Any investor who has an aunt, sister, daughter, or friend who struggles with infertility is more likely to understand the case for a business in the space. But that's a very personal take on a business case.

"It has to be meaningful, personally, to the person that you're speaking to, and I can't think of any other category where that is the case."

Is it faster? Is it cheaper? Is it easier?

An increasing number of femtech companies are selling to insurers and employers. "Take a company like Milk Stork, which started with consumers," says Braun Scherl. Milk Stork is a breast milk–shipping company, led by Kate Torgersen. "Now you have women going into their HR department saying, if you want me to travel, you have to pay for me to ship my milk back."

Braun Scherl points out that femtech entrepreneurs have to become activists, as legislation can be a hurdle. Claire Coder, the founder and CEO of Aunt Flow, the organization that stocks businesses and schools in the United States with organic tampons and pads, is actively involved in shaping legislation.

When Braun Scherl advises femtech companies, she says, "The biggest, biggest, biggest challenge is: Are you solving a problem that needs solving? And is the way you're solving it better? Is it cheaper? Is it faster? Is it easier? Ideally it has to be 'ER' in one way or another."

Warby Parker, the glasses company, has perfected this strategy. They have pulled apart the process of how glasses are supplied. Too expensive? They manufacture them. Not enough choices? They send you five frames. Too hard to get an appointment? They have virtual try-on. They never claimed to be the first company to sell people glasses; rather they have improved an existing process that left much to be desired. This logic needs to be applied to femtech.

The founders of today's successful smart breast pumps had a deeper understanding of the customers' problem—perhaps deeper than what most customers could even articulate. "It's not just interviewing women and saying nursing is a pain in the ass," says Braun Scherl. That would be a superficial view of the unmet needs. What's more important is the underlying problem, paddling below the surface like the legs of a swan. She describes it as "I feel immobile. I feel trapped. I feel like a prisoner of my own body. I can't get to work. All of those things are insights that could have resulted in a better pump." It's about revealing those deeper insights.

17

BUSINESS & SOCIETY

WHAT IF FEMTECH WINS?

It's a Monday morning. I have a side hustle as an adjunct professor teaching students from the NYU Stern School of Business who come to London for a year. Walking to my lecture, I usually get stopped by security, because I forgot to wear the body of a sixty-year-old man once again. My bad. It reminds me of how deep-seated our societal perceptions are.

Whenever I welcome a new group of business students, I talk about my work as a journalist. I show them the *Wired* article about vaginas and investors. At first they giggle. But then they are interested. One day, when these students run the world of business, my hope is that they won't deny women around the world the innovation we need, just because they are embarrassed to talk about vaginas on a Monday morning.

In this world of the future, businesses, researchers, healthcare professionals, investors, and educators have come together across disciplines to bring about wider societal changes. Because business and society always reflect each other.

324 THE VAGINA BUSINESS

The old model of focusing on shareholder value and maximizing profits at any cost while ignoring wealth inequalities and the planet is as outdated as the pre-Copernicus belief that the Earth is the center of the universe, orbited by the sun and planets.

Research is no longer structured by the male default. It's impossible to publish data in a reputable, peer-reviewed journal that's not sex disaggregated, just like it's not possible to publish a study without revealing the sample size. The height of achievement for any scientist is no longer to be published in *Nature*, but it's a new journal I'll call *The Journal of Female Bodies and Health Research*.

The collaborative effort of researchers continues to fill the gender data gap in health, forever changing the landscape of healthcare. Each country around the world has launched a women's health strategy. Healthcare is universal and accessible to all. Medicine has become more preventative and holistic.

For medical professionals, it's mandatory to be trained in contraceptive options, sexual health, women-specific health issues, and menopause. Women no longer experience delayed diagnoses across 770 diseases. Women's pain is taken seriously. All medical professionals pride themselves on making women feel comfortable and heard. They know exactly how to diagnose and treat endometriosis, PCOS, fibroids, and similar conditions without side effects. Women are no longer expected to put themselves last.

Investors vie to invest in femtech ventures. Marc Andreessen and Ben Horowitz have launched a femtech fund called aFemTechz. This has led to hordes of tech bros in the Valley bragging about the ten-bagger menopause company in their portfolio and the cutting-edge contraceptive for men they invested in. At annual shareholder meetings in Omaha, Warren Buffet has begun to take credit for ending pregnancy-related disparities. We let them brag.

We have turned Eve's curse into a blessing. Giving birth is safe for everyone. When talking about birth, nobody would dream of saying "Leave your dignity at the door." Birth is appreciated as the great achievement that it is. No woman is pressured into or denied an epidural, an elective cesarean, or another procedure of her choice for financial or cultural reasons.

Abortions are legal and safe. There are many contraceptive options, and they are accessible to everybody. Contraceptives have been researched rigorously, and they have few or no side effects. Medical professionals no longer recommend the contraceptive pill as if it's a five-a-day.

Period products are available for free in bathrooms, just like toilet paper. There is no period poverty. No period product is made to ever become landfill. No period product ends up as trash in the ocean—they're all biodegradable. Their ingredients are transparent, have been tested, and are safe.

Sex education includes consent and sexual pleasure as a central element of our overall health. There is no orgasm gap. There is no abusive porn; it has been replaced by social sex. Everybody can draw a clitoris.

In job interviews, nobody asks women "So, how do plan to combine work and family?" Because the question is now relevant to all of us. Shared parental leave is well paid and normalized. There are free nurseries and flexible work patterns. Workplaces no longer pretend that we don't have families and interests outside of work.

The term "digital health" is as necessary as "liquid water," because all health is digital. The term "femtech" no longer exists because tech serves all of us equally well.

Women make up half the workforce, and there is no gender pay gap. Jade is as likely to raise money and run a big company as John. Women are no longer "having it all" in the sense of having a career while raising children—we are "sharing it all," with our partners, with our workplace, and with the communities we have built. Of course, we do not live in this utopian world yet, but it's good to have a north star.

For tech to serve women, society must make women's health a priority. The start-ups and institutions we have—what products they create, how they are run, and whether they are good or bad actors—is always going to reflect the values we hold as a society.

I have gone on this journey through the world of femtech to shine a spotlight on what is possible. I want more innovation for all of us because we deserve better. It's a revolution, and this is only the beginning.

ACKNOWLEDGMENTS

Almost forty years ago, a woman with determined eyes and big curly hair decided to set up a publishing house in her spare bedroom in Naperville, Illinois. Just like the entrepreneurs in this book, she encountered many obstacles. The bank didn't want to give her a loan and directed all questions at her husband, so she bootstrapped the company. Established booksellers refused to take her calls, but she persevered. Today, Dominique Raccah, the CEO of Sourcebooks, heads up the largest woman-founded publishing house in North America, and it's thanks to her idealism and entrepreneurship that this book has a lead publisher.

Thank you to my editor Erin McClary, your energy, enthusiasm, and insight have made all the difference. Thanks to Anna Michels, Jillian Rahn, Laura Boren, Tara Jaggers, Emily Proano, Kayleigh George, Liz Kelsch, Kiera Jamison, Connor Stait, and the whole teams at Sourcebooks and Icon Books for your time and talent.

To my wonderful literary agent Hattie Grünewald, who

appreciated my writing at a time when people couldn't tell "femtech" from "fintech." Thanks to Rory Scarfe, Liane-Louise Smith, Adam Reed, Rhian Parry, and the team of wizards at The Blair Partnership in London.

To my brilliant literary agent Jaidree Braddix, who called editors to tell them "I've sent you a book proposal, but it might be in your spam because it has vagina in the title!" Thanks to the team at Park & Fine in New York, the most stylish people I've ever seen.

I'd like to thank my partner, my love, but he's too humble, he says "don't thank me, thank your mother!"

None of this would be possible without my mother. Not just because she gave birth to me, but because she risked everything for us to flee the former Soviet Union when I was a toddler, so that I could grow up in the safety of the West. Despite the difficult circumstances of our immigration, she raised me to believe that I could achieve anything – even if I wanted to be an author who lives in London or New York. Your love of life, bravery, creativity, and openness about female sexual pleasure have always been a guiding light for me. Thanks to my superstar grandparents, my whole family, and my partner's parents and sister, for all your love and support.

My friends are one of my biggest blessings. Thank you Elly for your all-round brilliance, Shira for your courage and outspokenness, Jess for your brutal honesty and excellent support, Emma for your spiritual companionship, Daniella for your thoughtful advice, Amie for your jokes and dances, Gaby for your gentle empathy, Vicky for your smart questions, Alla for always lifting me up, and Tom for no longer being embarrassed by the subject.

Thanks to my editors in the world of journalism and to my colleagues and students at NYU Stern in London and New York.

Thanks to the Alfred P. Sloan Foundation and The Society of Authors for awarding me grants that allowed me focus and travel to take this book as far as possible. Thanks to the London Library's Emerging Writers Cohort 2020/21, especially Claire Berliner, the salonnière, who brought us together.

Thanks to the femtech community and every person I have met and spoken to on this journey. I may be the composer but you're the orchestra.

And now to you, yes you, dear reader: thank you for joining me on this ride. Thank you for your curiosity and your time. Does it come as a surprise if I tell you that the book title has been controversial? I had to put up a fight to have this title on the cover. Just like investors, booksellers are squeamish—some might hide this book away; some might refuse to promote it. I rely on you to spread the word.

If this book has taught you as much as it taught me, gift it to your friends, start a book club, post about it on social media and feel free to tag me, if you like. I will be sharing news about the book and about femtech on www.marinagerner.com. Let's continue to make this world a better place, one venture, one research project, and one conversation at a time. As Gloria Steinem said, the way to overcome stigma is by talking about it.

NOTES

Introduction: Skin in the Game

"Hormonal contraception": Farah Kabir, cofounder of HANX, interview with author, December 2020.

My article was published: Marina Gerner, "We Need to Talk About Investors' Problem with Vaginas," *Wired*, August 10, 2020, https://www.wired.co.uk /article/vagina-pitches-vcs-sexism.

Women make 80 percent: Sabrina Matoff-Stepp et al., "Women as Health Care Decision-Makers: Implications for Health Care Coverage in the United States," *Journal of Health Care for the Poor and Underserved* 25, no. 4 (November 2014), https://www.ncbi.nlm.nih.gov/pubmed/25418222.

It was only in 1933: U.S. Congress Public Law No 103–43. National Institutes of Health Revitalization Act of 1993, 10 June 1993.

Women were long excluded: Rebecca M. Shansky, "Are Hormones a 'Female Problem' for Animal Research?," *Science* 364 (2019), https://www.science.org /doi/abs/10.1126/science.aaw7570.

Women are 50 percent more likely: British Heart Foundation, August 30, 2016, https://www.bhf.org.uk/what-we-do/news-from-the-bhf/news-archive/2016 /august/women-are-50-per-cent-more-likely-than-men-to-be-given-incorrect -diagnosis-following-a-heart-attack.

Across 770 types: David Westergaard et al., "Population-Wide Analysis of Differences in Disease Progression Patterns in Men and Women," *Nature Communications* 10, 666 (2019), https://www.ncbi.nlm.nih.gov/pubmed /30737381.

Female-specific diseases: "Why Polycystic Ovarian Syndrome Is Often Misdiagnosed," *Women's Healthcare of Princeton*, December 1, 2019, https://www.princetongyn.com/blog/why-polycystic-ovarian-syndrome-is-often-misdiagnosed.

It can take close to a decade: "It Takes an Average of 7.5 years to Get a Diagnosis of Endometriosis—It Shouldn't," Endometriosis UK, accessed August 24, 2022, https://www.endometriosis-uk.org/it-takes-average-7.5-years-get-diagnosis-endometriosis-it-shouldnt.

Even Oprah: Oprah Winfrey, *Oprah Daily*, September 18, 2019, "Oprah Reveals How Heart Palpitations Led Her to Discover She Was Approaching Menopause," https://www.oprahdaily.com/life/health/a29109829/oprah-menopause-symptoms/.

The dosage of most drugs: Irving Zucker and Brian J. Prendergast, "Sex Differences in Pharmacokinetics Predict Adverse Drug Reactions in Women," *Biology of Sex Differences* 11, 32 (2020), https://doi.org/10.1186/s13293-020-00308-5, https://www.ncbi.nlm.nih.gov/pubmed/32503637.

Only 4 percent of all healthcare research: Kelly Knickerbocker, "What Is Femtech?," *PitchBook* (blog), January 27, 2023, https://pitchbook.com/blog/what-is-femtech.

In the UK, only 2.5 percent: "UK Health Research Analysis 2014," UK Clinical Research Collaboration, accessed May 12, 2021, http://www.hrcsonline.net/pages/uk-health-research-analysis-2014.

In a speech: Virginia Woolf, "Professions for Women" (speech, Women's Service League, London, UK,1 931), https://www.literaturecambridge.co.uk/news/professions-women.

"But there's no direct Japanese word": Amina Sugimoto, CEO and cofounder of Fermata Inc., interview with author, August 2022.

"When I first saw the product": Tracy MacNeal, CEO of Materna Medical, interview with author, August 2021.

Gloria Steinem imagined: Gloria Steinem, "If Men Could Menstruate," *Ms. Magazine*, October 1978, https://www.tandfonline.com/doi/epdf/10.1080/23293691.2019.1619050?needAccess=true&role=button.

In an experiment: Tomi-Ann Roberts et al., "'Feminine Protection': The Effects of Menstruation on Attitudes Towards Women," *Psychology of Women Quarterly* 26 (2002).

In a survey: Ingrid Johnston-Robledo et al., "Reproductive Shame: Self-Objectification and Young Women's Attitudes Toward Their Reproductive Functioning," *Women & Health* 46, no. 1 (2007), https://doi.org/10.1300/J013v46n01_03.

Two-thirds of women: "Young Women Too Self-Conscious to Seek Medical Help,"

Ovarian Cancer Action, 2015, accessed November 1, 2020, http://ovarian.org
.uk/news-and-campaigning/article/young-women-too-self-conscious-to-seek
-medical-help.

"After I gave birth": Gloria Kolb, CEO and cofounder of Elidah, interview with
author, July 2022.

"Nobody tells you": Mridula Pore, co-CEO and cofounder of Peppy, Future of
Health Tech webinar organized by Women of Wearables, August 26, 2020.

"People are realizing": Rob Perkins, cofounder of OMGYes For Goodness Sake,
interview with author, August 2022.

"Shortly before the meeting": Juliana Garaizar, lead investor at Portfolia and board
member of the Angel Capital Association, from investor's perspective: fireside
chat organized by Women of Wearables, May 13, 2020.

It was Sigmund Freud: Sigmund Freud, *Three Essays on the Theory of Sexuality*.
Translated by James Strachey. New York: Basic Books, 1962, p. 86.

43 percent of women: R. C. Rosen, "Prevalence and Risk Factors of Sexual
Dysfunction in Men and Women," *Current Psychiatry Report* 2, no. 3 (June
2000), https://doi.org/10.1007/s11920-996-0006-2.

"I became very interested": Dr. Lyndsey Harper, CEO and founder of Rosy,
interview with author, November 2020.

"The convulsions made": Lora Haddock DiCarlo, CEO and founder of Lora
DiCarlo, interview with author, September 2021.

"I had this moment": Eirini Rapti, CEO and cofounder of Inne, interview with
author, November 2022.

"…learned first-hand": Colette Courtion, CEO and founder of Joylux, Future of
Health Tech webinar organized by Women of Wearables, August 26, 2020.

"…a central bridge": Martha Nussbaum, "Compassion: The Basic Social
Emotion," *Social Philosophy and Policy* 13, no. 1 (1996), https://
www.cambridge.org/core/article/compassion-the-basic-social-emotion
/A1D501ADE7B92CA7427273FFBB449B03.

Femtech market potential: Dr. Brittany Barreto, Jessica Karr, Mia Farnham,
Su Wern Khor, Mariana Keymolen, Sangeetha Ranadeeve, Kala Pham,
Brianna Cochran, Alley Lyles, and Dr. Julie Hakim, "FemTech Landscape
2021 Annual Report," FemTech Focus; FemHealth Insights (2021), https://
femtechfocus.org/wp-content/uploads/2021/09/FemTech-Landscape
-2021_v3.pdf.

Until recently: Matthew Boyle and Jeff Green, "Work Shift: Women CEOs (Finally)
Outnumber Those Named John," April 25, 2023, https://www.bloomberg
.com/news/newsletters/2023-04-25/women-ceos-at-big-companies-finally
-outnumber-those-named-john.

That's because women: Dana Kanze et al., "Evidence That Investors Penalize Female

Founders for Lack of Industry Fit," *Science Advances* 6, no. 48 (2020), https://www.science.org/doi/abs/10.1126/sciadv.abd7664.

Consumers replicate: Elise Tak, Shelley J. Correll, and Sarah A. Soule, "Gender Inequality in Product Markets: When and How Status Beliefs Transfer to Products," *Social Forces* 98, no. 2 (2019), https://doi.org/10.1093/sf/soy125, https://doi.org/10.1093/sf/soy125.

We are at: Edelman Trust Barometer, Global Report, 2023. https://www.edelman.com/trust/2023/trust-barometer.

Chapter 1: Launch

"Raising money in women's health": Tracy MacNeal, CEO of Materna Medical, interview with author, August 2021.

The speculum: Rose Eveleth, "Why No One Can Design a Better Speculum," *The Atlantic,* November 17, 2014, https://www.theatlantic.com/health/archive/2014/11/why-no-one-can-design-a-better-speculum/382534.

The forceps: "Chamberlen-Type Obstetrical Forceps, Europe, 1680–1750," Science Museum, London, https://wellcomecollection.org/works/zvcs8x7b.

If these muscles weaken: "Treatment: Pelvic Organ Prolapse," National Health Service UK, 24 March 24, 2021, https://www.nhs.uk/conditions/pelvic-organ-prolapse/treatment.

It's estimated that nine in ten: "Perineal Tears During Childbirth," Royal College of Obstetricians & Gynaecologists, May 12, 2022, https://www.rcog.org.uk/for-the-public/perineal-tears-and-episiotomies-in-childbirth/perineal-tears-during-childbirth.

It has been shown that perineal massage: C. I. Aquino et al., "Perineal Massage During Labor: A Systematic Review and Meta-Analysis of Randomized Controlled Trials," *Journal of Maternal Fetal Neonatal Medicine* 33, no. 6 (March 2020), https://doi.org/10.1080/14767058.2018.1512574.

When episiotomies are done as routine: John Kelly and Alison Young, "Episiotomies Are Painful, Risky and Not Routinely Recommended. Dozens of Hospitals Are Doing Too Many," *USA Today,* May 21, 2019, https://eu.usatoday.com/in-depth/news/investigations/deadly-deliveries/2019/05/21/episiotomy-vs-tearing-moms-cut-in-childbirth-despite-guidelines/3668035002.

Not only new technology: J. Huang et al., "A Review and Comparison of Common Maternal Positions During the Second Stage of Labor," *International Journal of Nursing Sciences* 6, no. 4 (October 10, 2019), https://doi.org/10.1016/j.ijnss.2019.06.007.

"And I did not know that 50 percent": The American College of Obstetricians, Gynecologists, and the American Urogynecologic Society, "Pelvic Organ

Prolapse," *Urogynecology* 25, no. 6 (2019), https://journals.lww.com/fpmrs /Fulltext/2019/11000/Pelvic_Organ_Prolapse.1.aspx.

"And we're almost six times": V. L. Handa et al., "Pelvic Floor Disorders 5–10 Years After Vaginal or Cesarean Childbirth," *Obstetrics & Gynecology* 118, no. 4 (October 2011), https://doi.org/10.1097/AOG.0b013e3182267f2f.

"They go and do it": Roopan Gill, cofounder and executive director of Vitala Global Foundation, interview with author, January 2022.

They result in 35 million: "Investing in Sexual and Reproductive Health in Low- and Middle-Income Countries Factsheet," Guttmacher Institute, July 2020, https:// www.guttmacher.org/fact-sheet/investing-sexual-and-reproductive-health-low -and-middle-income-countries.

In countries with bans: "Unintended Pregnancy and Abortion Worldwide Factsheet," Guttmacher Institute, March 2022, https://www.guttmacher.org/fact -sheet/induced-abortion-worldwide.

The WHO only recommends: "Recommendations on Self-Care Interventions: Self-Management of Medical Abortion, 2022 Update," World Health Organization, September 21, 2022, https://www.who.int/publications/i/item/WHO-SRH-22.1.

Research has shown that misoprostol alone: Elizabeth G. Raymond, Margo S. Harrison, and Mark A. Weaver, "Efficacy of Misoprostol Alone for First-Trimester Medical Abortion: A Systematic Review," *Obstetrics & Gynecology* 133, no. 1 (2019), https://journals.lww.com/greenjournal/Fulltext/2019/01000/Efficacy _of_Misoprostol_Alone_for_First_Trimester.19.aspx.

"You don't really": Tania Boler, CEO and founder of Elvie, interview with author, November 2021.

Pelvic organ prolapse: "Pelvic Organ Prolapse Fact Sheet," Office on Women's Health, February 22, 2021, https://www.womenshealth.gov/a-z-topics/pelvic -organ-prolapse.

Chapter 2: Money

A start-up can be: Eric Ries, *The Lean Startup* (New York: Crown Business, 2011), 27.

At conferences: Joe Miller, Özlem Türeci, and Uğur Şahin, *The Vaccine: Inside the Race to Conquer the COVID-19 Pandemic* (London: Welbeck, 2021), chap. 1.

It was only when: Amos Tversky and Daniel Kahneman, "The Framing of Decisions and the Psychology of Choice," *Science* 211, no. 4481 (1981), https://www .science.org/doi/abs/10.1126/science.7455683.

"I walk into this room": Colette Courtion, CEO and founder of Joylux, interview with author, July 2020.

While the proportion: Gené Teare, "EoY 2019 Diversity Report: 20 Percent of

Newly Funded Startups in 2019 Have a Female Founder," Crunchbase News, January 21, 2020, https://news.crunchbase.com/venture/eoy-2019-diversity -report-20-percent-of-newly-funded-startups-in-2019-have-a-female-founder.

Venture capital investors: Dan Primarck, "More Women Are Top VC Decision- Makers, But Parity Is a Long Way Off," *Axios,* July 21, 2020, https://www.axios .com/2020/07/21/women-venture-capital-gender-equality.

"Most people are": Maya Ackerman, Associate Professor of Computer Science and Engineering at Santa Clara University, interview with author, March 2021.

In 2021, Ackerman led: Christopher Cassion et al., "Investors Embrace Gender Diversity, Not Female CEOs: The Role of Gender in Startup Fundraising," Intelligent Technologies for Interactive Entertainment (2021), https://doi.org /https://doi.org/10.1007/978-3-030-76426-5_10.

Supporting this point: Dana Kanze et al., "We Ask Men to Win and Women Not to Lose: Closing the Gender Gap in Startup Funding," *Academy of Management Journal* 61, no. 2 (2018), https://doi.org/10.5465/amj.2016.1215.

This goes some way: PitchBook, "US VC Female Founders Dashboard," October 2, 2023, https://pitchbook.com/news/articles/the-vc-female-founders -dashboard.

"The apples used": Crystal Etienne, CEO and founder of Ruby Love, interview with author, March 2021.

In 2019, she raised: Estrella Jaramillo, "This Founder Bootstrapped to $10M, Now Raises Series A to Disrupt Period Apparel," *Forbes,* July 29, 2019, https://www .forbes.com/sites/estrellajaramillo/2019/07/29/founder-bootstrapped-to-10 -m-now-raises-series-a-to-disrupt-period-apparel.

I have come across two: Afton Vechery, cofounder and former CEO of Modern Fertility, and Katherine Ryder, founder and CEO of Maven Clinic, Femtech Forum panel organized by Women of Wearables, June 25, 2020.

"My best advice": Lora Haddock DiCarlo, CEO and founder of Lora DiCarlo, interview with author, July 2020.

Researchers at the Kauffman Foundation: Juliana Garaizar, "The Rising Tide: A 'Learning-by-Investing' Initiative to Bridge the Gender Gap," Kauffman Fellows (2016), https://www.kauffmanfellows.org/wp-content/uploads/KFR_Vol7 /Juliana_Garaizar_vol7.pdf.

Researchers at the University of California: Michael Ewens and Richard R. Townsend, "Are Early-Stage Investors Biased Against Women?," *Journal of Financial Economics* 135, no. 3 (2020), https://www.sciencedirect.com/science /article/pii/S0304405X19301758.

I join a group: "Women's Committee Book Club, Economic History Society— Female Entrepreneurs," April 14, 2021, https://ehs.org.uk/event/womens -committee-book-club-female-entrepreneurs/.

Madame Saget: *Female Entrepreneurs in the Long Nineteenth Century: A Global Perspective. Palgrave Studies in Economic History*, ed. Jennifer Aston and Catherine Bishop (Cham. UK: Palgrave Macmillan, 2020), 126–127.

Julia Ridgeway: Susan Ingalls Lewis, *Unexceptional Women: Female Proprietors in Mid-Nineteenth-Century Albany, New York, 1830–1885* (Columbus, OH: Ohio State University Press, 2009), chap. 7, 131–134.

Elizabeth Gold: *Female Entrepreneurs*, 178–179.

Rebecca Lukens: Lewis, *Unexceptional Women*, 118.

In groundbreaking research: Carry van Lieshout, "The Age of Entrepreneurship: New Insights into Female Business Proprietors in Victorian Britain," *Economic History Society*, 2019, https://ehs.org.uk/the-age-of-entrepreneurship-new-insights-into -female-business-proprietors-in-victorian-britain.

The proportion of female shareholders: Janette Rutterford et al., "Who Comprised the Nation of Shareholders? Gender and Investment in Great Britain, c. 1870–1935," *The Economic History Review* 64, no. 1 (2011), p. 169.

Looking at company records: Janette Rutterford, "The Rise of the Small Investors in the US and the UK, 1900 to 1960," Business History after Chandler, Association of Business Historians Annual Conference, University of Birmingham, UK, July 4–5, 2008, 11 and 15.

"Yes, it's likely": Jane Hamlett, email exchange with author, March 2021.

"Oh yes": Janette Rutterford, interview with author, March 2021.

By the twentieth century: Josephine Maltby and Janette Rutterford, "Gender and Finance," in *The Oxford Handbook of the Sociology of Finance*, ed. Karin Knorr Cetina and Alex Preda (Oxford University Press, 2012), 516.

"It is fun": Alice Zheng, principal at RH Capital, interview with author, February 2022.

Given the numbers: "Global Gender Gap Report 2021," World Economic Forum, March 2021, http://www3.weforum.org/docs/WEF_GGGR_2021.pdf.

"On the trading floor": Lizzy Goldman, investment associate at Olive Tree Ventures, interview with author, April 2021.

"There is a lot": Antonio Miguel, founder and managing partner at MAZE, interview with author, April 2021.

"the most triumphant city": Fernand Braudel, *Perspective of the World: Civilization and Capitalism, 15th–18th Century*, vol. 3 (University of California Press, 1992), 30.

"I started meeting": Deena Shakir, General Partner at Lux Capital, interview with author, August 2022.

For that reason: Paul A. Gompers et al., "How Do Venture Capitalists Make Decisions?," *Journal of Financial Economics* 135, no. 1 (January 1, 2020), https://www.sciencedirect.com/science/article/pii/S0304405X19301680.

Yet these companies: Scott Kupor, "Secrets of Sand Hill Road" (London: Ebury, 2019), 3.

"We have Maven": Leslie Schrock, angel investor, entrepreneur, and author of Bumpin' and Fertility Rules, interview with author, June 2023.

"We need even more": Halle Tecco, angel investor, and founder of Rock Health, Natalist and Cofertility, email exchange with author, June 2023.

In 2023, women's health: Eva Epker, "2024 Could be Women's Health's Long-Awaited, Much-Needed Standout Year," Forbes, January 15, 2024, https://www .forbes.com/sites/evaepker/2024/01/15/2024-could-be-womens-healths -long-awaited-much-needed-standout-year/?sh=7963438f1d0d

Chapter 3: Research

"You are the research team": Nicole Woitowich, Research Assistant Professor of Medical Social Sciences at Northwestern University's Feinberg School of Medicine, interview with author, December 2021 and January 2022.

In 1928, Alexander Fleming: "The Discovery and Development of Penicillin 1928–1945," American Chemical Society, 1999, https://www.acs.org/education /whatischemistry/landmarks/flemingpenicillin.html.

In the 1950s, the German drug: "Thalidomide," Science Museum UK, December 11, 2019, https://www.sciencemuseum.org.uk/objects-and-stories/medicine /thalidomide.

In the United States, there was a parallel: P. Zamora-León, "Are the Effects of DES Over? A Tragic Lesson from the Past," International Journal of Environmental Research and Public Health 18, no. 19 (September 20, 2021), https://doi.org /10.3390/ijerph181910309.

In 1977, the FDA's General: "General Considerations for the Clinical Evaluation of Drugs," U.S. Department of Health and Human Services, Food and Drug Administration, Center for Drug Evaluation and Research (1977), https:// www.fda.gov/media/71495/download.

The guidelines were "widely misinterpreted": Ameeta Parekh, "Women in Clinical Drug Trials: United States Food and Drug Administration Update on Policies and Practices," in Handbook of Clinical Gender Medicine, ed. Paula DeCola Karin Schenck-Gustafsson, Donald Pfaff, David Pisetsky (Karger AG, 2012), p. 467.

Out of ten prescription drugs: "Drug Safety: Most Drugs Withdrawn in Recent Years Had Greater Health Risks for Women," U.S Government Accountability Office (2001), https://www.gao.gov/products/gao-01-286r.

According to a 2020 study: Irving Zucker, and Brian J. Prendergast, "Sex Differences in Pharmacokinetics Predict Adverse Drug Reactions in

Women," *Biology of Sex Differences* 11, 32 (2020), https://www.ncbi.nlm.nih.gov/pubmed/32503637.

"When female physicians join": Ruth B. Merkatz, "Women in Clinical Trials: An Introduction," *Food and Drug Law Journal* 48, no. 2 (1993): 164, http://www.jstor.org/stable/26659478.

"I believe that women": R. B. Merkatz and S. W. Junod, "Historical Background of Changes in FDA Policy on the Study and Evaluation of Drugs in Women," *Academic Medicine* 69, no. 9 (1994): 703, https://journals.lww.com/academicmedicine/Fulltext/1994/09000/Historical_background_of_changes_in_FDA_policy_on.4.aspx.

Then, she quoted Simone de Beauvoir: Merkatz and Junod, "Historical Background of Changes in FDA Policy on the Study and Evaluation of Drugs in Women," 706.

In 2016, the NIH announced: M. E. Arnegard et al., "Sex as a Biological Variable: A 5-Year Progress Report and Call to Action," *Journal of Women's Health* 29, no. 6 (June 2020), https://doi.org/10.1089/jwh.2019.8247.

Every five years: S. E. Geller et al., "The More Things Change, the More They Stay the Same: A Study to Evaluate Compliance with Inclusion and Assessment of Women and Minorities in Randomized Controlled Trials," *Academic Medicine* 93, no. 4 (April 2018), https://doi.org/10.1097/acm.0000000000002027.

This bias sets in early: N. C. Woitowich, A. Beery, and T. Woodruff, "A 10-Year Follow-Up Study of Sex Inclusion in the Biological Sciences," *Elife* 9 (June 9, 2020), https://doi.org/10.7554/eLife.56344.

Besides, a 2023 study: D. R. Levy et al., "Mouse Spontaneous Behavior Reflects Individual Variation Rather Than Estrous State," *Current Biology* 33, no. 7 (April 10, 2023), https://doi.org/10.1016/j.cub.2023.02.035.

"Individual males": Rebecca Shansky, email exchange with author, April 2023.

A team led by Cassidy Sugimoto: C. R. Sugimoto et al., "Factors Affecting Sex-Related Reporting in Medical Research: A Cross-Disciplinary Bibliometric Analysis," *Lancet* 393, no. 10171 (February 9, 2019), https://doi.org/10.1016/s0140-6736(18)32995-7.

"It's a really low bar": Katie Schubert, president and CEO of the Society for Women's Health Research (SWHR), interview with author, September 2022.

"When a doctor gives you a drug": Dr. Marjorie Jenkins, keynote at the FemTechnology Summit, June 2022.

According to the WHAM report: Matthew D. Baird et al., "The WHAM report: The Case to Fund Women's Health Research," Rand Corporation (2021), https://thewhamreport.org/report.

In the UK, childbirth: "UK Health Research Analysis 2014," UK Clinical Research Collaboration, accessed May 12, 2021, http://www.hrcsonline.net/pages/uk-health-research-analysis-2014.

Despite the fact only 19 percent: "Why Do We Still Not Know What Causes PMS?," *ResearchGate,* August 12, 2016, https://www.researchgate.net/blog/why-do-we-still-not-know-what-causes-pms.

It's also a matter of who: Rembrand Koning, Sampsa Samila, and John-Paul Ferguson, "Who Do We Invent for? Patents by Women Focus More on Women's Health, but Few Women Get to Invent," *Science* 372, no. 6548 (2021), https://www.science.org/doi/abs/10.1126/science.aba6990.

Studies find that both: L. Zhang et al., "Gender Biases in Estimation of Others' Pain," *Journal of Pain* 22, no. 9 (September 2021), https://doi.org/10.1016/j.jpain.2021.03.001.

At emergency departments: E. H. Chen et al., "Gender Disparity in Analgesic Treatment of Emergency Department Patients with Acute Abdominal Pain," *Academic Emergency Medicine* 15, no. 5 (May 2008), https://doi.org/10.1111/j.1553-2712.2008.00100.x.

and women with chest pain: D. Banco et al., "Sex and Race Differences in the Evaluation and Treatment of Young Adults Presenting to the Emergency Department with Chest Pain," *Journal of American Heart Association* 11, no. 10 (May 17, 2022), https://doi.org/10.1161/jaha.121.024199.

"The reason there is": Alicia Chong Rodriguez, founder and CEO of Bloomer Tech, and Aceil Halay, Chief Operations Officer at Bloomer Tech, interview with author, May 2020 and September 2021.

They found that women: B. N. Greenwood, S. Carnahan, and L. Huang, "Patient-Physician Gender Concordance and Increased Mortality Among Female Heart Attack Patients," *Proceedings of the National Academy of Sciences of the United States of America* 115, no. 34 (August 21, 2018), https://doi.org/10.1073/pnas.1800097115.

"I used to be": Petronela Sandulache, founder and CEO of CorDiFio Health, interview with author, October 2021.

"Women don't fit into": Alyson McGregor, Associate Professor of Emergency Medicine at the Warren Alpert Medical School, Brown University and author of *Sex Matters: How Male-Centric Medicine Endangers Women's Health,* interview with author, March 2022.

Trans women who take estrogen: Alyson McGregor, "Sex Matters: How Male-Centric Medicine Endangers Women's Health" (London: Quercus, 2020), 149.

Chapter 4: Unmet Needs

Since 2000, their alumni: "Our Impact: 2016 Stanford Biodesign Alumni Survey," Stanford Biodesign, 2016, https://biodesign.stanford.edu/our -impact.html.

"At Biodesign, we try": Josh Makower, Boston Scientific Applied Bioengineering Professor of Medicine and of Bioengineering at the Stanford University Schools of Medicine and Engineering and the Director of the Stanford Byers Center for Biodesign, interview with author, January 2022 and August 2022.

"I'm the daughter of two feminists": Holly Rockweiler, cofounder and CEO of Madorra, interview with author, August 2021.

Years before the current wave: Christina Farr, "Breast Pump Start-Up Naya Health Shuts Down After Failing to Raise Money," CNBC, January 3, 2019, https:// www.cnbc.com/2019/01/03/naya-health-the-breast-pump-company-that -went-dark-has-officially-shut-down.html.

Moxxly is another: Natasha Mascarenhas, "Breast Pump Maker Moxxly Quietly Shuts Down," Crunchbase News, August 8, 2018, https://news.crunchbase.com /business/breast-pump-maker-moxxly-quietly-shuts-down.

Seattle-based Poppy: Avni Patel Thompson, "What Shutting Down Your Startup Feels Like," Y Combinator, January 2019, https://www.ycombinator.com/library /5P-what-shutting-down-your-startup-feels-like.

The Cusp: Brian Rinker, "Femtech startup The Cusp abruptly shuts down," *San Francisco Business Times,* December 11, 2020, https://www.bizjournals.com /sanfrancisco/news/2020/12/11/femtech-startup-the-cusp-abruptly-shuts -down.html.

Trellis: https://www.yelp.com/biz/trellis-new-york-2, accessed January 16, 2023.

In 2022, allegations emerged: Erin Brodwin, "FemTec's Missteps: Missed Payments and Unhappy Customers," *Axios,* October 6, 2022, https://www.axios.com /pro/health-tech-deals/2022/10/06/femtec-health-struggles-layoffs-debt -acquisitions; Erin Brodwin, "End of the Line for FemTec Health," *Axios,* May 23, 2023, https://www.axios.com/2023/05/23/femtec-health-winds-down.

"These immature egg cells": Ovascience, "Form 10-K Annual Report" (SEC, 2015), https://www.sec.gov/Archives/edgar/data/1544227/000154422716000008 /ovas-20151231x10k.htm.

By 2016: Karen Weintraub, "Turmoil at Troubled Fertility Company Ovascience," *MIT Technology Review,* December 29, 2016, https://www.technologyreview .com/2016/12/29/106805/turmoil-at-troubled-fertility-company-ovascience.

"I started to mentor": Brittany Barreto, CEO of FemHealth Insights and host of the FemTech Focus podcast, interview with author, April 2023.

One of the first figures: Frost & Sullivan contributors, "Femtech Market—Digitizing

Women's Health," Frost.com, June 25, 2019, https://store.frost.com/industries /femtech-market-research.html.

Precedence Research: August 19, 2022, https://www.precedenceresearch.com /femtech-market.

Elsewhere, the global: Future Market Insights Global & Consulting contributors, January 5, 2023, https://www.futuremarketinsights.com/reports/feminine -hygiene-products-market.

and the menopause market: Emma Hinchliffe, "Menopause Is a $600 Billion Opportunity, Report Finds," *Fortune,* October 26, 2020, https://fortune.com /2020/10/26/menopause-startups-female-founders-fund-report.

Chapter 5: Period Apps, the OG

In 2016, Ida Tin: https://www.youtube.com/watch?v=4JZ62DUUh3o. An interview with Ida Tin: Hannah Ward-Glenton, "Meet the Woman Who Invented a Whole New Subsection of Tech Set to Be Worth $1 Trillion," CNBC, March 6, 2023, https://www.cnbc.com/2023/03/06/meet-the-woman-who-invented-a -whole-new-subsection-of-tech-set-to-be-worth-1-trillion.html.

Deep in the archives: William M. Emmons III, "Tambrands, Inc.: The Femtech Soviet Joint Venture (A)," Harvard Business School Case 390–159 (August 1991, revised March 1993).

Though we are still: Steinem, "If Men Could Menstruate."

The app's foray: Julia Carrie Wong, "Birth Control App Reported to Swedish Officials After 37 Unwanted Pregnancies," *The Guardian,* January 17, 2018, https://www .theguardian.com/technology/2018/jan/17/birth-control-app-natural-cycle -pregnancies.

Condoms: "How Effective Is Contraception at Preventing Pregnancy?," National Health Service UK, April 17, 2020, https://www.nhs.uk/conditions /contraception/how-effective-contraception.

According to a study: E. Berglund Scherwitzl et al., "Perfect-Use and Typical-Use Pearl Index of a Contraceptive Mobile App," *Contraception* 96, no. 6 (December 2017), https://doi.org/10.1016/j.contraception.2017.08.014.

The British advertising regulator: "ASA Ruling on NaturalCycles Nordic AB Sweden t/a Natural Cycles," Advertising Standards Authority, August 29, 2018, https://www.asa.org.uk/rulings/naturalcycles-nordic-ab-sweden-a17–393896. html.

As Olivia Sudjic: Olivia Sudjic, "'I Felt Colossally Naive': The Backlash Against the Birth Control App," *The Guardian,* July 21, 2018, https://www.theguardian.com /society/2018/jul/21/colossally-naive-backlash-birth-control-app.

"There was just": Laura Shipp, doctoral researcher in cybersecurity and femtech at Royal Holloway, University of London, interview with author, August 2022.

In Shipp's 2020 study: Laura Shipp and Jorge Blasco, "How Private Is Your Period? A Systematic Analysis of Menstrual App Privacy Policies," *Proceedings on Privacy Enhancing Technologies* 4 (2020).

"Not selling user data": Lucy Purdon, Senior Tech Policy Fellow at Mozilla Foundation, interview with author, June 2023.

In the UK: Lucy Purdon, "The NHS Data Breach Demonstrates the Urgent Need for Reforming the Online Advertising Industry–Femtech Can Show the Way," Femtech World, May 31, 2023, https://www.femtechworld.co.uk/opinion /the-nhs-data-breach-demonstrates-the-urgent-need-for-reforming-the-online -advertising-industry-femtech-can-show-the-way.

The evidence used: Gennie Gebhart and Daly Barnett, "Should You Really Delete Your Period Tracking App?," Electronic Frontiers Foundation, June 30, 2022, https://www. eff.org/deeplinks/2022/06/should-you-really-delete-your-period-tracking-app.

In 2023, an investigation: Shanti Das, "NHS Data Breach: Trusts Shared Patient Details with Facebook Without Consent," *The Guardian,* May 27, 2023, https:// www.theguardian.com/society/2023/may/27/nhs-data-breach-trusts-shared -patient-details-with-facebook-meta-without-consent.

An investigation by The Markup: Simon Fondrie-Teitler Todd Feathers, Angie Waller, and Surya Mattu, "Facebook Is Receiving Sensitive Medical Information from Hospital Websites," *The Markup,* June 16, 2022, https://themarkup.org /pixel-hunt/2022/06/16/facebook-is-receiving-sensitive-medical-information -from-hospital-websites.

In a collaboration: Jonathan R. Bull et al., "Real-World Menstrual Cycle Characteristics of More Than 600,000 Menstrual Cycles," *npj Digital Medicine* 2, no. 1 (2019), https://doi.org/10.1038/s41746-019-0152-7.

The WHO defines: M. Duane et al., "Fertility Awareness-Based Methods for Women's Health and Family Planning," *Frontiers in Medicine (Lausanne)* 9 (2022), https://doi.org/10.3389/fmed.2022.858977.

Only 3 percent of women: C. B. Polis and R. K. Jones, "Multiple Contraceptive Method Use and Prevalence of Fertility Awareness Based Method Use in the United States, 2013–2015," *Contraception* 98, no. 3 (September 2018), https:// doi.org/10.1016/j.contraception.2018.04.013.

More recently, researchers: J. L. Fitzpatrick et al., "Chemical Signals from Eggs Facilitate Cryptic Female Choice in Humans," *Proceedings of the Royal Sciences B, Biological Sciences* 287, no. 1928 (June 10, 2020), https://doi.org/10.1098 /rspb.2020.0805.

The second-highest chance: Emily Oster, *Expecting Better* (London: Orion, 2018), 14.

One study of the Clearblue: Janet E. Robinson, Melanie Wakelin, and Jayne E. Ellis, "Increased Pregnancy Rate with Use of the Clearblue Easy Fertility Monitor," *Fertility and Sterility* 87, no. 2 (February 2007), https://www.ncbi.nlm.nih.gov/pubmed/17074329.

In 2018, researchers asked: Sarah Johnson, Lorrae Marriott, and Michael Zinaman, "Can Apps and Calendar Methods Predict Ovulation with Accuracy?," *Current Medical Research and Opinion* 34, no. 9 (September 2018), https://www.ncbi.nlm.nih.gov/pubmed/29749274.

"Our answer is": Carrie Walter and Audrey Tsang, co-CEOs at Clue, interview with author, September 2022.

For Clue's FDA approval: Victoria Jennings et al., "Perfect- and Typical-Use Effectiveness of the Dot Fertility App over 13 Cycles: Results from a Prospective Contraceptive Effectiveness Trial," *The European Journal of Contraception & Reproductive Health Care* 24, no. 2 (2019), https://doi.org/10.1080/13625187.2019.1581164.

"I invented Proov": Amy Beckley, CEO and founder of Proov, interview with author, October 2022.

"I was always on the Pill": Eirini Rapti, CEO and founder of Inne, interview with author, November 2022.

"It could be": Kristina Cahojova, CEO and founder of kegg interview with author, October 2022.

"CO2 correlates": Lisa Krapinger-Rüther, co-CEO of breathe ilo GmbH, interview with author, December 2022.

At this point, the research: L. M. Colenso-Semple et al., "Current Evidence Shows No Influence of Women's Menstrual Cycle Phase on Acute Strength Performance or Adaptations to Resistance Exercise Training," *Front Sports Act Living* 5 (2023), https://doi.org/10.3389/fspor.2023.1054542; E. Sung et al., "Effects of Follicular Versus Luteal Phase–Based Strength Training in Young Women," *Springerplus* 3 (2014), https://doi.org/10.1186/2193-1801-3-668.

Chapter 6: Sextech

"It would feel like": Anna Lee, cofounder and head of engineering at Lioness, interview with author, August 2022 and February 2023.

The Lioness team raised: "Lioness Smart Vibrator: Literally See Your Orgasms," accessed July 13, 2022, https://www.indiegogo.com/projects/lioness-smart-vibrator-literally-see-your-orgasms#/.

There are three primary types: J. Pfaus et al., "Women's Orgasms Determined by Autodetection of Pelvic Floor Muscle Contractions Using the Lioness 'Smart'

Vibrator," *The Journal of Sexual Medicine* 19, no. 8, Supplement 3 (2022), https://www.sciencedirect.com/science/article/pii/S1743609522013285.

There's also an earlier orgasm study from the 1980s: J. G. Bohlen et al., "The Female Orgasm: Pelvic Contractions," *Archives of Sexual Behavior* 11, no. 5 (October 1982), https://doi.org/10.1007/bf01541570.

Taking a closer look: O. A. Raheem et al., "The Association of Erectile Dysfunction and Cardiovascular Disease: A Systematic Critical Review," *American Journal of Men's Health* 11, no. 3 (May 2017), https://doi .org/10.1177/1557988316630305.

The term "sextech": Cindy Gallop, "What Is Sextech and Why Is Everyone Ignoring It?," *Hot Topics*, accessed April 6, 2022, https://hottopics.ht/14192/what-is -sextech-and-why-is-everyone-ignoring-it.

"We have not even": Cindy Gallop, CEO and founder of MakeLoveNotPorn, interview with author, April 2022.

VDom, an inflatable smart prosthetic: Glenise Kinard-Moore at "Wearables & Healthcare Female Founder Stories" webinar organized by Women of Wearables, February 11, 2011.

"I felt for so long": Byrony Cole, founder of SexTech School and host of *Future of Sex* podcast, interview with author, April 2022.

He found that 80 percent: "The Kinsey Scale," first published in *Sexual Behavior in the Human Male* (1948), accessed June 14, 2022, https://kinseyinstitute.org /research/publications/kinsey-scale.php.

In studies that would: Thomas Maier, *Masters of Sex* (New York: Basic Books, 2009), chap. 11.

It goes some way: D. A. Frederick et al., "Differences in Orgasm Frequency Among Gay, Lesbian, Bisexual, and Heterosexual Men and Women in a U.S. National Sample," *Archives of Sexual Behavior* 47, no. 1 (January 2018), https://doi.org /10.1007/s10508-017-0939-z.

"What do you do?": Rob Perkins, cofounder of OMGYes For Goodness Sake, interview with author, August 2022.

The WHO has declared: "Redefining Sexual Health for Benefits Throughout Life," World Health Organization Departmental News, February 11, 2022, https:// www.who.int/news/item/11-02-2022-redefining-sexual-health-for-benefits -throughout-life.

Research has found: M. Zaneva et al., "What Is the Added Value of Incorporating Pleasure in Sexual Health Interventions? A Systematic Review and Meta-Analysis," *PLoS One* 17, no. 2 (2022), https://doi.org/10.1371/journal.pone .0261034.

"My younger brother": Heather Morrison, cofounder and CEO of Bump'n, interview with author, May 2022.

"But they didn't know": Morenike Fajemisin, cofounder and CEO of WHISPA, interview with author, October 2022.

And yet, the country: "Abortion in Nigeria Fact Sheet," Guttmacher Institute, October 2015, https://www.guttmacher.org/fact-sheet/abortion-nigeria.

Meanwhile the use of modern contraceptives: O. Fadeyibi et al., "Household Structure and Contraceptive Use in Nigeria," *Frontiers in Global Women's Health* 3 (2022), https://doi.org/10.3389/fgwh.2022.821178.

Chapter 7: The Future of Contraception

Women try an average: Brittni Frederiksen et al., "Women's Sexual and Reproductive Health Services: Key Findings from the 2020 KFF Women's Health Survey," Kaiser Family Foundation, April 21, 2021, https://www.kff.org/womens-health -policy/issue-brief/womens-sexual-and-reproductive-health-services-key -findings-from-the-2020-kff-womens-health-survey.

But for 91 percent: Lauren N. Lessard et al., "Contraceptive Features Preferred by Women at High Risk of Unintended Pregnancy," Guttmacher Institute, September 1, 2012, https://www.guttmacher.org/journals/psrh/2012/09 /contraceptive-features-preferred-women-high-risk-unintended-pregnancy.

In fact, 58 percent: Rachel K. Jones, *"Beyond Birth Control: The Overlooked Benefits of Oral Contraceptive Pills,"* Guttmacher Institute, November 2011, https://www.guttmacher.org/pubs/Beyond-Birth-Control.pdf.

One consequence that: W. V. Williams et al., "Hormonally Active Contraceptives, Part II: Sociological, Environmental, and Economic Impact," *Linacre Quarterly* 88, no. 3 (August 2021), https://doi.org/10.1177/00243639211005121.

"Martinis and voodoo": Saundra Pelletier, "Investing and Fundraising in Health Tech and Femtech," organized by Women of Wearables, June 17, 2021.

"I was given": Saundra Pelletier, CEO of Evofem Biosciences, interview with author, November 9, 2021.

The product is 93 percent: Phexxi Pearl Index, accessed November 2, 2021, https:// www.plannedparenthood.org/learn/birth-control/spermicide/phexxi.

"I started working": Frederik Petursson Madsen, CEO and cofounder of Cirqle Biomedical, interview with author, September 2022.

A study from 2016: Charlotte Skovlund et al., "Association of Hormonal Contraception with Depression," *JAMA Psychiatry* 73 (2016), https://doi.org /10.1001/jamapsychiatry.2016.2387.

A second study: C. W. Skovlund et al., "Association of Hormonal Contraception with Suicide Attempts and Suicides," *American Journal of Psychiatry* 175, no. 4 (April 1, 2018), https://doi.org/10.1176/appi.ajp.2017.17060616.

However, a large-scale: E. Toffol et al., "Use of Hormonal Contraception and

Attempted Suicide: A Nested Case-Control Study," *European Psychiatry* (September 1, 2022); no. 65, Supplement 1: S122–3. eCollection June 2022, https://doi.10.1192/j.eurpsy.2022.339.

It included 322 women: N. Zethraeus et al., "A First-Choice Combined Oral Contraceptive Influences General Well-Being in Healthy Women: A Double-Blind, Randomized, Placebo-Controlled Trial," *Fertility and Sterility* 107, no. 5 (May 2017), https://doi.org/10.1016/j.fertnstert.2017.02.120.

"The women were talking": Kevin Eisenfrats, CEO and cofounder of Contraline Inc., interview with author, March 2022.

In the 1990s: S. C. Zhao, "Vas Deferens Occlusion by Percutaneous Injection of Polyurethane Elastomer Plugs: Clinical Experience and Reversibility," *Contraception* 41, no. 5 (May 1990), https://doi.org/10.1016/0010–7824 (90)90055-z.

Here's an overview of previous attempts to create a contraceptive using the vas deferens: I. Khourdaji et al., "The Future of Male Contraception: A Fertile Ground," *Translational Andrology and Urology* 7, Supplement 2 (May 2018), https://doi.org/10.21037/tau.2018.03.23.

One survey of men: K. Heinemann et al., "Attitudes Toward Male Fertility Control: Results of a Multinational Survey on Four Continents," *Human Reproduction* 20, no. 2 (February 2005), https://doi.org/10.1093/humrep/deh574.

A survey of 1894 women: A. F. Glasier et al., "Would Women Trust Their Partners to Use a Male Pill?," *Human Reproduction* 15, no. 3 (March 2000), https://doi.org /10.1093/humrep/15.3.646.

In 2016, it was reported: Staff NPR, "Male Birth Control Study Killed After Men Report Side Effects," NPR, November 3, 2016, https://www.npr.org/sections /health-shots/2016/11/03/500549503/male-birth-control-study-killed-after -men-complain-about-side-effects.

In the same year: H. M. Behre et al., "Efficacy and Safety of an Injectable Combination Hormonal Contraceptive for Men," *The Journal of Clinical Endocrinology & Metabolism* 101, no. 12 (December 2016), https://doi.org/10.1210/jc.2016 –2141.

Chapter 8: FertilityTech

"You spend so many years": Maureen Brown, CEO and cofounder of Mosie Baby, interview with author, March 2023.

A previous study: Jeffrey M. Goldberg et al., "Comparison of Intrauterine and Intracervical Insemination with Frozen Donor Aperm: A Meta-Analysis," *Fertility and Sterility* 72, no. 5 (1999), https://doi.org/10.1016/S0015

-0282(99)00374-X, https://www.sciencedirect.com/science/article/pii/S001502829900374X.

"Nobody told me": Ravid Israel, founder of Embie, interviews with author, June 2022 and February 2023.

In the United States, some clinics: Ruth La Ferla, "Why Fertility Clinics Are Throwing 'Egg Freezing' Parties with Champagne and Canapés," *Independent,* September 10, 2018, https://www.independent.co.uk/life-style/health-and-families/egg-freezing-party-women-fertility-preservation-millennial-a8520996.html.

This chart illustrates: R. H. Goldman et al., "Predicting the Likelihood of Live Birth for Elective Oocyte Cryopreservation: A Counseling Tool for Physicians and Patients," *Human Reproduction* 32, no. 4 (April 1, 2017), https://doi.org/10.1093/humrep/dex008.

Research has shown: S. L. Broer et al., "Anti-Müllerian Hormone Predicts Menopause: A Long-Term Follow-Up Study in Normoovulatory Women," *The Journal of Clinical Endocrinology & Metabolism* 96, no. 8 (2011), https://doi.org/10.1210/jc.2010-2776.

It wasn't originally: T. Copp et al., "Anti-Mullerian Hormone (AMH) Test Information on Australian and New Zealand Fertility Clinic Websites: A Content Analysis," *BMJ Open* 11, no. 7 (July 7, 2021), https://doi.org/10.1136/bmjopen-2020-046927.

PCOS, for example: Jacob P. Christ and Marcelle I. Cedars. "Current Guidelines for Diagnosing PCOS," *Diagnostics* 13, no. 6 (March 15, 2023): 1113, https://doi.org/10.3390/diagnostics13061113.

According to the American Society: "Fact Sheet: Can I Freeze My Eggs to Use Later If I'm Not Sick?," The American Society for Reproductive Medicine (ASRM), 2014, accessed November 9, 2022, https://www.reproductivefacts.org/globalassets/rf/news-and-publications/bookletsfact-sheets/english-fact-sheets-and-info-booklets/can_i_freeze_my_eggs_to_use_later_if_im_not_sick_factsheet.pdf.

Out of 2.5 million IVF cycles: R. Sciorio et al., "One Follicle, One Egg, One Embryo: A Case Report of Successful Pregnancy Obtained from a Single Oocyte Collected," *JBRA Assisted Reproduction* 25, no. 2 (April 27, 2021), https://doi.org/10.5935/1518-0557.20200087.

It's often the case: Zeynep B. Gürtin and Emily Tiemann, "The Marketing of Elective Egg Freezing: A Content, Cost and Quality Analysis of UK Fertility Clinic Websites," *Reproductive Biomedicine & Society Online* 12 (2021), https://www.sciencedirect.com/science/article/pii/S24\05661820300289.

In 2012, both the American: N. Rimon-Zarfaty et al., "Between 'Medical' and 'Social' Egg Freezing: A Comparative Analysis of Regulatory Frameworks in

Austria, Germany, Israel, and the Netherlands," *Journal of Bioethical Inquiry* 18, no. 4 (December 2021), https://doi.org/10.1007/s11673-021-10133-z.

Egg freezing typically: "Fact Sheet: Can I Freeze My Eggs to Use Later If I'm Not Sick?" (Ibid.)

yet, research shows: S. D. Cascante et al., "Fifteen Years of Autologous Oocyte Thaw Outcomes from a Large University-Based Fertility Center," *Fertility and Sterility* 118, no. 1 (July 2022), https://doi.org/10.1016/j.fertnstert.2022.04.013.

As well as in the UK: "Press release: Age Is the Key Factor for Egg Freezing Success Says New HFEA Report, As Overall Treatment Numbers Remain Low," Human Fertilisation and Embryology Authority News Release, December 20, 2018, https://www.hfea.gov.uk/about-us/news-and-press-releases/2018-news -and-press-releases/press-release-age-is-the-key-factor-for-egg-freezing-success -says-new-hfea-report-as-overall-treatment-numbers-remain-low.

The main motivation: M. C. Inhorn et al., "Ten Pathways to Elective Egg Freezing: A Binational Analysis," *Journal of Assisted Reproduction and Genetics* 35, no. 11 (November 2018), https://doi.org/10.1007/s10815-018-1277-3.

"It's definitely harder": Timothy Hickman, president of the Society of Assisted Reproductive Technology and medical director and cofounder of CCRM Houston, interview with author, September 2022.

The air quality: R. Sciorio, E. Rapalini, and S. C. Esteves, "Air Quality in the Clinical Embryology Laboratory: A Mini-Review," *Therapeutic Advances in Reproductive Health* 15 (January–December 2021), https://doi.org/10.1177 /2633494121990684.

It has been shown: D. Preece et al., "Red Light Improves Spermatozoa Motility and Does Not Induce Oxidative DNA Damage," *Scientific Reports* 7 (April 20, 2017), https://doi.org/10.1038/srep46480.

and that a petri dish: A. P. Sommer et al., "Genesis on Diamonds II: Contact with Diamond Enhances Human Sperm Performance by 300," *Annals of Translational Medicine* 4, no. 20 (October 2016), https://doi.org/10.21037 /atm.2016.08.18.

In 2023, researchers at Osaka: K. Murakami et al., "Generation of Functional Oocytes from Male Mice in Vitro," *Nature* 615, no. 7954 (March 2023), https://doi.org/10.1038/s41586-023-05834-x.

Chapter 9: FamilyTech

"Our nation has": Representative Lauren Underwood, Black Maternal Health Conference organized by the Motherlab and Tufts University Medical School, April 8, 2022.

The pregnancy related: William M. Callaghan, "Overview of Maternal Mortality

in the United States," *Seminars in Perinatology* 36, no. 1 (2012), https://www
.sciencedirect.com/science/article/pii/S0146000511001480.

Out of all pregnancy-related: "Maternal Mortality in the United States: A
Primer," The Commonwealth Fund (December 16, 2020), https://www
.commonwealthfund.org/publications/issue-brief-report/2020/dec/maternal
-mortality-united-states-primer.

The most frequent: Susanna Trost, Jennifer Beauregard, Gyan Chandra, et al.,
"Pregnancy-Related Deaths: Data from Maternal Mortality Review Committees
in 36 US States, 2017–2019," Atlanta, GA: Centers for Disease Control and
Prevention, U.S. Department of Health and Human Services (2022).

"Dr. Hernandez and I": Rasheeta Chandler, Associate Professor of the Nell Hodgson
School of Nursing at Emory University and Fellow of the American Academy of
Nurse Practitioners; Natalie Hernandez, Assistant Professor in the Department
of Community Health and Preventive Medicine and the Interim Director of the
Center for Maternal Health Equity at Morehouse School of Medicine; interview
with author, February 2022.

More than half: Laura Harker, "Efforts Advance to Put More Health Care Providers
in Reach of Georgians," Georgia Budget & Policy Institute, May 8, 2019, https://
gbpi.org/georgias-ongoing-efforts-to-improve-health-provider-capacity.

Black women living in rural: Shirley Sylvester, "Science in Action: Collaborating
in Georgia to Improve Black Maternal Health," Johnson & Johnson, February
16, 2021, https://chwi.jnj.com/news-insights/science-in-action-collaborating-in
-georgia-to-improve-black-maternal-health.

Differences in health insurance: Latoya Hill, Samantha Artiga, and Usha Ranji,
"Racial Disparities in Maternal and Infant Health: Current Status and Efforts to
Address Them," Kaiser Family Foundation (2022), https://www.kff.org/racial
-equity-and-health-policy/issue-brief/racial-disparities-in-maternal-and-infant
-health-current-status-and-efforts-to-address-them.

One of the key: "Improving Postpartum Care," Georgia Department of Community
Health, July 2021.

"You have this increasing": Eric Dy, founder and CEO of Bloomlife Inc., interview
with author, October 2022.

In the United States, 36 percent: Jacqueline Howard, "36% of US Counties Are
'Maternity Care Deserts,' Raising Risks for Women and Babies, New Report
Finds," CNN, October 11, 2022, https://edition.cnn.com/2022/10/11/health
/maternity-care-deserts-march-of-dimes-report/index.html.

The goal is: R. Morgan Griffin, "Nonstress Test (NST)," WebMD, August 9, 2022,
https://www.webmd.com/baby/nonstress-test-nst.

This practice has: Brittany M. Byerley and David M. Haas, "A Systematic Overview of
the Literature Regarding Group Prenatal Care for High-Risk Pregnant Women,"

BMC Pregnancy and Childbirth 17, no. 1 (2017), https://doi.org/10.1186/s12884-017-1522-2.

"There was a lot": Rosanne Longmore, CEO of Coroflo, interview with author, October 2022.

The WHO recommends: "Exclusive Breastfeeding for Six Months Best for Babies Everywhere," World Health Organization, January 15, 2011, https://www.who.int/news/item/15-01-2011-exclusive-breastfeeding-for-six-months-best-for-babies-everywhere.

In Europe, 13 percent: World Health Organization data, La Leche League International, and other national sources analyzed by Coroflo.

For an in-depth analysis: Emily Oster, *Cribsheet* (London: Profile Books, 2019), chap. 4.

"I was the first": Michelle Kennedy, cofounder and CEO of Peanut, interview with author, February 2023.

some say it's: J. Holt-Lunstad, T. B. Smith, and J. B. Layton, "Social Relationships and Mortality Risk: A Meta-Analytic Review," *PLoS Med* 7, no. 7 (July 27, 2010), https://doi.org/10.1371/journal.pmed.1000316.

An article on the fifteen cigarettes comparison: Andrea Wigfield, Jan Gurung, and Laura Makey, "Is Loneliness Really As Damaging to Your Health as Smoking 15 Cigarettes a Day?," *The Conversation,* May 12, 2023, https://theconversation.com/is-loneliness-really-as-damaging-to-your-health-as-smoking-15-cigarettes-a-day-204959.

"If you look at a typical family": Aditi Hazra-Ganju, cofounder and COO of Saathealth, interview with author, February 2022.

A suburb of informal: Shruti Ravindran, "This Slum Has the Worst Air Pollution in Mumbai," Vice News, March 27, 2015, https://www.vice.com/en/article/59anzd/this-slum-has-the-worst-air-pollution-in-mumbai.

Women around the world: Jennifer Ervin et al., "Gender Differences in the Association Between Unpaid Labour and Mental Health in Employed Adults: A Systematic Review," *The Lancet Public Health* 7, no. 9 (2022), https://doi.org/10.1016/S2468-2667(22)00160-8.

India has one of: Alessandra Costagliola, "Labor Participation and Gender Inequalities in India: Traditional Gender Norms in India and the Decline in the Labor Force Participation Rate (LFPR)," *The Indian Journal of Labour Economics* 64, no. 3 (2021), https://doi.org/10.1007/s41027-021-00329-7.

Play is central: Regina M. Milteer et al., "The Importance of Play in Promoting Healthy Child Development and Maintaining Strong Parent-Child Bond: Focus on Children in Poverty," *Pediatrics* 129, no. 1 (2012), https://doi.org/10.1542/peds.2011-295.

Chapter 10: MenopauseTech

"**Did you know**": comedian Karen Mills, accessed April 23, 2023, https://www
.tiktok.com/@karenmillscomedy.

Though for up to 80 percent: R. E. Nappi et al., "Global Cross-Sectional Survey
of Women with Vasomotor Symptoms Associated with Menopause: Prevalence
and Quality of Life Burden," *Menopause* 28, no. 8 (May 24, 2021), https://doi
.org/10.1097/gme.0000000000001793.

In the Western: S. Palacios et al., "Age of Menopause and Impact of Climacteric
Symptoms by Geographical Region," *Climacteric* 13, no. 5 (October 2010),
https://doi.org/10.3109/13697137.2010.507886.

globally it's between: "Menopause Fact Sheet," World Health Organization,
October 17, 2022, https://www.who.int/news-room/fact-sheets/detail
/menopause.

About 1 percent: "Early and premature menopause," National Health Service
Scotland, March 22, 2023, https://www.nhsinform.scot/healthy-living
/womens-health/later-years-around-50-years-and-over/menopause-and-post
-menopause-health/early-and-premature-menopause.

There are more than: Elizabeth Gordon, Jillian Levovitz, Carley
Prentice, Brittany Barreto, and Yedidiah Teitelbaum, "2022 Femtech
Landscape," FemHealth Insights (March 2023), https://mailchi.mp
/femhealthinsights/2022-landscape-report.

Around 1.2 billion women: "Menopause-Like Symptoms May Strike Before the
Menopause Transition," North American Menopause Society, January 11,
2023, https://www.menopause.org/docs/default-source/press-release
/late-reproductive-stage-symptoms-vs-menopause.pdf.

In 2002, the WHI: A. Cagnacci and M. Venier, "The Controversial History of
Hormone Replacement Therapy," *Medicina (Kaunas)* 55, no. 9 (September 18,
2019), https://doi.org/10.3390/medicina55090602.

"The benefits of HRT": "Benefits and Risks—Hormone Replacement Therapy
(HRT)," National Health Service UK, September 9, 2019, https://www.nhs.uk
/conditions/hormone-replacement-therapy-hrt/risks.

some research has found: Lynne Robinson, "HRT: The History—Women's
Health Concern Fact Sheet" (November 2020), https://www.womens-health
-concern.org/wp-content/uploads/2022/11/10-whc-fatsheet-hrt-the-history
-nov22-a.pdf.

In the UK, a survey: "Menopause Support Survey Reveals Shocking Disparity in
Menopause Training in Medical Schools," Menopause Support, May 13, 2021,
https://menopausesupport.co.uk/?p=14434.

In the United States, it is estimated: J. M. Kling et al., "Menopause Management
Knowledge in Postgraduate Family Medicine, Internal Medicine, and Obstetrics

and Gynecology Residents: A Cross-Sectional Survey," *Mayo Clinic Proceedings* 94, no. 2 (February 2019), https://doi.org/10.1016/j.mayocp.2018.08.033.

All the while one in ten: Kate Ng, "One in 10 Women Have Quit Their Job Due to Menopause," *Independent,* May 2, 2022, https://www.independent.co.uk/life-style/women/menopause-women-quit-jobs-hrt-b2069754.html.

One survey of 453: P. Sharma and S. Kapoor, "Impact of Husband's Attitude Towards Menopause on Severity of Menopausal Symptoms Among Women in India: Pankhuri Sharma," *European Journal of Public Health* 24, Supplement 2 (2014), https://doi.org/10.1093/eurpub/cku161.065.

One study conducted in China: Y. Zhang et al., "A Cross-Cultural Comparison of Climacteric Symptoms, Self-Esteem, and Perceived Social Support Between Mosuo Women and Han Chinese Women," *Menopause* 23, no. 7 (July 7, 2016), https://doi.org/10.1097/gme.0000000000000621.

Delving into research: "Startup Grind Hosts David Cohen Tanugi," YouTube, January 2, 2018, https://www.youtube.com/watch?v=O7pDlHjhxpg.

"They ended up hiring me": Elizabeth Gazda, CEO of Embr Labs, interview with author, July 2022.

In Europe, 69 percent: Nappi et al., "Global Cross-Sectional Survey of Women with Vasomotor Symptoms Asociated with Menopause: Prevalence and Quality of Life Burden."

African American women: E. W. Freeman et al., "Hot Flashes in the Late Reproductive Years: Risk Factors for African American and Caucasian Women," *Journal of Women's Health & Gender-Based Medicine* 10, no. 1 (January–February 2001), https://doi.org/10.1089/152460901750067133.

In a small study of 39: J. Composto et al., "Thermal Comfort Intervention for Hot-Flash Related Insomnia Symptoms in Perimenopausal and Postmenopausal-aged Women: An Exploratory Study," *Behavioral Sleep Medicine* 19, no. 1 (January–February 2021), https://doi.org/10.1080/15402002.2019.1699100.

Women have a lower bone mass: A. Singh and A. R. Varma, "Whole-Body Vibration Therapy as a Modality for Treatment of Senile and Postmenopausal Osteoporosis: A Review Article," *Cureus* 15, no. 1 (January 2023), https://doi.org/10.7759/cureus.33690.

Bone health might: "General Facts: What Women Need to Know," Bone Health & Osteoporosis Foundation, accessed July 20, 2022, https://www.bonehealthandosteoporosis.org/preventing-fractures/general-facts/what-women-need-to-know.

And tragically, a study: "Kaiser Permanente: Women Who Break a Hip at Increased Risk of Dying Within a year, Study Finds," Science Daily News Release, September 26, 2011, https://www.sciencedaily.com/releases/2011/09/110926165857.htm.

A team led by Professor Clinton Rubin: M. E. Chan, G. Uzer, and C. T. Rubin, "The Potential Benefits and Inherent Risks of Vibration as a Non-Drug Therapy for the Prevention and Treatment of Osteoporosis," *Current Osteoporosis Report* 11, no. 1 (March 2013), https://doi.org/10.1007/s11914-012-0132-1.

Though vibration: author email exchange with Lora V. Bleacher at NASA's Office of Communications and with Professor Rubin and Professor Chan, July 2022.

"Vibration is essentially simulating exercise": Laura Yecies, CEO of Bone Health Technologies, interview with author, July 2022.

"I jumped into": Sherrie Palm, founder and CEO of Association for Pelvic Organ Prolapse Support (APOPS) and author of four books on the topic, most recently *The Biggest Secret in Women's Health: Stigma, Indifference, Outrage, and Optimism*, interview with author, February 2023.

"vaginal vault at the top": J. L. Lowder, "Apical Vaginal Support: The Often Forgotten Piece of the Puzzle," *Modern Medicine* 114, no. 3 (May–June 2017).

Chapter 11: Final Frontier

"I still remember": Gloria Kolb, CEO and cofounder of of Elidah, interview with author, July 2022.

It is estimated: "RCOG Calling for Action to Reduce Number of Women Living with Poor Pelvic Floor Health," Royal College of Obstetricians & Gynaecologists News Release, February 2, 2023, https://www.rcog.org.uk/news/rcog-calling-for-action-to-reduce-number-of-women-living-with-poor-pelvic-floor-health.

In the United States: Linh N. Tran and Yana Puckett, "Urinary Incontinence," August 8, 2022, https://www.ncbi.nlm.nih.gov/books/NBK559095.

Only 30 percent of women: Megan B. Shannon et al., "Attendance at Prescribed Pelvic Floor Physical Therapy in a Diverse, Urban Urogynecology Population," *PM&R* 10, no. 6 (2018), https://www.sciencedirect.com/science/article/pii/S1934148217314156.

with only 13 percent of women: Susan S. Silbey, "Why Do So Many Women Who Study Engineering Leave the Field?," *Harvard Business Review,* August 23, 2016, https://hbr.org/2016/08/why-do-so-many-women-who-study-engineering-leave-the-field.

and 16.5 percent in the UK: "Statistics of women in engineering in the UK," Women's Engineering Society, March 2022, https://www.wes.org.uk/about/what-we-do/resources/statistics.

The overall number: Carla Dugas and Valori H. Slane, "Miscarriage," StatPearls, June 27, 2022, https://www.ncbi.nlm.nih.gov/books/NBK532992.

"A lot of people think": Lina Chan, the CEO and cofounder of Parla, interview with author, August 2022.

Yet only 31 percent of women: Coni Longden-Jefferson, "Results of Our Study with the Wellcome Trust," Parla, October 2, 2019, https://myparla.com/health-hub/fertility/adia-and-the-wellcome-trust-results-of-our-study.

About 85 percent of women: "Taboos Grant Programme: Parla Report, Executive Summary" submitted to Wellcome Trust, seen by the author in September 2022.

"I've had endometriosis": Noémie Elhadad, Associate Professor and Chair of the Department of Biomedical Informatics at Columbia University, interview with author, February 2023.

On average, it takes: L. R. Frankel, "A 10-Year Journey to Diagnosis with Endometriosis: An Autobiographical Case Report," *Cureus* 14, no. 1 (January 2022), https://doi.org/10.7759/cureus.21329.

In 2020, the U.S. government: "U.S. House Approves Doubling Funding for Endometriosis Research for $26 Million Annually," Endofound.org, July 31, 2020, https://www.endofound.org/u.s.-house-approves-doubling-funding-for-endometriosis-research-to-26-million-annually.

In the same year: "Estimates of Funding for Various Research, Condition, and Disease Categories," NIH, March 31, 2023, https://report.nih.gov/funding/categorical-spending#/.

Besides the $26 million: Tracey Lindeman, Bleed: Destroying Myths and Misogyny in Endometriosis Care (Toronto: ECW Press, 2023) 218.

Endometriosis has been: P. G. Signorile et al., "New Evidence of the Presence of Endometriosis in the Human Fetus," *Reproductive Biomedicine Online* 21, no. 1 (July 2010), https://doi.org/10.1016/j.rbmo.2010.04.002.

Elsewhere, studies have: Jingying Wang et al., "Detecting Postpartum Depression in Depressed People by Speech Features," paper presented at the Human Centered Computing, Cham, UK, 2018.

"There's nothing wrong": "Endometriosis—The Mystery Disease of Women | Cécile Real | TEDxBinnenhof," Tedx Talks, April 14, 2016, YouTube Video, 7:39, https://www.youtube.com/watch?v=6HeQ4iEqAUk.

"I've cofounded": Cécile Réal, CEO and cofounder of Endodiag, interview with author, March 2023.

Chapter 12: Community

"Come closer": Gloria Steinem and Dr. Ann Olivarius, panel event organized by the Trouble Club at Soho House NYC, April 15, 2022.

"You must promise": Gloria Steinem, *My Life on the Road* (London: Oneworld, 2016), dedication page.

After Black power, women's liberation: Gloria Steinem, "After Black Power, Women's Liberation," *New York Magazine,* April 7, 1969.

Such "consciousness-raising" circles: Vivian Gornick, "Chapter 20: Consciousness," in *Taking a Long Look* (London: Verso, 2022), chap. 20.

In the United States, women control: Olivia Howard, Pooneh Baghai, Lakshmi Prakash, and Jill Zucker, "Women As the Next Wave of Growth in US Wealth Management," McKinsey, July 29, 2020, https://www.mckinsey.com/industries/financial-services /our-insights/women-as-the-next-wave-of-growth-in-us-wealth-management.

Vibrators were presented: Sady Doyle, "Orgasmic Design: How Vibrators Have Become Ambitious Tech Products," *The Guardian,* January 9, 2016, https:// www.theguardian.com/world/2016/jan/09/vibrator-design-tech-product -orgasm.

"We have very diverse members": Marija Butkovic, CEO and founder of Women of Wearables, interview with author, September 2022.

"France is still": Christel Bony, president at SexTech for Good, and Delphine Moulu, cofounder at Femtech France, interview with author, December 2022.

Chapter 13: Big in Japan

Walking through: Femtech Fes organized by Fermata, Tokyo, October 14–16, 2022.

"I was working in policy": Amina Sugimoto, CEO and cofounder of Fermata Inc., interview with author, August 2022.

"I'm half British, half Japanese": Hiromi Marissa Ozaki, known as Sputniko!, interview with author, October 2022.

In 2018, it was revealed: Vanessa Romo, "Tokyo Medical School Busted for Rigging Women's Tests Admits Rejected Applicants," NPR, November 7, 2018, https:// www.npr.org/2018/11/07/665445268/tokyo-medical-school-busted-for -rigging-womens-tests-admits-rejected-applicants.

Even though Japan's health ministry: Justin McCurry, "Japan Urged to Abolish Third-Party Consent from Abortion Law," *The Guardian,* September 27, 2021, https://www.theguardian.com/world/2021/sep/27/japan-urged-to-abolish -third-party-consent-from-abortion-law.

Chapter 14: The Insidious Side

"'Hygienic,' 'clean'": "Die Höhle der Löwen," Vox, April 12, 2021, https://www .vox.de/cms/die-hoehle-der-loewen-2021-am-12-april-pitchen-sause-bierkruste -pinky-lucky-loop-und-werksta-tt-4736120.html. Translated by the author.

There's the "anti-cholera belt": "Design for Cholera Belt," National Archives, accessed January 27, 2023. https://www.nationalarchives.gov.uk/education /resources/coping-with-cholera/a-cholera-belt.

The link between poor sanitation: Julie Halls, *Inventions That Didn't Change the World* (London: Thames and Hudson, 2014), 147.

The second design: F. Parsons, "Corset with Expansible Busts," The National Archives, London (April 11, 1881), https://discovery.nationalarchives.gov.uk /details/r/C14038289.

Today, we know: Julie Halls, "Video: Inventions That Didn't Change the World: A History of Victorian Curiosities," National Archives, London, November 11, 2014. https://media.nationalarchives.gov.uk/index.php/inventions-didnt-change -world-presentation/

"Ancient feminine wisdom": "Home Electronic Vaginal Steam Seat 130% Funded in One Day," PRWeb, June 20, 2019, https://www.prweb.com/releases/leiamoon _brings_the_time_honored_tradition_of_vaginal_steaming_to_modern _women_at_home/prweb16355481.htm; "Leiamoon: Your Home Electronic Steam Seat," Kickstarter, last updated December 31, 2022, https://www .kickstarter.com/projects/leiamoonsteamseat/leiamoon-your-home-electronic -steam-seat.

Vaginal steaming gained widespread attention: Ann Robinson, "Sorry, Gwyneth Paltrow, But Steaming Your Vagina Is a Bad Idea," *The Guardian,* January 30, 2015, https://www.theguardian.com/lifeandstyle/2015/jan/30/sorry-gwyneth -paltrow-but-steaming-your-vagina-is-a-bad-idea.

It's well documented: A. Jenkins, D. Money, and K. C. O'Doherty, "Is the Vaginal Cleansing Product Industry Causing Harm to Women?," *Expert Review of Anti-Infective Therapy* 19, no. 3 (March 2021), https://doi.org/10.1080/14787210 .2020.1822166; S. E. Crann et al., "Vaginal Health and Hygiene Practices and Product Use in Canada: A National Cross-Sectional Survey," *BMC Women's Health* 18, no. 1 (March 2018), https://doi.org/10.1186/s12905-018-0543-y; B. H. Cottrell, "An Updated Review of Evidence to Discourage Douching," *MCN American Journal of Maternal/Child Nursing* 35, no. 2 (March–April 2010), https://doi.org/10.1097/NMC.0b013e3181cae9da.

For this false claim: Amy B. Wang, "Gwyneth Paltrow's Goop Touted the 'Benefits' of Putting a Jade Egg in Your Vagina. Now It Must Pay," *Washington Post,* September 5, 2018, https://www.washingtonpost.com/health/2018/09/05 /gwyneth-paltrows-goop-touted-benefits-putting-jade-egg-your-vagina-now-it -must-pay.

In a study of over 5000: J. Gunter and S. Parcak, "Vaginal Jade Eggs: Ancient Chinese Practice or Modern Marketing Myth?," *Female Pelvic Medical Reconstructive Surgery* 25, no. 1 (January–Febuary 2019), https://doi.org/10.1097/spv .0000000000000643.

While the artifact itself: Maris Fessenden, "Medieval Chastity Belts Are a Myth,"

Smithsonian Magazine, August 20, 2015, https://www.smithsonianmag.com /smart-news/medieval-chastity-belts-are-myth-180956341.

This claim can: Rachel Maines, *The Technology of Orgasm: "Hysteria," the Vibrator, and Women's Sexual Satisfaction* (Baltimore, MD: Hopkins University Press, 1999), chap. 1.

In 2018, two academics: Hallie Lieberman and Eric Schatzberg, "A Failure of Academic Quality Control: The Technology of Orgasm," *Journal of Positive Sexuality* 4, no. 2 (2018).

The decision to regulate medical devices: Catherine M. Klapperich, "From the Dalkon Shield to Britney Spears' IUD: Why Diverse Teams Need to Be Involved in Contraceptive Design," *The Brink, Pioneering Research from Boston University,* July 1, 2021, https://www.bu.edu/articles/2021/from-the -dalkon-shield-to-britney-spears-iud-why-diverse-teams-need-to-be-involved-in -contraceptive-design.

The Dalkon Shield: Robin Marantz Henig, "The Dalkon Shield Disaster: Review of 'At Any Cost; Corporate Greed, Women and the Dalkon Shield' by Morton Mintz," *Washington Post,* November 17, 1985, https://www.washingtonpost .com/archive/entertainment/books/1985/11/17/the-dalkon-shield-disaster /6c58f354-fa50–46e5–877a-10d96e1de610.

Essure was a type of: Reuters Staff, "Bayer to Pay $1.6 Billion to Resolve U.S. Claims for Essure Birth-Control Device," Reuters, August 20, 2020, https://www.reuters .com/article/us-bayer-essure-idUKKBN25G24Y.

In 2018, Bayer removed: Kirby Dick, *"The Bleeding Edge,"* Netflix, July 27, 2018.

The FDA's 510(k) process: Editorial Board, "80,000 Deaths. 2 Million Injuries. It's Time for a Reckoning on Medical Devices," *New York Times,* May 4, 2019, https://www.nytimes.com/2019/05/04/opinion/sunday/medical-devices.html.

While the FDA has the responsibility: "Can Supplements Save Your Sex Life?," Harvard Health Publishing, February 8, 2019, https://www.health.harvard.edu /staying-healthy/can-supplements-save-your-sex-life.

"Compounded bioidentical hormones": Nanette Santoro, MD, and Professor and E. Stewart Taylor Chair of Obstetrics & Gynecology at the University of Colorado, email exchange with author, February 2022.

But a 2021 study: X. Jiang et al., "Safety Assessment of Compounded Non-FDA-Approved Hormonal Therapy Versus FDA-Approved Hormonal Therapy in Treating Postmenopausal Women," *Menopause* 28, no. 8 (May 10, 2021), https://doi.org/10.1097/gme.0000000000001782.

The FDA and FTC issued: "FDA and FTC Send Warning Letters to Five Companies for Illegally Selling Dietary Supplements Claiming to Treat Infertility," U.S. Food and Drug Administration, May 26, 2021, https://www.fda.gov/food/cfsan -constituent-updates/fda-and-ftc-send-warning-letters-five-companies-illegally -selling-dietary-supplements-claiming-treat.

Joining the group: "Can Supplements Save Your Sex Life?"

In an investigation for Undark: Alison Motluk, "For a Change of Heart, Would-Be Egg Donors Face Threats and Bills," *Undark,* February 24, 2020, https://undark .org/2020/02/24/egg-donor-harrassment-threats-legal-bills.

Then there are apps: Drew Harwell, "Is Your Pregnancy App Sharing Your Intimate Data with Your Boss?," *Washington Post,* April 10, 2019, https://www.washingtonpost .com/technology/2019/04/10/tracking-your-pregnancy-an-app-may-be-more -public-than-you-think.

Misinformation about abortions: Claire Provost and Nadini Archer, "Exclusive: Trump-Linked Religious 'Extremists' Target Women with Disinformation Worldwide," openDemocracy, February 10, 2020, https://www.opendemocracy .net/en/5050/trump-linked-religious-extremists-global-disinformation -pregnant-women.

But, as an example: "Vaginal Rejuvenation Market Worth over $5bn by 2026," GMI, September 22, 2020, https://www.gminsights.com/pressrelease/vaginal -rejuvenation-market.

The global "intimate wash": "Intimate Wash Care Products Market Worth USD 6.07 Bn by 2029," GlobeNewswire, January 17, 2023, https://www.globenewswire .com/en/news-release/2023/01/17/2589849/0/en/Intimate-Wash-Care -Products-Market-Worth-USD-6–07-Bn-by-2029-Business-Environment- Analysis-Global-Industry-Analysis-and-Forecast-to-2029.html.

Chapter 15: Vigilantes

"They always skip a beat": Brad Haines and Nicole Schwartz, Internet of Dongs, interview with author, November 2022.

In 2016, We-Vibe: Alex Hern, "Vibrator Maker Ordered to Pay Out C$4m for Tracking Users' Sexual Activity," *The Guardian,* March 14, 2017, https://www .theguardian.com/technology/2017/mar/14/we-vibe-vibrator-tracking-users -sexual-habits.

Companies should provide: "Vendor Best Practices," Internet of Dongs, 2023, https://internetofdon.gs/vendor-best-practices.

In 2021, an American Catholic blog: Liam Stack, "Catholic Officials on Edge After Reports of Priests Using Grindr," *New York Times,* August 20, 2021, https://www.nytimes.com/2021/08/20/nyregion/pillar-grindr-catholic -church.html.

A study of court files: Afsaneh Rigot, "Digital Crime Scenes: The Role of Digital Evidence in the Persecution of LGBTQ People in Egypt, Lebanon, and Tunisia,"

Berkman Klein Center (March 7, 2022), https://cyber.harvard.edu/publication /2022/digital-crime-scenes.

"My patient came": Katherine T. Chen, Associate Professor and Vice Chair of Education at the ob-gyn department at the Icahn School of Medicine at Mount Sinai, interview with author, September 2022.

Her team downloaded: M. D. Soffer and K. T. Chen, "In Search of Accurate Fetal Heart Rate Monitoring Mobile Applications," *Telemed Journal of E-Health* 25, no. 9 (September 2019), https://doi.org/10.1089/tmj.2018.0104.

In a second study: G. Frid, K. Bogaert, and K. T. Chen, "Mobile Health Apps for Pregnant Women: Systematic Search, Evaluation, and Analysis of Features," *Journal of Medical Internet Research* 23, no. 10 (October 18, 2021), https:// doi.org/10.2196/25667.

In a third study: K. Chyjek, S. Farag, and K. T. Chen, "Rating Pregnancy Wheel Applications Using the APPLICATIONS Scoring System," *Obstetrics & Gynecology* 125, no. 6 (June 2015), https://doi.org/10.1097/aog .0000000000000842.

In another study: M. L. Moglia et al., "Evaluation of Smartphone Menstrual Cycle Tracking Applications Using an Adapted APPLICATIONS Scoring System," *Obstetrics & Gynecology* 127, no. 6 (June 2016), https://doi.org/10.1097/aog .0000000000001444.

They have ranked: N. T. Sudol et al., "In Search of Mobile Applications for Patients with Pelvic Floor Disorders," *Female Pelvic Medicine & Reconstructive Surgery* 25, no. 3 (May–June 2019), https://doi.org/10.1097/spv.0000000000000527.

"I usually say": Amanda Hearn, Founder of Put A Cup In It (PACII), interview with author, October 2022.

It is estimated: "Why Are Period Products an Environmental Concern?," City to Sea, February 25, 2020, https://www.citytosea.org.uk/campaign/plastic-free -periods/periods-and-the-environment.

As tampons, they carry: M. A. Mitchell et al., "A Confirmed Case of Toxic Shock Syndrome Associated with the Use of a Menstrual Cup," *Canadian Journal of Infectious Disease and Medical Microbiology* 26, no. 4 (July–August 2015), https://doi.org/10.1155/2015/560959.

"Try and avoid": Alexandra Scranton, Director of Science and Research at Women's Voices for the Earth, interview with author, June 2023.

Nanosilver, for example: "Nanosilver in Period Care Products Fact Sheet," Women's Voices for the Earth, April 2019, https://womensvoices.org/nanosilver-in -period-care-products.

Therefore high levels: "Do Your Tampons Contain PFAS 'Forever Chemicals?' They Might.—Report," Mamavation, October 26, 2022, https://www.mamavation .com/beauty/pfas-tampons.html.

For an in-depth analysis: "What's in Your Period Product? An Investigation of Ingredients Disclosed on Product Labels," Women's Voices for the Earth (May 2022), https://womensvoices.org/report-whats-in-your-period-product.

Depending on the chemical: David E. Tourgeman et al., "Serum and Tissue Hormone Levels of Vaginally and Orally Administered Estradiol," *American Journal of Obstetrics and Gynecology* 180, no. 6 (1999), https://www.sciencedirect.com/science/article/pii/S0002937899700426.

As an early customer: The Lowdown Live event, London, September 29, 2022.

"It took me a couple of years": Alice Pelton, CEO and cofounder of The Lowdown, interview with author, November 2022.

But how pronounced is this shift: Lowdown Recommender responses, shared with author in November 2022.

Chapter 16: Impressions

"We call it the Guccigator": Cindy Gallop, CEO and founder of MakeLoveNotPorn, interview with author, April 2022.

"I adore being single": Emma Page, "Cindy Gallop: 'I Cannot Wait to Die Alone,'" *Stuff,* April 11, 2021, https://www.stuff.co.nz/life-style/love-sex/300266587/cindy-gallop-i-cannot-wait-to-die-alone.

Instead of asking for advice: Tomas Chamorro-Premuzic and Cindy Gallop, "7 Pieces of Bad Career Advice Women Should Ignore," *Harvard Business Review,* April 15, 2021, https://hbr.org/2021/04/7-pieces-of-bad-career-advice-women-should-ignore.

"On the New York subway": Amanda Duberman, "Here Are the Images Deemed Too Sexual for the New York City Subway," *Huffington Post,* May 17, 2018, https://www.huffpost.com/entry/new-york-subway-unbound-ad-campaign_n_5afda776e4b0a59b4e019cca.

"There is an obvious double standard": Lora DiCarlo, "Open Letter from Lora DiCarlo: Our Sex Toy Won a CES Robotics Innovation Award Then They Took It Back," News Release, January 8, 2018, https://www.prnewswire.com/news-releases/open-letter-from-lora-dicarlo-our-sex-toy-won-a-ces-robotics-innovation-award-then-they-took-it-back-300774435.html.

A media outcry followed: Valeriya Safronova, "What's So 'Indecent' About Female Pleasure?," *New York Times,* January 18, 2018, https://www.nytimes.com/2019/01/18/style/sex-toy-ces.html.

The scandal brought attention: Lora Haddock DiCarlo, CEO and founder of Lora DiCarlo, interview with author, September 2021.

"I thought the venture capital model": Jackie Rotman, founder and CEO of Center for Intimacy Justice (CIJ), interview with author, June 2023.

In their first report: Jackie Rotman, *Facebook's Censorship of Health Ads for Women and People of Diverse Genders*, Center for Intimacy Justice, accessed April 27, 2023, https://www.intimacyjustice.org/report.

The report was picked up: Valeriya Safronova, "Why Did Facebook Reject These Ads?," *New York Times*, January 11, 2022, https://www.nytimes.com/2022/01/11/style/facebook-womens-sexual-health-advertising.html.

It now states: "Adult Products or Services—Ad Policy," *Meta*, accessed June 14, 2023, https://transparency.fb.com/en-gb/policies/ad-standards/content-specific-restrictions/adult-products-or-services.

"We have come an extraordinary way": Rachel Braun Scherl, cofounder and managing partner at Spark Solutions for Growth, interview with author, March 2023.

Serena Williams, the tennis star: Serena Williams, "How Serena Williams Saved Her Own Life," *ELLE*, April 5, 2022, https://www.elle.com/life-love/a39586444/how-serena-williams-saved-her-own-life.

BIBLIOGRAPHY

"80,000 Deaths. 2 Million Injuries. It's Time for a Reckoning on Medical Devices."
    New York Times. May 4, 2019. https://www.nytimes.com/2019/05/04
    /opinion/sunday/medical-devices.html.

"Abortion in Nigeria Fact Sheet." Guttmacher Institute, October 2015, https://www
    .guttmacher.org/fact-sheet/abortion-nigeria.

"Adult Products or Services—Ad Policy." *Meta*. Accessed 2023. https://transparency
    .fb.com/en-gb/policies/ad-standards/content-specific-restrictions/adult
    -products-or-services.

American College of Obsteticians and Gynecologists, and American Urogynecologic
    Society. "Pelvic Organ Prolapse." *Urogynecology* 25, no. 6 (2019): 397–408.
    https://journals.lww.com/fpmrs/fulltext/2019/11000/pelvic_organ_prolapse
    .1.aspx.

Aquino, C. I., M. Guida, G. Saccone, Y. Cruz, A. Vitagliano, F. Zullo, and V. Berghella.
    "Perineal Massage During Labor: A Systematic Review and Meta-Analysis of
    Randomized Controlled Trials." *Journal of Maternal-Fetal & Neonatal Medicine*
    33, no. 6 (March 2020): 1051–63. https://doi.org/10.1080/14767058.2018
    .1512574.

Arnegard, M. E., L. A. Whitten, C. Hunter, and J. A. Clayton. "Sex as a Biological
    Variable: A 5-Year Progress Report and Call to Action." *Journal of Women's
    Health* 29, no. 6 (Jun 2020): 858–64. https://doi.org/10.1089/jwh.2019
    .8247.

"ASA Ruling on Naturalcycles Nordic Ab Sweden t/a Natural Cycles." Advertising
    Standards Authority, August 29, 2018, https://www.asa.org.uk/rulings
    /naturalcycles-nordic-ab-sweden-a17-393896.html.

Aston, Jennifer, and Catherine Bishop, eds. *Female Entrepreneurs in the Long Nineteenth Century: A Global Perspective. Palgrave Studies in Economic History.* Cham, UK: Palgrave Macmillan, 2020.

Baird, Matthew D., Melanie A. Zaber, Annie Chen, Andrew W. Dick, Chloe E. Bird, Molly Waymouth, Grace Gahlon, et al. "The Wham Report: The Case to Fund Women's Health Research," Rand Corporation (2021), https://thewhamreport .org/report.

Banco, D., J. Chang, N. Talmor, P. Wadhera, A. Mukhopadhyay, X. Lu, S. Dong, et al. "Sex and Race Differences in the Evaluation and Treatment of Young Adults Presenting to the Emergency Department with Chest Pain," *Journal of the American Heart Association* 11, no. 10 (May 17, 2022): E024199, https://doi .org/10.1161/jaha.121.024199.

Barreto, Brittany, PhD; Jessica Karr; Mia Farnham; Su Wern Khor; Mariana Keymolen; Sangeetha Ranadeeve; Kala Pham; Brianna Cochran; Alley Lyles; and Julie Hakim, MD. "Femtech Landscape 2021 Annual Report." Femtech Focus; Femhealth Insights (2021), https://femtechfocus.org/wp-content/uploads /2021/09/femtech-landscape-2021_v3.pdf.

"Bayer to Pay $1.6 Billion to Resolve U.S. Claims for Essure Birth-Control Device." Reuters. August 20, 2020, https://www.reuters.com/article/us-bayer-essure -idukkbn25g24y.

Behre, H. M., M. Zitzmann, R. A. Anderson, D. J. Handelsman, S. W. Lestari, R. I. McLachlan, M. C. Meriggiola, et al. "Efficacy and Safety of an Injectable Combination Hormonal Contraceptive for Men," *Journal of Clinical Endocrinology & Metabolism* 101, no. 12 (December 2016): 4779–88, https:// doi.org/10.1210/jc.2016–2141.

"Benefits and Risks—Hormone Replacement Therapy (HRT)." National Health Service UK, September 9, 2019, https://www.nhs.uk/conditions/hormone -replacement-therapy-hrt/risks.

Berglund Scherwitzl, E., O. Lundberg, H. Kopp Kallner, K. Gemzell Danielsson, J. Trussell, and R. Scherwitzl. "Perfect-Use and Typical-Use Pearl Index of a Contraceptive Mobile App," *Contraception* 96, no. 6 (December 2017): 420–25, https://doi.org/10.1016/j.contraception.2017.08.014.

Bohlen, J. G., J. P. Held, M. O. Sanderson, and A. Ahlgren. "The Female Orgasm: Pelvic Contractions." *Archives of Sexual Behavior* 11, no. 5 (October 1982): 367–86, https://doi.org/10.1007/bf01541570.

Boston Women's Health Book Collective and Judy Norsigian. *Our Bodies, Ourselves.* New York, NY: Simon & Schuster, 1973.

Boyle, Matthew, and Jeff Green. "Work Shift: Women CEOs (Finally) Outnumber Those Named John," 2023, https://www.bloomberg.com/news/newsletters/2023 -04-25/women-ceos-at-big-companies-finally-outnumber-those-named-john.

Braudel, Fernand. *Perspective of the World: Civilization and Capitalism, 15th–18th Century.* Vol. 3: University of California Press, 1992.

Brodwin, Erin. "End of the Line for Femtec Health." *Axios,* May 23, 2023, https://www.axios.com/2023/05/23/femtec-health-winds-down.

———. "Femtec's Missteps: Missed Payments and Unhappy Customers." *Axios,* October 6, 2022, https://www.axios.com/pro/health-tech-deals/2022/10/06/femtec-health-struggles-layoffs-debt-acquisitions.

Broer, S. L., M. J. C. Eijkemans, G. J. Scheffer, I. A. J. Van Rooij, A. De Vet, A. P. N. Themmen, J. S. E. Laven, et al. "Anti-Müllerian Hormone Predicts Menopause: A Long-Term Follow-Up Study in Normoovulatory Women." *The Journal of Clinical Endocrinology & Metabolism* 96, no. 8 (2011): 2532–39, https://doi.org/10.1210/jc.2010-2776.

Bull, Jonathan R., Simon P. Rowland, Elina Berglund Scherwitzl, Raoul Scherwitzl, Kristina Gemzell Danielsson, and Joyce Harper. "Real-World Menstrual Cycle Characteristics of More Than 600,000 Menstrual Cycles." *npj Digital Medicine* 2, no. 1 (2019): 83, https://doi.org/10.1038/s41746-019-0152-7.

Byerley, Brittany M., and David M. Haas. "A Systematic Overview of the Literature Regarding Group Prenatal Care for High-Risk Pregnant Women." *BMC Pregnancy and Childbirth* 17, no. 1 (2017): 329, https://doi.org/10.1186/s12884-017-1522-2.

Cagnacci, A., and M. Venier. "The Controversial History of Hormone Replacement Therapy." *Medicina (Kaunas)* 55, no. 9 (September 18, 2019), https://doi.org/10.3390/Medicina55090602.

Callaghan, William M. "Overview of Maternal Mortality in the United States." *Seminars in Perinatology* 36, no. 1 (2012): 2–6, https://www.sciencedirect.com/science/article/pii/s0146000511001480.

"Can Supplements Save Your Sex Life?" Harvard Health Publishing. February 8, 2019, https://www.health.harvard.edu/staying-healthy/can-supplements-save-your-sex-life.

Cascante, S. D., J. K. Blakemore, S. Devore, B. Hodes-Wertz, M. E. Fino, A. S. Berkeley, C. M. Parra, C. McCaffrey, and J. A. Grifo. "Fifteen Years of Autologous Oocyte Thaw Outcomes from a Large University-Based Fertility Center." *Fertility Sterility* 118, no. 1 (July 2022): 158–66, https://doi.org/10.1016/j.fertnstert.2022.04.013.

Cassion, Christopher, Yuhang Qian, Constant Bossou, and Margareta Ackerman. "Investors Embrace Gender Diversity, Not Female CEOs: The Role of Gender in Startup Fundraising." *Intelligent Technologies for Interactive Entertainment* (2021): 145–64, https://doi.org/https://doi.org/10.1007/978-3-030-76426-5_10.

"Chamberlen-Type Obstetrical Forceps, Europe, 1680–1750." Science Museum, London, UK, https://wellcomecollection.org/works/zvcs8x7b.

Chan, M. E., G. Uzer, and C. T. Rubin. "The Potential Benefits and Inherent Risks of Vibration as a Non-Drug Therapy for the Prevention and Treatment of Osteoporosis." *Current Osteoporosis Reports* 11, no. 1 (March 2013): 36–44, https://doi.org/10.1007/s11914-012-0132-1.

Chen, E. H., F. S. Shofer, A. J. Dean, J. E. Hollander, W. G. Baxt, J. L. Robey, K. L. Sease, and A. M. Mills. "Gender Disparity in Analgesic Treatment of Emergency Department Patients with Acute Abdominal Pain." *Academic Emergency Medicine* 15, no. 5 (May 2008): 414–8, https://doi.org/10.1111/j.1553-2712 .2008.00100.x.

Christ, Jacob P., and Marcelle I. Cedars. "Current Guidelines for Diagnosing PCOS." *Diagnostics* 13, no. 6 (2023). https://doi.org/10.3390/diagnostics13061113.

Chyjek, K., S. Farag, and K. T. Chen. "Rating Pregnancy Wheel Applications Using the Applications Scoring System." *Obstetrics & Gynecology* 125, no. 6 (June 2015): 1478–83, https://doi.org/10.1097/aog.0000000000000842.

Colenso-Semple, L. M., A. C. D'souza, K. J. Elliott-Sale, and S. M. Phillips. "Current Evidence Shows No Influence of Women's Menstrual Cycle Phase on Acute Strength Performance or Adaptations to Resistance Exercise Training." *Frontiers in Sports and Active Living* 5 (2023): 1054542, https://doi.org/10.3389/fspor .2023.1054542.

Composto, J., E. S. Leichman, K. Luedtke, and J. A. Mindell. "Thermal Comfort Intervention for Hot-Flash-Related Insomnia Symptoms in Perimenopausal and Postmenopausal-Aged Women: An Exploratory Study." *Behavioral Sleep Medicine* 19, no. 1 (January–February 2021): 38–47, https://doi.org/10.1080 /15402002.2019.1699100.

Copp, T., B. Nickel, S. Lensen, K. Hammarberg, D. Lieberman, J. Doust, B. W. Mol, and K. McCaffery. "Anti-Mullerian Hormone (Amh) Test Information on Australian and New Zealand Fertility Clinic Websites: A Content Analysis." *BMJ Open* 11, no. 7 (July 7 2021): E046927, https://doi.org/10.1136/bmjopen -2020-046927.

Costagliola, Alessandra. "Labor Participation and Gender Inequalities in India: Traditional Gender Norms in India and the Decline in the Labor Force Participation Rate (LFPR)." *The Indian Journal of Labor Economics* 64, no. 3 (2021): 531–42, https://doi.org/10.1007/s41027-021-00329-7.

Cottrell, B. H. "An Updated Review of Evidence to Discourage Douching." *MCN, The American Journal of Maternal-Child Nursing* 35, no. 2 (March–April 2010): 102–7; Quiz 08–9, https://doi.org/10.1097/nmc.0b013e3181cae9da.

Crann, S. E., S. Cunningham, A. Albert, D. M. Money, and K. C. O'Doherty. "Vaginal Health and Hygiene Practices and Product Use in Canada: A National Cross-Sectional Survey." *BMC Women's Health* 18, no. 1 (March 23, 2018): 52, https:// doi.org/10.1186/s12905-018-0543-y.

Criado-Perez, Caroline. *Invisible Women: Data Bias in a World Designed for Men.* London: Chatto & Windus, 2019.

Das, Shanti. "NHS Data Breach: Trusts Shared Patient Details with Facebook Without Consent." *The Guardian*, May 27, 2023, https://www.theguardian.com /society/2023/may/27/nhs-data-breach-trusts-shared-patient-details-with -facebook-meta-without-consent.

"Design for Cholera Belt." National Archives. Accessed January 27, 2023. https:// www.nationalarchives.gov.uk/education/resources/coping-with-cholera/a -cholera-belt/.

Dicarlo, Lora. "Open Letter from Lora Dicarlo: Our Sex Toy Won a CES Robotics Innovation Award Then They Took It Back." PR News News Release, January 8, 2018, https://www.prnewswire.com/news-releases/open-letter-from-lora -dicarlo-our-sex-toy-won-a-ces-robotics-innovation-award-then-they-took-it -back-300774435.html.

Dick, Kirby. *The Bleeding Edge* Netflix, July 27, 2018.

"Die Höhle Der Löwen." Vox, April 12, 2021, https://www.vox.de/cms/die-hoehle -der-loewen-2021-am-12-april-pitchen-sause-bierkruste-pinky-lucky-loop-und -werksta-tt-4736120.html.

"The Discovery and Development of Penicillin 1928–1945." American Chemical Society, 1999, https://www.acs.org/education/whatischemistry/landmarks /flemingpenicillin.html.

Doyle, Sady. "Orgasmic Design: How Vibrators Have Become Ambitious Tech Products." *The Guardian*, January 9, 2016. https://www.theguardian.com /world/2016/jan/09/vibrator-design-tech-product-orgasm.

"Drug Safety: Most Drugs Withdrawn in Recent Years Had Greater Health Risks for Women." U.S. Government Accountability Office (2001), https://www.gao.gov /products/gao-01-286r.

Duane, M., J. B. Stanford, C. A. Porucznik, and P. Vigil. "Fertility Awareness-Based Methods for Women's Health and Family Planning." *Frontiers in Medicine* 9 (2022): 858977, https://doi.org/10.3389/fmed.2022.858977.

Duberman, Amanda. "Here Are the Images Deemed Too Sexual for the New York City Subway." *Huffington Post*, May 17, 2018, https:// www.huffpost.com/entry/new-york-subway-unbound-ad-campaign_n _5afda776e4b0a59b4e019cca.

Dugas, Carla, and Valori H. Slane. "Miscarriage." StatPearls, June 27, 2022, https:// www.ncbi.nlm.nih.gov/books/nbk532992/.

"Early and Premature Menopause." National Health Service Scotland, March 22, 2023, https://www.nhsinform.scot/healthy-living/womens-health/later- years-around-50-years-and-over/menopause-and-post-menopause-health/ early-and-premature-menopause.

Edelman Trust Barometer, Global Report (2023). Accessed January 15, 2023. https://www.edelman.com/trust/2023/trust-barometer.

Emmons, William M., III. "Tambrands, Inc.: The Femtech Soviet Joint Venture (A)." Harvard Business School Case 390–159 (August 1991, revised March 1993).

"Endometriosis—The Mystery Disease of Women | Cécile Real | Tedxbinnenhof." Tedx Talks. April 14, 2016. Youtube Video, 7:39 https://www.youtube.com /watch?v=6HeQ4iEqAUk&t=64s.

Ervin, Jennifer, Yamna Taouk, Ludmila Fleitas Alfonzo, Belinda Hewitt, and Tania King. "Gender Differences in the Association Between Unpaid Labor and Mental Health in Employed Adults: A Systematic Review." *The Lancet Public Health* 7, no. 9 (2022): E775–E86, https://doi.org/10.1016/s2468-2667(22)00160-8.

Eveleth, Rose. "Why No One Can Design a Better Speculum." *The Atlantic*, 17 November 2014, https://www.theatlantic.com/health/archive/2014/11/why -no-one-can-design-a-better-speculum/382534/.

Ewens, Michael, and Richard R. Townsend. "Are Early Stage Investors Biased Against Women?" *Journal of Financial Economics* 135, no. 3 (2020): 653–77, https:// www.sciencedirect.com/science/article/pii/s0304405x19301758.

"Exclusive Breastfeeding for Six Months Best for Babies Everywhere." World Health Organization, January 15, 2011, https://www.who.int/news/item/15-01-2011 -exclusive-breastfeeding-for-six-months-best-for-babies-everywhere.

"Fact Sheet: Can I Freeze My Eggs to Use Later If I'm Not Sick?" The American Society for Reproductive Medicine (ASRM), 2014, https://www.reproductivefacts .org/globalassets/rf/news-and-publications/bookletsfact-sheets/english-fact -sheets-and-info-booklets/can_i_freeze_my_eggs_to_use_later_if_im_not _sick_factsheet.pdf.

Fadeyibi, O., M. Alade, S. Adebayo, T. Erinfolami, F. Mustapha, and S. Yaradua. "Household Structure and Contraceptive Use in Nigeria." *Frontiers in Global Women's Health* 3 (2022): 821178, https://doi.org/10.3389/fgwh.2022 .821178.

Farr, Christina. "Breast Pump Start-Up Naya Health Shuts Down After Failing to Raise Money." CNBC, January 3, 2019, https://www.cnbc.com/2019/01/03 /naya-health-the-breast-pump-company-that-went-dark-has-officially-shut -down.html.

"FDA and FTC Send Warning Letters to Five Companies for Illegally Selling Dietary Supplements Claiming to Treat Infertility." U.S. Food and Drug Administration. May 26, 2021. https://www.fda.gov/food/cfsan-constituent-updates/fda-and -ftc-send-warning-letters-five-companies-illegally-selling-dietary-supplements -claiming-treat.

Ferla, Ruth La. "Why Fertility Clinics Are Throwing 'Egg Freezing' Parties with Champagne and Canapés." *Independent*, September 10, 2018, https://www

.independent.co.uk/life-style/health-and-families/egg-freezing-party-women
-fertility-preservation-millennial-a8520996.html.

Fessenden, Maris. "Medieval Chastity Belts Are a Myth." *Smithsonian Magazine,*
August 20, 2015, https://www.smithsonianmag.com/smart-news/medieval
-chastity-belts-are-myth-180956341.

Fitzpatrick, J. L., C. Willis, A. Devigili, A. Young, M. Carroll, H. R. Hunter, and
D. R. Brison. "Chemical Signals from Eggs Facilitate Cryptic Female Choice in
Humans." *Proceedings of the Royal Society B, Biological Sciences* 287, no. 1928
(June 10, 2020): 20200805, https://doi.org/10.1098/rspb.2020.0805.

Frankel, L. R. "A 10-Year Journey to Diagnosis with Endometriosis: An
Autobiographical Case Report." *Cureus* 14, no. 1 (January 2022): E21329,
https://doi.org/10.7759/cureus.21329.

Frederick, D. A., H. K. S. John, J. R. Garcia, and E. A. Lloyd. "Differences in Orgasm
Frequency Among Gay, Lesbian, Bisexual, and Heterosexual Men and Women in
a U.S. National Sample." *Archives of Sexual Behavior* 47, no. 1 (January 2018):
273–88, https://doi.org/10.1007/s10508-017-0939-z.

Frederiksen, Brittni, Usha Ranji, Alina Salganicoff, and Michelle Long, "Women's
Sexual and Reproductive Health Services: Key Findings from the 2020
KFF Women's Health Survey." Kaiser Family Foundation, April 21, 2021,
https://www.kff.org/womens-health-policy/issue-brief/womens-sexual-and
-reproductive-health-services-key-findings-from-the-2020-kff-womens-health
-survey/.

Freeman, E. W., M. D. Sammel, J. A. Grisso, M. Battistini, B. Garcia-Espagna, and L.
Hollander. "Hot Flashes in the Late Reproductive Years: Risk Factors for African
American and Caucasian Women." *Journal of Women's Health and Gender-
Based Medicine* 10, no. 1 (January–February 2001): 67–76, https://doi.org/10
.1089/152460901750067133.

Freud, Sigmund. *Three Essays on the Theory of Sexuality.* Translated by James
Strachey. New York: Basic Books, 1962.

Frid, G., K. Bogaert, and K. T. Chen. "Mobile Health Apps for Pregnant Women:
Systematic Search, Evaluation, and Analysis of Features" *Journal of Medical
Internet Research* 23, no. 10 (October 18, 2021): E25667, https://doi.org/10.2196
/25667.

Friedan, Betty. *The Feminine Mystique.* New York: Norton, 1963.

Gallop, Cindy. "What Is Sextech and Why Is Everyone Ignoring It?" HotTopics, 2014,
https://hottopics.ht/14192/what-is-sextech-and-why-is-everyone-ignoring-it.

Gallop, Cindy, and Tomas Chamorro-Premuzic. "7 Pieces of Bad Career Advice
Women Should Ignore." *Harvard Business Review,* April 15, 2021, https://hbr
.org/2021/04/7-pieces-of-bad-career-advice-women-should-ignore.

Garaizar, Juliana. *The Rising Tide: A "Learning-By-Investing" Initiative to Bridge the Gender Gap.* Kauffman Fellows (2016), https://www.kauffmanfellows.org/wp-content/uploads/kfr_vol7/juliana_garaizar_vol7.pdf.

Gebhart, Gennie, and Daly Barnett. "Should You Really Delete Your Period Tracking App?" Electronic Frontiers Foundation, June 30, 2022, https://www.eff.org/deeplinks/2022/06/should-you-really-delete-your-period-tracking-app.

Geller, S. E., A. R. Koch, P. Roesch, A. Filut, E. Hallgren, and M. Carnes. "The More Things Change, the More They Stay the Same: A Study to Evaluate Compliance with Inclusion and Assessment of Women and Minorities in Randomized Controlled Trials." *Academic Medicine* 93, no. 4 (April 2018): 630–35, https://doi.org/10.1097/acm.0000000000002027.

"General Considerations for the Clinical Evaluation of Drugs." U.S. Department of Health and Human Services, Food and Drug Administration, Center for Drug Evaluation and Research (1977), https://www.fda.gov/media/71495/download.

"General Facts: What Women Need to Know." Bone Health & Osteoporosis Foundation, https://www.bonehealthandosteoporosis.org/preventing-fractures/general-facts/what-women-need-to-know.

Gerner, Marina. "We Need to Talk About Investors' Problem with Vaginas." *Wired*, 2020, https://www.wired.co.uk/article/vagina-pitches-vcs-sexism.

Glasier, A. F., R. Anakwe, D. Everington, C. W. Martin, Z. Van Der Spuy, L. Cheng, P. C. Ho, and R. A. Anderson. "Would Women Trust Their Partners to Use a Male Pill?" *Human Reproduction* 15, no. 3 (March 2000): 646–9, https://doi.org/10.1093/humrep/15.3.646.

"Global Gender Gap Report 2021." World Economic Forum (March 2021), http://www3.weforum.org/docs/wef_gggr_2021.pdf.

Goldberg, Jeffrey M., Edward Mascha, Tommaso Falcone, and Marjan Attaran. "Comparison of Intrauterine and Intracervical Insemination with Frozen Donor Sperm: A Meta-Analysis." *Fertility and Sterility* 72, no. 5 (1999): 792–95, https://www.sciencedirect.com/science/article/pii/s001502829900374x.

Goldman, R. H., C. Racowsky, L. V. Farland, S. Munné, L. Ribustello, and J. H. Fox. "Predicting the Likelihood of Live Birth for Elective Oocyte Cryopreservation: A Counseling Tool for Physicians and Patients." *Human Reproduction* 32, no. 4 (April 1, 2017): 853–59, https://doi.org/10.1093/humrep/dex008.

Gompers, Paul A., Will Gornall, Steven N. Kaplan, and Ilya A. Strebulaev. "How Do Venture Capitalists Make Decisions?" *Journal of Financial Economics* 135, no. 1 (2020): 169–90, https://www.sciencedirect.com/science/article/pii/s0304405x19301680.

Gornick, Vivian. "Chapter 20: Consciousness." Chap. 20 in *Taking a Long Look*. London: Verso, 2022.

Greenwood, B. N., S. Carnahan, and L. Huang. "Patient-Physician Gender

Concordance and Increased Mortality Among Female Heart Attack Patients." *Proceedings of the National Academy of Sciences of the United States of America* 115, no. 34 (August 21, 2018): 8569–74, https://doi.org/10.1073/pnas.1800097115.

Griffin, R. Morgan. "Nonstress Test (NST)." WebMD, August 9, 2022, https://www.webmd.com/baby/nonstress-test-nst.

Gunter, J., and S. Parcak. "Vaginal Jade Eggs: Ancient Chinese Practice or Modern Marketing Myth?" *Female Pelvic Medical Reconstructive Surgery* 25, no. 1 (January–February 2019): 1–2, https://doi.org/10.1097/spv.0000000000000643.

Gürtin, Zeynep B., and Emily Tiemann. "The Marketing of Elective Egg Freezing: A Content, Cost and Quality Analysis of UK Fertility Clinic Websites." *Reproductive Biomedicine & Society Online* 12 (2021): 56–68, https://www.sciencedirect.com/science/article/pii/s2405661820300289.

Halls, Julie. *Inventions That Didn't Change the World.* London: Thames and Hudson, 2014.

———. "Video: Inventions That Didn't Change the World: A History of Victorian Curiosities." National Archives, London, November 11, 2014.

Handa, V. L., J. L. Blomquist, L. R. Knoepp, K. A. Hoskey, K. C. McDermott, and A. Muñoz. "Pelvic Floor Disorders 5–10 Years After Vaginal or Cesarean Childbirth." *Obstetrics & Gynecology* 118, no. 4 (October 2011): 777–84, https://doi.org/10.1097/aog.0b013e3182267f2f.

Harker, Laura. "Efforts Advance to Put More Health Care Providers in Reach of Georgians." Georgia Budget & Policy Institute, May 8, 2019, https://gbpi.org/georgias-ongoing-efforts-to-improve-health-provider-capacity/.

Harwell, Drew. "Is Your Pregnancy App Sharing Your Intimate Data with Your Boss?" *Washington Post*, April 10, 2019, https://www.washingtonpost.com/technology/2019/04/10/tracking-your-pregnancy-an-app-may-be-more-public-than-you-think/.

Heinemann, K., F. Saad, M. Wiesemes, S. White, and L. Heinemann. "Attitudes Toward Male Fertility Control: Results of a Multinational Survey on Four Continents." *Human Reproduction* 20, no. 2 (February 2005): 549–56, https://doi.org/10.1093/humrep/deh574.

Henig, Robin Marantz. "The Dalkon Shield Disaster: Review of 'At Any Cost; Corporate Greed, Women and the Dalkon Shield', By Morton Mintz." *Washington Post*, November 17, 1985, https://www.washingtonpost.com/archive/entertainment/books/1985/11/17/the-dalkon-shield-disaster/6c58f354-fa50-46e5-877a-10d96e1de610/.

Hern, Alex. "Vibrator Maker Ordered to Pay Out C$4m for Tracking Users' Sexual Activity." *The Guardian*, March 14, 2017, https://www.theguardian.com/technology/2017/mar/14/we-vibe-vibrator-tracking-users-sexual-habits.

Hill, Latoya, Samantha Artiga, and Usha Ranji. "Racial Disparities in Maternal and Infant Health: Current Status and Efforts to Address Them." Kaiser Family Foundation (2022), https://www.kff.org/racial-equity-and-health-policy /issue-brief/racial-disparities-in-maternal-and-infant-health-current-status-and -efforts-to-address-them.

Hill, Sarah E. *How The Pill Changes Everything: Your Brain on Birth Control.* London: Orion, 2019.

Hinchliffe, Emma. "Menopause Is a $600 Billion Opportunity, Report Finds." *Fortune,* October 26, 2020, https://fortune.com/2020/10/26/menopause -startups-female-founders-fund-report/.

Holt-Lunstad, J., T. B. Smith, and J. B. Layton. "Social Relationships and Mortality Risk: A Meta-Analytic Review." *PLOS Medicine* 7, no. 7 (July 27, 2010): E1000316, https://doi.org/10.1371/journal.pmed.1000316.

"How Effective Is Contraception at Preventing Pregnancy?" National Health Service UK, April 17, 2020, https://www.nhs.uk/conditions/contraception/how -effective-contraception/.

Howard, Jacqueline. "36% of US Counties Are 'Maternity Care Deserts,' Raising Risks for Women and Babies, New Report Finds." CNN, October 11, 2022, https://edition.cnn.com/2022/10/11/health/maternity-care-deserts-march-of -dimes-report/index.html.

Huang, J., Y. Zang, L. H. Ren, F. J. Li, and H. Lu. "A Review and Comparison of Common Maternal Positions During the Second Stage of Labor." *International Journal of Nursing Sciences* 6, no. 4 (October 10, 2019): 460–67, https://doi .org/10.1016/j.ijnss.2019.06.007.

Inhorn, M. C., D. Birenbaum-Carmeli, L. M. Westphal, J. Doyle, N. Gleicher, D. Meirow, M. Dirnfeld, et al. "Ten Pathways to Elective Egg Freezing: A Binational Analysis." *Journal of Assisted Reproduction and Genetics* 35, no. 11 (November 2018): 2003–11, https://doi.org/10.1007/s10815-018-1277-3.

"Investing in Sexual and Reproductive Health in Low- and Middle-Income Countries Factsheet." Guttmacher Institute (July 2020), https://www.guttmacher.org /fact-sheet/investing-sexual-and-reproductive-health-low-and-middle-income -countries.

"It Takes an Average of 7.5 Years to Get a Diagnosis of Endometriosis—It Shouldn't." Endometriosis UK. Accessed August 24, 2022. https://www.endometriosis-uk .org/it-takes-average-75-years-get-diagnosis-endometriosis-it-shouldnt.

Jaramillo, Estrella. "This Founder Bootstrapped to $10m, Now Raises Series A to Disrupt Period Apparel." *Forbes,* July 29, 2019, https://www.forbes.com /sites/estrellajaramillo/2019/07/29/founder-bootstrapped-to-10-m-now -raises-series-a-to-disrupt-period-apparel/.

Jenkins, A., D. Money, and K. C. O'Doherty "Is the Vaginal Cleansing Product

Industry Causing Harm to Women?" *Expert Review of Anti-Infective Therapy* 19, no. 3 (March 2021): 267–69, https://doi.org/10.1080/14787210.2020 .1822166.

Jennings, Victoria, Liya T. Haile, Rebecca G. Simmons, Jeff Spieler, and Dominick Shattuck. "Perfect- and Typical-Use Effectiveness of the Dot Fertility App over 13 Cycles: Results from a Prospective Contraceptive Effectiveness Trial." *The European Journal of Contraception & Reproductive Health Care* 24, no. 2 (2019): 148–53, https://doi.org/10.1080/13625187.2019.1581164.

Jiang, X., A. Bossert, K. N. Parthasarathy, K. Leaman, S. S. Minassian, P. F. Schnatz, and M. B. Woodland. "Safety Assessment of Compounded Non-FDA-Approved Hormonal Therapy Versus FDA-Approved Hormonal Therapy in Treating Postmenopausal Women." *Menopause* 28, no. 8 (May 10, 2021): 867–74, https://doi.org/10.1097/gme.0000000000001782.

Jillian Levovitz, Elizabeth Gordon, Carley Prentice, Brittany Barreto, and Yedidiah Teitelbaum. "2022 Femtech Landscape." Femhealth Insights (March 2023), https://mailchi.mp/femhealthinsights/2022-landscape-report.

Johnson, Sarah, Lorrae Marriott, and Michael Zinaman. "Can Apps and Calendar Methods Predict Ovulation with Accuracy?" *Current Medical Research and Opinion* 34, no. 9 (September 2018): 1587–94, https://www.ncbi.nlm.nih.gov /pubmed/29749274.

Johnston-Robledo, Ingrid, Kristin Sheffield, Jacqueline Voigt, and Jennifer Wilcox-Constantine. "Reproductive Shame: Self-Objectification and Young Women's Attitudes Toward Their Reproductive Functioning." *Women & Health* 46, no. 1 (2007): 25–39, https://doi.org/10.1300/j013v46n01_03.

Jones, Rachel K. "Beyond Birth Control: The Overlooked Benefits of Oral Contraceptive Pills." Guttmacher Institute: New York, 2011.

"Kaiser Permanente: Women Who Break a Hip at Increased Risk of Dying Within a Year, Study Finds." *Science Daily* News Release, September 26, 2011, https:// www.sciencedaily.com/releases/2011/09/110926165857.htm.

Kanze, Dana, Mark A. Conley, Tyler G. Okimoto, Damon J. Phillips, and Jennifer Merluzzi. "Evidence That Investors Penalize Female Founders for Lack of Industry Fit." *Science Advances* 6, no. 48 (2020): Eabd7664, https://www .science.org/doi/abs/10.1126/sciadv.abd7664.

Kanze, Dana, Laura Huang, Mark A. Conley, and E. Tory Higgins. "We Ask Men to Win and Women Not to Lose: Closing the Gender Gap in Startup Funding." *Academy of Management Journal* 61, no. 2 (2018): 586–614, https://doi.org /10.5465/amj.2016.1215.

Kelly, John, and Alison Young. "Episiotomies Are Painful, Risky and Not Routinely Recommended. Dozens of Hospitals Are Doing Too Many." *USA Today*, May 21, 2019, https://eu.usatoday.com/in-depth/news/investigations/deadly

-deliveries/2019/05/21/episiotomy-vs-tearing-moms-cut-in-childbirth-despite
-guidelines/3668035002/.

Khourdaji, I., J. Zillioux, K. Eisenfrats, D. Foley, and R. Smith. "The Future of Male
Contraception: A Fertile Ground." *Translational Andrology and Urology* 7, no.
Supplement 2 (May 2018): S220-S35, https://doi.org/10.21037/tau.2018.03.23.

"The Kinsey Scale," Kinsey Insitute. Accessed June 14, 2022. https://kinseyinstitute
.org/research/publications/kinsey-scale.php.

Klapperich, Catherine M. "From the Dalkon Shield to Britney Spears' IUD: Why
Diverse Teams Need to Be Involved in Contraceptive Design." *The Brink,
Pioneering Research from Boston University*, 1 July 2021.

Kling, J. M., K. L. MacLaughlin, P. F. Schnatz, C. J. Crandall, L. J. Skinner, C. A. Stuenkel,
A. M. Kaunitz, et al. "Menopause Management Knowledge in Postgraduate
Family Medicine, Internal Medicine, and Obstetrics and Gynecology Residents:
A Cross-Sectional Survey." *Mayo Clinic Proceedings* 94, no. 2 (February 2019):
242–53, https://doi.org/10.1016/j.mayocp.2018.08.033.

Knickerbocker, Kelly. "What Is Femtech?" *PitchBook* (blog), 2023, https://
pitchbook.com/blog/what-is-femtech.

Koning, Rembrand, Sampsa Samila, and John-Paul Ferguson. "Who Do We Invent
For? Patents by Women Focus More on Women's Health, But Few Women Get to
Invent." *Science* 372, no. 6548 (2021): 1345–48, https://www.science.org/doi
/abs/10.1126/science.aba6990.

Kupor, Scott. *Secrets of Sand Hill Road* London: Ebury, 2019.

Lessard, Lauren N., Deborah Karasek, Sandi Ma, Philip Darney, Julianna Deardorff,
Maureen Lahiff, Dan Grossman, and Diana Greene Foster. "Contraceptive
Features Preferred by Women at High Risk of Unintended Pregnancy." Guttmacher
Institute, September 1, 2012, https://www.guttmacher.org/journals/psrh/2012
/09/contraceptive-features-preferred-women-high-risk-unintended-pregnancy.

Levy, D. R., N. Hunter, S. Lin, E. M. Robinson, W. Gillis, E. B. Conlin, R. Anyoha,
R. M. Shansky, and S. R. Datta. "Mouse Spontaneous Behavior Reflects
Individual Variation Rather Than Estrous State." *Current Biology* 33, no. 7 (April
10, 2023): 1358–64, https://doi.org/10.1016/j.cub.2023.02.035.

Lewis, Susan Ingalls. *Unexceptional Women: Female Proprietors in
Mid-Nineteenth-Century Albany, New York, 1830–1885.* Columbus, OH:
Ohio State University Press, 2009.

Lieberman, Hallie, and Eric Schatzberg. "A Failure of Academic Quality Control: The
Technology of Orgasm." *Journal of Positive Sexuality* 4, no. 2 (2018): 24–47.

Lieshout, Carry Van. "The Age of Entrepreneurship: New Insights into Female
Business Proprietors in Victorian Britain." Economic History Society, 2019,
https://ehs.org.uk/the-age-of-entrepreneurship-new-insights-into-female
-business-proprietors-in-victorian-britain.

Longden-Jefferson, Coni. *Results of Our Study with The Wellcome Trust*. Parla, October 2, 2019, https://myparla.com/health-hub/fertility/adia-and-the -wellcome-trust-results-of-our-study/.

Lowder, J. L. "Apical Vaginal Support: The Often Forgotten Piece of the Puzzle." *Modern Medicine* 114, no. 3 (May–June 2017): 171–75, https://pubmed.ncbi .nlm.nih.gov/30228575.

Maier, Thomas. *Masters of Sex*. New York: Basic Books, 2009.

Maines, Rachel. *The Technology of Orgasm: "Hysteria," The Vibrator, and Women's Sexual Satisfaction*. Baltimore, MD: Hopkins University Press, 1999.

"Male Birth Control Study Killed After Men Report Side Effects." NPR. November 3, 2016. https://www.npr.org/sections/health-shots/2016/11/03/500549503 /male-birth-control-study-killed-after-men-complain-about-side-effects.

Maltby, Josephine, and Janette Rutterford. "Gender and Finance." In *The Oxford Handbook of the Sociology of Finance*, ed. Karin Knorr Cetina and Alex Preda, 510–28. Oxford University Press, 2012.

Mascarenhas, Natasha. "Breast Pump Maker Moxxly Quietly Shuts Down." Crunchbase News, August 8, 2018. https://news.crunchbase.com/business /breast-pump-maker-moxxly-quietly-shuts-down.

"Maternal Mortality in the United States: A Primer." The Commonwealth Fund (December 16, 2020). https://www.commonwealthfund.org/publications /issue-brief-report/2020/dec/maternal-mortality-united-states-primer.

Matoff-Stepp, Sabrina, Bethany Applebaum, Jennifer Pooler, and Erin Kavanagh. "Women As Health Care Decision-Makers: Implications for Health Care Coverage in the United States." *Journal of Health Care—The Poor and Underserved* 25, no. 4 (November 2014): 1507–13. https://www.ncbi.nlm.nih .gov/pubmed/25418222.

McCullough, L. D., G. J. De Vries, V. M. Miller, J. B. Becker, K. Sandberg, and M. M. McCarthy. "NIH Initiative to Balance Sex of Animals in Preclinical Studies: Generative Questions to Guide Policy, Implementation, and Metrics." *Biology of Sex Differences* 5 (2014): 15, https://doi.org/10.1186/s13293-014-0015-5.

McCurry, Justin. "Japan Urged to Abolish Third-Party Consent from Abortion Law." *The Guardian*, September 27, 2021, https://www.theguardian.com/world /2021/sep/27/japan-urged-to-abolish-third-party-consent-from-abortion-law.

McGregor, Alyson. *Sex Matters: How Male-Centric Medicine Endangers Women's Health—And What We Can Do About It*. London: Quercus, 2020.

"Menopause Fact Sheet." World Health Organization, October 17, 2022, https:// www.who.int/news-room/fact-sheets/detail/menopause.

"Menopause Support Survey Reveals Shocking Disparity in Menopause Training in Medical Schools." Menopause Support, May 13, 2021, https:// menopausesupport.co.uk/?p=14434.

"Menopause-Like Symptoms May Strike Before the Menopause Transition." North American Menopause Society, January 11, 2023, https://www.menopause.org/docs /default-source/press-release/late-reproductive-stage-symptoms-vs-menopause.pdf.

Merkatz, R. B., and S. W. Junod. "Historical Background of Changes in FDA Policy on the Study and Evaluation of Drugs in Women." *Academic Medicine* 69, no. 9 (1994): 703–7, https://journals.lww.com/academicmedicine/fulltext/1994 /09000/historical_background_of_changes_in_fda_policy_on.4.aspx.

Merkatz, Ruth B. "Women in Clinical Trials: An Introduction." *Food and Drug Law Journal* 48, no. 2 (1993): 161–66, http://www.jstor.org/stable/26659478.

Miller, Joe. "Inside the Hunt for a Covid-19 Vaccine: How Biontech Made the Breakthrough." *Financial Times* (Frankfurt), November 13, 2020, https://www .ft.com/content/c4ca8496-a215–44b1-a7eb-f88568fc9de9.

Miller, Joe, Özlem Türeci, and Uğur Şahin. *The Vaccine: Inside the Race to Conquer the Covid-19 Pandemic.* London: Welbeck, 2021.

Milteer, Regina M., Kenneth R. Ginsburg, Deborah Ann Mulligan, Nusheen Ameenuddin, et al. "The Importance of Play in Promoting Healthy Child Development and Maintaining Strong Parent-Child Bond: Focus on Children in Poverty." *Pediatrics* 129, no. 1 (2012): E204-E13, https://doi.org/10.1542 /peds.2011–2953.

Mitchell, M. A., S. Bisch, S. Arntfield, and S. M. Hosseini-Moghaddam. "A Confirmed Case of Toxic Shock Syndrome Associated with the Use of a Menstrual Cup." *Canadian Journal of Infectious Disease and Medical Microbiology* 26, no. 4 (July–August 2015): 218–20, https://doi.org/10.1155/2015/560959.

Moglia, M. L., H. V. Nguyen, K. Chyjek, K. T. Chen, and P. M. Castaño. "Evaluation of Smartphone Menstrual Cycle Tracking Applications Using an Adapted Applications Scoring System." *Obstetrics & Gynecology* 127, no. 6 (June 2016): 1153–60, https://doi.org/10.1097/aog.0000000000001444.

Motluk, Alison. "For a Change of Heart, Would-Be Egg Donors Face Threats and Bills." *Undark*, February 24, 2020, https://undark.org/2020/02/24/egg-donor -harrassment-threats-legal-bills.

Murakami, K., N. Hamazaki, N. Hamada, G. Nagamatsu, I. Okamoto, H. Ohta, Y. Nosaka, et al. "Generation of Functional Oocytes from Male Mice in Vitro." *Nature* 615, no. 7954 (March 2023): 900–06, https://doi.org/10.1038/s41586 -023-05834-x.

"Nanosilver in Period Care Products Fact Sheet." Women's Voices for the Earth, April 2019, https://womensvoices.org/nanosilver-in-period-care-products.

Nappi, R. E., R. Kroll, E. Siddiqui, B. Stoykova, C. Rea, E. Gemmen, and N. M. Schultz. "Global Cross-Sectional Survey of Women with Vasomotor Symptoms Associated with Menopause: Prevalence and Quality of Life Burden." *Menopause* 28, no. 8 (May 24 2021): 875–82, https://doi.org/10.1097/gme.0000000000001793.

Ng, Kate. "One in 10 Women Have Quit Their Job Due to Menopause." *Independent*, May 2, 2022, https://www.independent.co.uk/life-style/women/menopause -women-quit-jobs-hrt-b2069754.html.

NHS. "Treatment: Pelvic Organ Prolapse." National Health Service UK, March 24, 2021, https://www.nhs.uk/conditions/pelvic-organ-prolapse/treatment/.

Nussbaum, Martha. "Compassion: The Basic Social Emotion." *Social Philosophy and Policy* 13, no. 1 (1996): 27–58, https://doi.org/10.1017/s0265052500001515, https://www.cambridge.org/core/article/compassion-the-basic-social-emotion /a1d501ade7b92ca7427273ffbb449b03.

Osborne, Jari. "Picture This." National Film Board of Canada, 2017, https://www .nfb.ca/film/picture_this.

Oster, Emily. *Cribsheet*. London: Profile Books, 2019.

———. *Expecting Better*. London: Orion, 2018.

"Our Impact: 2016 Stanford Biodesign Alumni Survey." Stanford Byers Center for Biodesign, 2016, https://biodesign.stanford.edu/our-impact.html.

Ovascience. *Form 10- Annual Report* (SEC: 2015), https://www.sec.gov/Archives /edgar/data/1544227/000154422716000008/ovas-20151231x10k.htm.

Page, Emma. "Cindy Gallop: 'I Cannot Wait to Die Alone.'" *Stuff*, April 11, 2021, https://www.stuff.co.nz/life-style/love-sex/300266587/cindy-gallop-i-cannot -wait-to-die-alone.

Palacios, S., V. W. Henderson, N. Siseles, D. Tan, and P. Villaseca. "Age of Menopause and Impact of Climacteric Symptoms by Geographical Region." *Climacteric* 13, no. 5 (October 2010): 419–28, https://doi.org/10.3109/13697137.2010.507886.

Parekh, Ameeta. "Women in Clinical Drug Trials: United States Food and Drug Administration Update on Policies and Practices." In *Handbook of Clinical Gender Medicine*, ed. Paula Decola Karin Schenck-Gustafsson, Donald Pfaff, and David Pisetsky. Basel: Karger, 2012.

Parsons, F. "Corset with Expansible Busts." The National Archives, London, April 11, 1881, https://discovery.nationalarchives.gov.uk/details/r/c14038289.

"Pelvic Organ Prolapse Fact Sheet." Office on Women's Health, February 22, 2021, https://www.womenshealth.gov/a-z-topics/pelvic-organ-prolapse.

"Perineal Tears During Childbirth." Royal College of Obstetricians & Gynaecologists, 2022, https://www.rcog.org.uk/for-the-public/perineal-tears-and-episiotomies -in-childbirth/perineal-tears-during-childbirth/.

"Period Product Manufacturers Disclose Ingredients, But Health Groups Want More Data." American Chemical Society News Release, October 19, 2022, https:// www.acs.org/pressroom/presspacs/2022/acs-presspac-october-19–2022/ period-product-manufacturers-disclose-ingredients.html.

Pfaus, J., D. Hartmann, E. Wood, J. Wang, and E. Klinger. "Women's Orgasms Determined by Autodetection of Pelvic Floor Muscle Contractions Using

The Lioness 'Smart' Vibrator." *The Journal of Sexual Medicine* 19, no. 8, Supplement 3 (2022): S2–S3, https://www.sciencedirect.com/science/article /pii/s1743609522013285.

Polis, C. B., and R. K. Jones. "Multiple Contraceptive Method Use and Prevalence of Fertility Awareness Based Method Use in the United States, 2013–2015" *Contraception* 98, no. 3 (September 2018): 188–92, https://doi.org/10.1016/j .contraception.2018.04.013.

Pooneh Baghai, Olivia Howard, Lakshmi Prakash, and Jill Zucker. "Women As the Next Wave of Growth in US Wealth Management." McKinsey, July 29, 2020, https://www.mckinsey.com/industries/financial-services/our-insights/women -as-the-next-wave-of-growth-in-us-wealth-management.

Preece, D., K. W. Chow, V. Gomez-Godinez, K. Gustafson, S. Esener, N. Ravida, B. Durrant, and M. W. Berns. "Red Light Improves Spermatozoa Motility and Does Not Induce Oxidative DNA Damage." *Scientific Reports* 7 (April 20, 2017): 46480, https://doi.org/10.1038/srep46480.

"Press Release: Age Is the Key Factor for Egg Freezing Success, Says New HFEA Report, As Overall Treatment Numbers Remain Low." Human Fertilisation and Embryology Authority News Release, December 20, 2018, https://www.hfea .gov.uk/about-us/news-and-press-releases/2018-news-and-press-releases/press -release-age-is-the-key-factor-for-egg-freezing-success-says-new-hfea-report-as -overall-treatment-numbers-remain-low/.

Primarck, Dan. "More Women Are Top VC Decision-Makers, But Parity Is a Long Way Off." *Axios*, 2020, https://www.axios.com/2020/07/21/women-venture -capital-gender-equality.

Provost, Claire, and Nadini Archer. "Exclusive: Trump-Linked Religious 'Extremists' Target Women with Disinformation Worldwide." openDemocracy, February 10, 2020, https://www.opendemocracy.net/en/5050/trump-linked-religious -extremists-global-disinformation-pregnant-women.

Purdon, Lucy. "The NHS Data Breach Demonstrates the Urgent Need for Reforming the Online Advertising Industry—Femtech Can Show the Way." Femtech World, May 31, 2023, https://www.femtechworld.co.uk/opinion/the-nhs-data-breach -demonstrates-the-urgent-need-for-reforming-the-online-advertising-industry -femtech-can-show-the-way.

Raheem, O. A., J. J. Su, J. R. Wilson, and T. C. Hsieh. "The Association of Erectile Dysfunction and Cardiovascular Disease: A Systematic Critical Review" *American Journal of Men's Health* 11, no. 3 (May 2017): 552–63, https://doi .org/10.1177/1557988316630305.

Ravindran, Shruti. "This Slum Has the Worst Air Pollution in Mumbai." Vice News, March 27, 2015, https://www.vice.com/en/article/59anzd/this-slum-has-the -worst-air-pollution-in-mumbai.

Raymond, Elizabeth G., Margo S. Harrison, and Mark A. Weaver. "Efficacy of Misoprostol Alone for First-Trimester Medical Abortion: A Systematic Review." *Obstetrics & Gynecology* 133, no. 1 (2019), https://journals.lww.com /greenjournal/fulltext/2019/01000/efficacy_of_misoprostol_alone_for_first _trimester.19.aspx.

"RCOG Calling for Action to Reduce Number of Women Living with Poor Pelvic Floor Health." Royal College of Obstetricians & Gynaecologists News Release, February 2, 2023, https://www.rcog.org.uk/news/rcog-calling-for-action-to -reduce-number-of-women-living-with-poor-pelvic-floor-health.

"Recommendations on Self-Care Interventions: Self-Management of Medical Abortion, 2022 Update." World Health Organization, September 21, 2022, https://www.who.int/publications/i/item/who-srh-22.1.

"Redefining Sexual Health for Benefits Throughout Life." World Health Organization Departmental News, February 11, 2022, https://www.who.int/news/item/11 -02-2022-redefining-sexual-health-for-benefits-throughout-life.

Ries, Eric. *The Lean Startup.* New York: Crown Business, 2011.

Rigot, Afsaneh. "Digital Crime Scenes: The Role of Digital Evidence in the Persecution of LGBTQ People in Egypt, Lebanon, and Tunisia." Berkman Klein Center, March 7, 2022. https://cyber.harvard.edu/publication/2022/digital -crime-scenes.

Rimon-Zarfaty, N., J. Kostenzer, L. K. Sismuth, and A. De Bont. "Between 'Medical' and 'Social' Egg Freezing: A Comparative Analysis of Regulatory Frameworks in Austria, Germany, Israel, and the Netherlands." *Journal of Bioethical Inquiry* 18, no. 4 (December 2021): 683–99, https://doi.org/10.1007/s11673-021-10133-z.

Rinker, Brian. "Femtech Startup The Cusp Abruptly Shuts Down." *San Francisco Business Times,* December 11, 2020, https://www.bizjournals.com/sanfrancisco /news/2020/12/11/femtech-startup-the-cusp-abruptly-shuts-down.html.

Roberts, Tomi-Ann, Jamie L. Goldenberg, Cathleen Power, and Tom Pyszczynski. "'Feminine Protection': The Effects of Menstruation on Attitudes Toward Women." *Psychology of Women Quarterly* 26 (2002): 131–39.

Robinson, Ann. "Sorry, Gwyneth Paltrow, But Steaming Your Vagina Is a Bad Idea." *The Guardian,* January 30, 2015, https://www.theguardian.com/lifeandstyle /2015/jan/30/sorry-gwyneth-paltrow-but-steaming-your-vagina-is-a-bad-idea.

Robinson, Janet E., Melanie Wakelin, and Jayne E. Ellis. "Increased Pregnancy Rate with Use of the Clearblue Easy Fertility Monitor." *Fertility and Sterility* 87, no. 2 (February 2007): 329–34, https://www.ncbi.nlm.nih.gov/pubmed/17074329.

Robinson, Lynne. "HRT: The History—Women's Health Concern Fact Sheet." Women's Health Concern, November 2020. https://www.womens-health -concern.org/wp-content/uploads/2022/11/10-WHC-FACTSHEET-HRT -The-history-NOV22-A.pdf.

Romo, Vanessa. "Tokyo Medical School Busted for Rigging Women's Tests Admits Rejected Applicants." NPR, November 7, 2018, https://www.npr.org/2018/11/07/665445268/tokyo-medical-school-busted-for-rigging-womens-tests-admits-rejected-applicants.

Rosen, R. C. "Prevalence and Risk Factors of Sexual Dysfunction in Men and Women." Current Psychiatry Reports 2, no. 3 (June 2000): 189–95, https://doi.org/10.1007/s11920-996-0006-2.

Rotman, Jackie. "Facebook's Censorship of Health Ads for Women and People of Diverse Genders." Center for Intimacy Justice (2021), https://www.intimacyjustice.org/report.

Rutterford, Janette. "The Rise of the Small Investors in the US and the UK, 1900 to 1960." Business History After Chandler, Association of Business Historians Annual Conference, University of Birmingham, UK, July 4–5, 2008.

Rutterford, Janette, David R. Green, Josephine Maltby, and Alastair Owens. "Who Comprised the Nation of Shareholders? Gender and Investment in Great Britain, c. 1870–1935." The Economic History Review 64, no. 1 (2011): 168.

Safronova, Valeriya. "What's So 'Indecent' About Female Pleasure?" New York Times, January 18, 2018, https://www.nytimes.com/2019/01/18/style/sex-toy-ces.html.

———. "Why Did Facebook Reject These Ads?" New York Times, January 11, 2022, https://www.nytimes.com/2022/01/11/style/facebook-womens-sexual-health-advertising.html.

Sciorio, R., E. Angelaki, N. Al-Azemi, and A. Elmardi. "One Follicle, One Egg, One Embryo: A Case Report of Successful Pregnancy Obtained from a Single Oocyte Collected." JBRA Assisted Reproduction 25, no. 2 (April 27, 2021): 314–17, https://doi.org/10.5935/1518-0557.20200087.

Sciorio, R., E. Rapalini, and S. C. Esteves. "Air Quality in the Clinical Embryology Laboratory: A Mini-Review." Therapeutic Advances in Reproductive Health 15 (January–December 2021), https://doi.org/10.1177/2633494121990684.

Shannon, Megan B., Madeleine Genereux, Cynthia Brincat, William Adams, Linda Brubaker, Elizabeth R. Mueller, and Colleen M. Fitzgerald. "Attendance at Prescribed Pelvic Floor Physical Therapy in a Diverse, Urban Urogynecology Population." PM&R 10, no. 6 (2018): 601–06, https://www.sciencedirect.com/science/article/pii/s1934148217314156.

Shansky, Rebecca M. "Are Hormones a 'Female Problem' for Animal Research?" Science 364 (2019): 825–26, https://www.science.org/doi/abs/10.1126/science.aaw7570.

Sharma, P., and S. Kapoor. "Impact of Husband's Attitude Toward Menopause on Severity of Menopausal Symptoms Among Women in India: Pankhuri Sharma." European Journal of Public Health 24, Supplement 2 (2014), https://doi.org/10.1093/eurpub/cku161.065.

Shipp, Laura, and Jorge Blasco. "How Private Is Your Period? A Systematic Analysis of Menstrual App Privacy Policies." *Proceedings on Privacy Enhancing Technologies* 4 (2020): 491–510.

Signorile, P. G., F. Baldi, R. Bussani, M. D'Armiento, M. De Falco, M. Boccellino, L. Quagliuolo, and A. Baldi. "New Evidence of the Presence of Endometriosis in the Human Fetus." *Reproductive Biomedicine Online* 21, no. 1 (July 2010): 142–7, https://doi.org/10.1016/j.rbmo.2010.04.002.

Silbey, Susan S. "Why Do So Many Women Who Study Engineering Leave the Field?" *Harvard Business Review*, August 23, 2016, https://hbr.org/2016/08/why-do-so-many-women-who-study-engineering-leave-the-field.

Singh, A., and A. R. Varma. "Whole-Body Vibration Therapy as a Modality for Treatment of Senile and Postmenopausal Osteoporosis: A Review Article." *Cureus* 15, no. 1 (January 2023): E33690, https://doi.org/10.7759/cureus.33690.

Skovlund, C. W., L. S. Mørch, L. V. Kessing, T. Lange, and Ø. Lidegaard. "Association of Hormonal Contraception with Suicide Attempts and Suicides." *American Journal of Psychiatry* 175, no. 4 (April 1, 2018): 336–42, https://doi.org/10.1176/appi.ajp.2017.17060616.

Skovlund, Charlotte, Lina Mørch, Lars Kessing, and Øjvind Lidegaard. "Association of Hormonal Contraception with Depression." *JAMA Psychiatry* 73 (2016), https://doi.org/10.1001/jamapsychiatry.2016.2387.

Soffer, M. D., and K. T. Chen. "In Search of Accurate Fetal Heart Rate Monitoring Mobile Applications." *Telemedicine and E-Health* 25, no. 9 (September 2019): 870–77, https://doi.org/10.1089/tmj.2018.0104.

Sommer, A. P., S. Jaganathan, M. R. Maduro, K. Hancke, W. Janni, and H. J. Fecht. "Genesis on Diamonds II: Contact with Diamond Enhances Human Sperm Performance by 300." *Annals of Translational Medicine* 4, no. 20 (October 2016): 407, https://doi.org/10.21037/atm.2016.08.18.

Sputniko! "Menstruation Machine—Takashi's Take," 2010, https://sputniko.com/menstruation-machine.

Stack, Liam. "Catholic Officials on Edge After Reports of Priests Using Grindr." *New York Times*, August 20, 2021, https://www.nytimes.com/2021/08/20/nyregion/pillar-grindr-catholic-church.html.

"Startup Grind Hosts David Cohen Tanugi." YouTube, January 2, 2018, https://www.youtube.com/watch?v=o7pdlhjhxpg.

"Statistics of Women in Engineering in the UK." Women's Engineering Society, March 2022, https://www.wes.org.uk/about/what-we-do/resources/statistics.

Steinem, Gloria. "After Black Power, Women's Liberation." *New York Magazine*, April 7, 1969.

———. "If Men Could Menstruate." *Ms.* magazine, 1978, https://www.tandfonline.com/doi/epdf/10.1080/23293691.2019.1619050?needaccess=true&role=button.

———. *My Life on the Road*. London: Oneworld, 2016.

Sudjic, Olivia. "'I Felt Colossally Naive': The Backlash Against the Birth Control App." *The Guardian*, July 21, 2018, https://www.theguardian.com/society /2018/jul/21/colossally-naive-backlash-birth-control-app.

Sudol, N. T., E. Adams-Piper, R. Perry, F. Lane, and K. T. Chen. "In Search of Mobile Applications for Patients with Pelvic Floor Disorders." *Female Pelvic Medicine & Reconstructive Surgery* 25, no. 3 (May–June 2019): 252–56, https://doi.org /10.1097/spv.0000000000000527.

Sugimoto, C. R., Y. Y. Ahn, E. Smith, B. Macaluso, and V. Larivière. "Factors Affecting Sex-Related Reporting in Medical Research: A Cross-Disciplinary Bibliometric Analysis." *Lancet* 393, no. 10171 (February 9, 2019): 550–59, https://doi.org /10.1016/s0140-6736(18)32995-7.

Sung, E., A. Han, T. Hinrichs, M. Vorgerd, C. Manchado, and P. Platen. "Effects of Follicular Versus Luteal Phase-Based Strength Training in Young Women." *Springerplus* 3 (2014): 668, https://doi.org/10.1186/2193-1801-3-668.

Sylvester, Shirley. "Science in Action: Collaborating in Georgia to Improve Black Maternal Health." Johnson & Johnson, February 16, 2021, https://chwi.jnj.com /news-insights/science-in-action-collaborating-in-georgia-to-improve-black -maternal-health.

Tak, Elise, Shelley J. Correll, and Sarah A Soule. "Gender Inequality in Product Markets: When and How Status Beliefs Transfer to Products." *Social Forces* 98, no. 2 (2019): 548–77, https://doi.org/10.1093/sf/soy125, https://doi.org/10 .1093/sf/soy125.

Teare, Gené. "EoY 2019 Diversity Report: 20% of Newly Funded Startups in 2019 Have a Female Founder." Crunchbase News, 2020, https://news.crunchbase .com/venture/eoy-2019-diversity-report-20-percent-of-newly-funded-startups -in-2019-have-a-female-founder.

"Thalidomide." Science Museum. December 11, 2019. https://www.sciencemuseum .org.uk/objects-and-stories/medicine/thalidomide.

Thompson, Avni Patel. "What Shutting Down Your Startup Feels Like." Y Combinator, January 2019, https://www.ycombinator.com/library/5p-what -shutting-down-your-startup-feels-like.

Todd Feathers, Simon Fondrie-Teitler, Angie Waller, and Surya Mattu. "Facebook Is Receiving Sensitive Medical Information from Hospital Websites." *The Markup*, June 16, 2022, https://themarkup.org/pixel-hunt/2022/06/16/facebook-is -receiving-sensitive-medical-information-from-hospital-websites.

Toffol, E., T. Partonen, A. Latvala, A. But, O. Heikinheimo, and J. Haukka. "Use of Hormonal Contraception and Attempted Suicide: A Nested Case-Control Study." Supplement 1, *European Psychiatry* 65 (June 2022): S122–3. https:// doi.org/10.1192%2Fj.eurpsy.2022.339.

Tourgeman, David E., Elisabet Gentzchein, Frank Z. Stanczyk, and Richard J. Paulson. "Serum and Tissue Hormone Levels of Vaginally and Orally Administered Estradiol." *American Journal of Obstetrics and Gynecology* 180, no. 6 (1999): 1480–83, https://www.sciencedirect.com/science/article/pii /s0002937899700426.

Tran, Linh N., and Yana Puckett. "Urinary Incontinence." National Library of Medicine, August 8, 2022, https://www.ncbi.nlm.nih.gov/books/nbk559095/.

Treisman, Rachel. "Thinx Settled a Lawsuit over Chemicals in Its Period Underwear. Here's What to Know." NPR, January 19, 2023., https://www.npr.org/2023/01 /19/1150023002/thinx-period-underwear-lawsuit-settlement.

Trost S. L., J. Beauregard, F. Njie, et al. "Pregnancy-Related Deaths: Data from Maternal Mortality Review Committees in 36 US States, 2017–2019." Atlanta, GA: Centers for Disease Control and Prevention, U.S. Department of Health and Human Services (2022): https://www.cdc.gov/reproductivehealth/maternal-mortality /docs/pdf/Pregnancy-Related-Deaths-Data-MMRCs-2017–2019-H.pdf.

Tversky, Amos, and Daniel Kahneman. "The Framing of Decisions and the Psychology of Choice." *Science* 211, no. 4481 (1981): 453–58, https://www .science.org/doi/abs/10.1126/science.7455683.

"UK Health Research Analysis 2014." UK Clinical Research Collaboration, 2014, http://www.hrcsonline.net/pages/uk-health-research-analysis-2014.

"Unintended Pregnancy and Abortion Worldwide Factsheet." Guttmacher Institute, March 2022, https://www.guttmacher.org/fact-sheet/induced-abortion -worldwide.

"US VC Female Founders Dashboard." PitchBook, October 2, 2023, https:// pitchbook.com/news/articles/the-vc-female-founders-dashboard.

"Vendor Best Practices." Internet of Dongs, 2023, https://internetofdon.gs/vendor -best-practices.

Wang, Amy B. "Gwyneth Paltrow's Goop Touted the 'Benefits' of Putting a Jade Egg in Your Vagina. Now It Must Pay." *Washington Post*, September 5, 2018, https://www.washingtonpost.com/health/2018/09/05/gwyneth-paltrows -goop-touted-benefits-putting-jade-egg-your-vagina-now-it-must-pay/.

Wang, Jingying, Xiaoyun Sui, Bin Hu, Jonathan Flint, Shuotian Bai, Yuanbo Gao, Yang Zhou, and Tingshao Zhu. "Detecting Postpartum Depression in Depressed People by Speech Features." Paper Presented at The Human Centered Computing Third International Conference 2017, Springer, Cham, Switzerland, 2018.

Ward-Glenton, Hannah. "Meet the Woman Who Invented a Whole New Subsection of Tech Set to Be Worth $1 Trillion." CNBC, March 6, 2023, https://www.cnbc .com/2023/03/06/meet-the-woman-who-invented-a-whole-new-subsection-of -tech-set-to-be-worth-1-trillion.html.

Weintraub, Karen. "Turmoil at Troubled Fertility Company Ovascience." *MIT Technology Review*, December 29, 2016, https://www.technologyreview.com /2016/12/29/106805/turmoil-at-troubled-fertility-company-ovascience.

Westergaard, David, Pope Moseley, Freja K. H. Sorup, Pierra Baldi, and Soren Brunak. "Population-Wide Analysis of Differences in Disease Progression Patterns in Men and Women." *Nature Communications* 10, 666 (2019), https://www.ncbi .nlm.nih.gov/pubmed/30737381.

"What's in Your Period Product? An Investigation of Ingredients Disclosed on Product Labels." Women's Voices for the Earth, May 2022, https://womensvoices .org/report-whats-in-your-period-product/.

"Why Are Period Products an Environmental Concern?" City to Sea, February 25, 2020, https://www.citytosea.org.uk/campaign/plastic-free-periods/periods-and -the-environment/.

"Why Do We Still Not Know What Causes PMS?" *Researchgate* (blog), August 12, 2016, https://www.researchgate.net/blog/why-do-we-still-not-know-what -causes-pms.

"Why Polycystic Ovarian Syndrome Is Often Misdiagnosed." *Women's Healthcare of Princeton* (blog), December 1, 2019, https://www.princetongyn.com/blog /why-polycystic-ovarian-syndrome-is-often-misdiagnosed.

Wigfield, Andrea, Jan Gurung, and Laura Makey. "Is Loneliness Really As Damaging to Your Health As Smoking 15 Cigarettes a Day?" *The Conversation*, May 12, 2023, https://theconversation.com/is-loneliness-really-as-damaging-to-your -health-as-smoking-15-cigarettes-a-day-204959.

Williams, Serena. "How Serena Williams Saved Her Own Life." *ELLE*, April 5, 2022, https://www.elle.com/life-love/a39586444/how-serena-williams-saved-her -own-life.

Williams, W. V., J. Brind, L. Haynes, M. D. Manhart, H. Klaus, A. Lanfranchi, G. Migeon, et al. "Hormonally Active Contraceptives, Part II: Sociological, Environmental, and Economic Impact." *Linacre Quarterly* 88, no. 3 (August 2021): 291–316, https://doi.org/10.1177/00243639211005121.

Winfrey, Oprah. "Oprah Reveals How Heart Palpitations Led Her to Discover She Was Approaching Menopause." Oprah Daily, 2019, https://www.oprahdaily.com /life/health/a29109829/oprah-menopause-symptoms.

Woitowich, N. C., A. Beery, and T. Woodruff. "A 10-Year Follow-Up Study of Sex Inclusion in the Biological Sciences." *Elife* 9 (June 9, 2020), https://doi.org/10 .7554/elife.56344.

"Women Are 50% More Likely Than Men to Be Given Incorrect Diagnosis Following a Heart Attack." British Heart Foundation (2016), https://www.bhf.org.uk/what -we-do/news-from-the-bhf/news-archive/2016/august/women-are-50-per-cent -more-likely-than-men-to-be-given-incorrect-diagnosis-following-a-heart-attack.

"Women's Committee Book Club, Economic History Society—Female Entrepreneurs." April 14, 2021. https://ehs.org.uk/event/womens-committee -book-club-female-entrepreneurs/.

Wong, Julia Carrie. "Birth Control App Reported to Swedish Officials After 37 Unwanted Pregnancies." *The Guardian*, January 17, 2018, https://www .theguardian.com/technology/2018/jan/17/birth-control-app-natural-cycle -pregnancies.

Woolf, Virginia. "Professions for Women." A Speech at the Women's Service League (1931), https://www.literaturecambridge.co.uk/news/professions-women.

Zamora-León, P. "Are the Effects of DES Over? A Tragic Lesson from the Past." *International Journal of Environmental Research and Public Health* 18, no. 19 (September 30, 2021), https://doi.org/10.3390/ijerph181910309.

Zaneva, M., A. Philpott, A. Singh, G. Larsson, and L. Gonsalves. "What Is the Added Value of Incorporating Pleasure in Sexual Health Interventions? A Systematic Review and Meta-Analysis." *PLOS One* 17, no. 2 (2022): e0261034, https://doi .org/10.1371/journal.pone.0261034.

Zethraeus, N., A. Dreber, E. Ranehill, L. Blomberg, F. Labrie, B. Von Schoultz, M. Johannesson, and A. L. Hirschberg. "A First-Choice Combined Oral Contraceptive Influences General Well-Being in Healthy Women: A Double-Blind, Randomized, Placebo-Controlled Trial." *Fertility and Sterility* 107, no. 5 (May 2017): 1238–45, https://doi.org/10.1016/j.fertnstert.2017.02.120.

Zhang, L., E. A. R. Losin, Y. K. Ashar, L. Koban, and T. D. Wager. "Gender Biases in Estimation of Others' Pain." *Journal of Pain* 22, no. 9 (September 2021): 1048–59, https://doi.org/10.1016/j.jpain.2021.03.001.

Zhang, Y., X. Zhao, R. Leonhart, M. Nadig, A. Hasenburg, M. Wirsching, and K. Fritzsche. "A Cross-Cultural Comparison of Climacteric Symptoms, Self-Esteem, and Perceived Social Support Between Mosuo Women and Han Chinese Women." *Menopause* 23, no. 7 (July 2016): 784–91, https://doi.org/10.1097 /gme.0000000000000621.

Zhao, S. C. "Vas Deferens Occlusion by Percutaneous Injection of Polyurethane Elastomer Plugs: Clinical Experience and Reversibility." *Contraception* 41, no. 5 (May 1990): 453–9, https://doi.org/10.1016/0010-7824(90)90055-z.

Zucker, Irving, and Brian J. Prendergast. "Sex Differences in Pharmacokinetics Predict Adverse Drug Reactions in Women." *Biology of Sex Differences* 11, 32 (2020). https://www.ncbi.nlm.nih.gov/pubmed/32503637.

INDEX

D

Dalkon Shield, 281–282
data. *See also* cybersecurity
  collecting, 292
  funding and, 37
  GDPR, 121, 122
  privacy and, 108
  selling, 286
data breaches, 294
data gap, gender, xiii, 69, 74, 75, 324
death, pregnancy-related, 194–200
demand generation, 21
Department of Defense, U.S., 234
depression, 77, 79
depression, postpartum, 208, 241, 260
diagnosis, women and, xiv, 78
diagnostic tools, 244–245
diethylstilbestrol, 63
dilators, 88, 219
diseases, female-specific. *See* endometriosis; polycystic ovary syndrome (PCOS)
Dodson, Betty, 254
drugs
  dosage of, xiv
  health risks for women and, 64
  metabolization of, 68
  regulatory approval of, 3
due dates, calculating, 112

E

ECG (electrocardiogram), 75
economic gender gap, 43
ectopic pregnancy, 235
edging, 141
egg freezing, 183–193
  age and, 191
  AMH test, 187–188
  business model for, 285
  cost of, 189
  development of, 190–191
  egg production and, 188
  limited data on, 193
  number needed for success, 186
  procedure for, 191

I

S

ABOUT THE AUTHOR

© Ivan Weiss

Marina Gerner is an award-winning financial journalist and columnist. Her work has been published in the *Economist, Wall Street Journal,* the *Times, Financial Times, The Guardian,* and *Wired.* She is an adjunct professor at the NYU Stern School of Business and has a PhD from the London School of Economics. Her ideas and research for this book have been awarded grants from the prestigious Alfred P. Sloan Foundation and The Society of Authors. She was born in Kyiv, has lived in Frankfurt and New York, and is based in London.